MW00576873

Getting Started with Windows Server Security

Develop and implement a secure Microsoft infrastructure platform using native and built-in tools

Santhosh Sivarajan

[PACKT] PUBLISHING enterprise
professional expertise distilled

BIRMINGHAM - MUMBAI

Getting Started with Windows Server Security

First published: February 2015

Production reference: 1210215

Published by Packt Publishing Ltd.
Livery Place
35 Livery Street
Birmingham B3 2PB, UK.

ISBN 978-1-78439-872-9

www.packtpub.com

Credits

Author
Santhosh Sivarajan

Reviewers
Jack Cobben
Yuri Diogenes
Richard Diver
Richard M. Hicks

Commissioning Editor
Kunal Parikh

Acquisition Editor
Rebecca Youé

Content Development Editor
Shweta Pant

Technical Editor
Tanvi Bhatt

Copy Editors
Shivangi Chaturvedi
Adithi Shetty

Project Coordinator
Shipra Chawhan

Proofreaders
Maria Gould
Paul Hindle
Chris Smith

Indexer
Mariammal Chettiyar

Graphics
Abhinash Sahu

Production Coordinator
Melwyn D'sa

Cover Work
Melwyn D'sa

About the Author

Santhosh Sivarajan is a recognized subject matter expert in the Microsoft technology arena. He has extensive experience in designing, migrating, developing, and implementing enterprise solutions using Microsoft products and technologies. He holds a master's degree in computer information systems from the University of Houston, Texas. His certifications include MCITP, MCTS, MCSE, MCSA, Network+, CCNA, ITIL, and many more. He is also a certified migration expert in Quest Migration Manager products.

His blog (`http://blogs.sivarajan.com`) and SS Technology Forum (`http://www.sivarajan.com/forum`) are well known in the industry for providing free technical information and support. You can follow Santhosh on Twitter via `@santhosh_sivara`.

He is the author of the book *Migration from Windows Server 2008 to Windows Server 2012, Packt Publishing*. He has also published hundreds of articles on various technology sites.

Microsoft has recognized Santhosh with the Microsoft Most Valuable Professional (MVP) award multiple times for his exceptional contribution to the technical community. He lives in Sugarland, Texas, with his wife, Anjali, who is also an IT professional, and their 3-year-old daughter, Gayathri.

Acknowledgments

First and foremost, I would like to thank God for giving me the power to believe in myself and pursue my dreams.

My IT enterprise journey started from Camp Doha with the US Army (now known as Camp Arifjan) in Kuwait. The support and encouragement from the ADPE group and other army personnel at Camp Doha helped me start my career with a strong foundation. I am dedicating this book to my old friends and colleagues in Camp Doha.

Of course, I could not have completed this book without the support and encouragement of my family, especially my wife, Anjali, and my daughter, Gayathri, for giving up some of our time together so that I could share my ideas through this book.

I am grateful to all my friends and colleagues for their support throughout my career. A special thanks to my Microsoft MVP friends for listening to me and supporting my ideas. A special thanks to the book reviewers, Yuri Diogenes, Richard Hicks, Richard Diver, and Jack Cobben, for providing their constructive criticism and feedback. I would also like to express my gratitude and thanks to the entire Packt Publishing team for this opportunity and their support throughout this process.

About the Reviewers

Jack Cobben is no stranger to the challenges enterprises can experience when managing large deployments of Windows systems and Citrix implementations, with over 13 years of systems management experience in his free time he writes for his own blog, `www.jackcobben.nl`, and is active on Citrix support forums. He loves to test new software and share his knowledge in any way he can. You can follow him on Twitter via `@jackcobben`.

Jack has reviewed several other books such as *Citrix XenDesktop 7 Cookbook, Getting Started with Citrix Provisioning Services 7.0, Getting Started with XenDesktop 7.x*, and other titles for Packt Publishing.

> A big thanks to my wife and twins for letting me have the time to review this book.

While he works for Citrix, Citrix didn't help with, or support, this book in any way or form.

Yuri Diogenes has a master's degree in cyber security, specializing in cyber intel and forensics investigation from UTICA College and an MBA from FGV (Brazil). He is also certified in CISSP, CASP, E|CEH, E|CSA, CompTIA, Security+, CompTIA Cloud Essentials Certified, CompTIA Network+, CompTIA Cloud+, CompTIA Mobility+, Azure Specialist, MCSE, and MCTS. Yuri is a senior member of the ISSA Forth Worth/TX chapter, a member of CSA Brazil, and a speaker at Hacker Halted, TechEd US, TechEd Europe, and TechEd Brazil. He is also a coauthor of *Windows Server 2012 Security from End to Edge and Beyond from Syngress, Microsoft Forefront Threat Management Gateway (TMG) Administrator's Companion* by Microsoft Press, as well as three other books about Forefront (UAG, TMG, and FPE) by Microsoft Press, and a cloud essentials certification book and security+ book (both in Portuguese) by Novaterra Publisher. You can follow Yuri on Twitter via `@yuridiogenes`.

I would like to thank the Packt Publishing team for the opportunity to partner in this project, the author of this book for taking my feedback and addressing it, and to my wife, Alexsandra, and daughters, Yanne and Ysis, for always supporting me. Love you!

Richard Diver is a solutions architect with 15 years of experience across multiple industries and technologies, with a focus on Microsoft infrastructure, mobility, and identity management solutions. His previous book contributions include topics such as Sysinternals Tools, Windows Intune, and Office 365.

Richard M. Hicks (MCP, MCSE, MCTS, and MCITP Enterprise Administrator) is a network and information security expert specializing in Microsoft technologies. As a six-time Microsoft Most Valuable Professional (MVP) in the Enterprise Security discipline, he has traveled around the world, speaking to network engineers, security administrators, and IT professionals about Microsoft edge security and remote access solutions.

Richard has nearly two decades of experience working in large-scale corporate computing environments and has designed and deployed perimeter defense and secure remote access solutions for some of the largest companies in the world. He blogs extensively about Microsoft edge security and remote access solutions and is a contributing author at popular sites such as CloudComputingAdmin.com, WindowsSecurity.com, ISAserver.org, and the Petri IT Knowledgebase. In addition, he is a Pluralsight author and has served as the technical reviewer on several Windows Server and network security books.

Richard is the technical services director for Celestix Networks, a Microsoft OEM partner developing Microsoft-based edge security and remote access solutions. He's an avid fan of Major League Baseball, in particular, the Los Angeles Angels (of Anaheim!) and also enjoys craft beer and single malt Scotch whisky. He was born and raised in beautiful, sunny Southern California. He still resides there with Anne, the love of his life and wife of 27 years, along with their four children. You can keep up with Richard by visiting `http://www.richardhicks.com/`.

www.PacktPub.com

Support files, eBooks, discount offers, and more

For support files and downloads related to your book, please visit www.PacktPub.com.

Did you know that Packt offers eBook versions of every book published, with PDF and ePub files available? You can upgrade to the eBook version at www.PacktPub.com and as a print book customer, you are entitled to a discount on the eBook copy. Get in touch with us at service@packtpub.com for more details.

At www.PacktPub.com, you can also read a collection of free technical articles, sign up for a range of free newsletters and receive exclusive discounts and offers on Packt books and eBooks.

PACKTLIB™

https://www2.packtpub.com/books/subscription/packtlib

Do you need instant solutions to your IT questions? PacktLib is Packt's online digital book library. Here, you can search, access, and read Packt's entire library of books.

Why subscribe?

- Fully searchable across every book published by Packt
- Copy and paste, print, and bookmark content
- On demand and accessible via a web browser

Free access for Packt account holders

If you have an account with Packt at www.PacktPub.com, you can use this to access PacktLib today and view 9 entirely free books. Simply use your login credentials for immediate access.

Instant updates on new Packt books

Get notified! Find out when new books are published by following @PacktEnterprise on Twitter or the *Packt Enterprise* Facebook page.

Table of Contents

Preface

Welcome to *Getting Started with Windows Server Security* is a critical component for any organization. It can be implemented in various levels. Every organization has its own security polices based on their business and technical requirements. These policies must apply to end-to-end devices and services to effectively secure your IT infrastructure. As a security administrator, it is your responsibility to convert these business requirements into technical requirements. This book provides various methods to analyze your requirements and convert them based on the best practices and industry standards.

This book will walk you through different security tools and their configurations and implementation details based on my real-world experience. The goal is to have a protected and secure Microsoft Server infrastructure platform at the end of this journey. To achieve this goal in an efficient way, this book is divided into various chapters. Each chapter will provide you step-by-step instructions to secure your server infrastructure based on the installed components and applications on the server. For a security or Windows Server administrator, this book can be used as a reference manual when securing or hardening your server infrastructure.

What this book covers

Chapter 1, Operating System and Baseline Security, provides the details to translate your business requirements into a technical policy and implement these security policies in a Microsoft infrastructure environment. This chapter also covers instructions on creating and implementing Windows baseline polices using Microsoft Security Configuration Wizard.

Chapter 2, Native MS Security Tools and Configuration, provides an overview of various Microsoft tools and explains how they can be used in an enterprise to support your compliance and security needs. This chapter converts the configuration and implementation details of the Microsoft Security Compliance Manager, Attack Surface Analyzer, application control, and other auditing policies.

Chapter 3, Server Roles and Protocols, provides the details and methods to select correct server types and roles and identify and control unwanted services based on your requirements. It also provides a PowerShell-based solution to create and analyze baseline images based on the application or server type.

Chapter 4, Application Security, provides various options to create a secure server infrastructure platform for your application using Microsoft technologies. This chapter also covers the details to secure file and data servers, print servers, Hyper-V, web servers and encryption, and BitLocker technologies.

Chapter 5, Network Service Security, provides the details of protecting and controlling Microsoft network services. This chapter provides step-by-step instructions on securing Active Directory, Domain Controller, DNS, DHCP and configuration, and implementation details of gMSA and EMET.

Chapter 6, Access Control, provides an overview of the new access control mechanisms in Windows Server 2012. The step-by-step installation and configuration details of Dynamic Access Control are also included in this chapter.

Chapter 7, Patch Management, provides the details of maintaining the security and integrity of your Windows server using various Microsoft technologies. The step-by-step instructions on implementing and administering WSUS are also included in this chapter.

Chapter 8, Auditing and Monitoring, provides different options to audit and monitor your server infrastructure using various technologies. The details of auditing polices, GPOs, event forwarding, event alerting, and Best Practices Analyzer are also included in this chapter.

What you need for this book

The configuration and implementation details provided in this book are based on the Windows Server 2012 and Windows Server 2012 R2 operation systems. So, you need to have one of these operating systems at hand. You will also need to have the following software to successfully implement the solutions described in this book:

- Windows PowerShell
- Microsoft Security Configuration Wizard

- Microsoft Security Compliance Manger
- Surface Attack Analyzer
- AppLocker
- BitLocker
- Group Policy Objects
- Best Practices Analyzer

Who this book is for

This book is for server or security administrators who wants to advance their knowledge in Microsoft security and are responsible for the security and administration of the Microsoft Windows Server infrastructure.

Conventions

In this book, you will find a number of styles of text that distinguish between different kinds of information. Here are some examples of these styles, and an explanation of their meaning.

Code words in text, database table names, folder names, filenames, file extensions, pathnames, dummy URLs, user input, and Twitter handles are shown as follows: "Once you perform the rollback operation, the XML files get deleted from the `rollbackfiles` folder."

Any command-line input or output is written as follows:

```
Get-ADComputer -Filter * -Properties * |  Select Name, OperatingSystem
|out-file C:\Reports\ServerInfo.txt
```

New terms and **important words** are shown in bold. Words that you see on the screen, in menus or dialog boxes for example, appear in the text like this: "Click on **Finish** on the **Completing the Security Configuration Wizard** screen to complete the rollback operation."

[Warnings or important notes appear in a box like this.]

[Tips and tricks appear like this.]

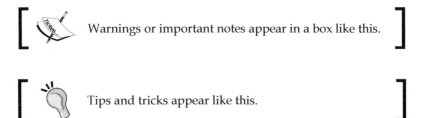

Reader feedback

Feedback from our readers is always welcome. Let us know what you think about this book—what you liked or may have disliked. Reader feedback is important for us to develop titles that you really get the most out of.

To send us general feedback, simply send an e-mail to `feedback@packtpub.com`, and mention the book title via the subject of your message.

If there is a topic that you have expertise in and you are interested in either writing or contributing to a book, see our author guide on `www.packtpub.com/authors`.

Customer support

Now that you are the proud owner of a Packt book, we have a number of things to help you to get the most from your purchase.

Errata

Although we have taken every care to ensure the accuracy of our content, mistakes do happen. If you find a mistake in one of our books—maybe a mistake in the text or the code—we would be grateful if you would report this to us. By doing so, you can save other readers from frustration and help us improve subsequent versions of this book. If you find any errata, please report them by visiting `http://www.packtpub.com/submit-errata`, selecting your book, clicking on the **errata submission form** link, and entering the details of your errata. Once your errata are verified, your submission will be accepted and the errata will be uploaded on our website, or added to any list of existing errata, under the Errata section of that title. Any existing errata can be viewed by selecting your title from `http://www.packtpub.com/support`.

Piracy

Piracy of copyright material on the Internet is an ongoing problem across all media. At Packt, we take the protection of our copyright and licenses very seriously. If you come across any illegal copies of our works, in any form, on the Internet, please provide us with the location address or website name immediately so that we can pursue a remedy.

Please contact us at `copyright@packtpub.com` with a link to the suspected pirated material.

We appreciate your help in protecting our authors, and our ability to bring you valuable content.

Questions

You can contact us at `questions@packtpub.com` if you are having a problem with any aspect of the book, and we will do our best to address it.

1
Operating System and Baseline Security

Server or network security doesn't start from a configuration or implementation level. In order to achieve the maximum result, it has to start from a policy or framework level. Also, your security and hardening policy must apply to all your end-to-end devices and services for it to effectively secure your IT infrastructure. The network or server components can be a part of this policy. Since the emphasis of this book is more towards the server security aspect, I will focus more on server security configuration instead of a broad security. Physical security is more important than any other security. For the purpose of this book, my assumption is that a policy, framework, and physical security are already in place. So our security conversation starts from a server level.

In this chapter, my plan is to walk you through a security tool, **Security Configuration Wizard** (**SCW**), and it's configuration details, and explain how you can use this tools in your environment to make the existing or new server infrastructure more secure. This tool will provide you with a common platform to create a policy template and apply these polices in an automated fashion, regardless of how they are defined and where they are coming from.

Microsoft Windows Server

The Microsoft Windows Server operating system has gone through several changes over the last decade. One of the major changes that you will notice in the latest versions of Windows is that of the improvement and integration of security. It is clear that server sęcurity is essential in one form or another in the enterprise world. Since the latest version of Windows is Windows Sever 2012 R2, I will be using this operating system as my base operating system in this book.

All solutions listed in the book are validated on a Windows 2012 environment. However, most of the methods and configuration details included in this book can also be used in the previous versions of Windows.

According to Microsoft, the Windows Server 2012 operating system is "secure by default". In some aspects, this is true. However, you need to tweak or customize it based on your business and technical requirements to achieve the maximum benefit.

If you are thinking about using the Windows Server 2012 operation system for applications, data, network services, and so on, the actual server hardening or security process starts from the selection of the type of operating system. In Windows Server 2012, you can use the Server Core installation to minimize the security threat. The details and benefits of Server Core can be found at `http://msdn.microsoft.com/en-us/library/hh846323(v=vs.85).aspx`. Since Server Core installation contains only a few services, processes, and so on, it can minimize the number of malicious attacks (attack surface) on the server. These server attacks can lead to a major enterprise-wide attack. So, if your service runs on the Server Core operating system, it is recommend to select Server Core for this application.

> Keep in mind that Server Core can support only a few services. The details of these supported services can be found at `http://msdn.microsoft.com/en-us/library/hh846323(v=vs.85).aspx`.

The next step in this process is to select the correct (or minimum) server roles for your server. The details of selecting and configuring server roles based on your requirements are included in *Chapter 3, Server Roles and Protocols*.

From an operating system perspective, in order to achieve maximum security using native and built-in solutions, the security aspect can be summarized using the following diagram:

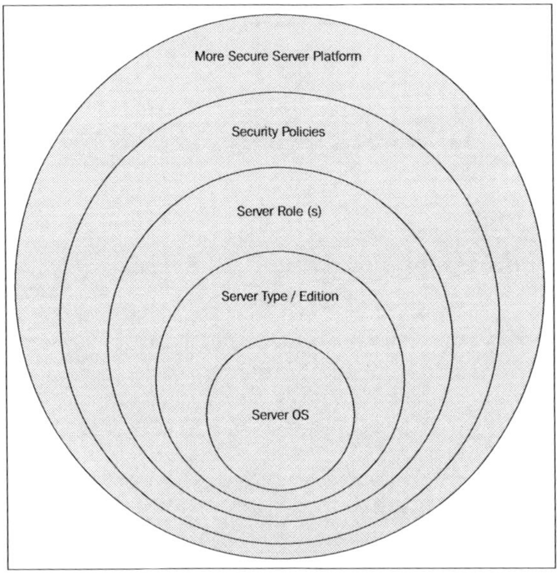

Windows Server 2012 operating system installation, configuration, and conversion details can be found in *Instant Migration from Windows Server 2008 and 2008 R2 to 2012 How-to, Packt Publishing*.

Baseline and security

According to its definition, baseline is something you can measure all the time and compare it to identify the difference between the current state and the starting point. In general, the business and technical requirements reflect the core of a baseline policy. It can also be a combination of your business requirements and industry-best practices. As a security administrator, your job is to translate these polices into a technical policy that you can apply in your IT environment.

Different companies and industries follow different standards and policies to secure their IT infrastructure. The following are some of the popular standards that are widely used in the industry:

- **National Institute of Standards and Technology** (**NIST**): `http://www.nist.gov/`
- **Center for Internet Security** (**CIS**): `http://www.cisecurity.org/`
- **Security Technical Implementation Guides** (**STIGs**): `http://iase.disa.mil/stigs`
- **National Security Agency** (**NSA**) **Configuration Guides**: `https://www.nsa.gov/ia/mitigation_guidance/security_configuration_guides/index.shtml`
- **Microsoft Security Baselines**

The details of these agencies and their recommendations can be reviewed on their websites.

Out of the box, Windows Server 2012 and higher provides a few security tools that can be used as a starting point for your Windows Server security configuration. We will start this journey with a built-in security tool called Microsoft **Security Configuration Wizard** (**SCW**). This is a very powerful role-based tool that is included with Windows Server 2012 or higher. You can easily translate your business security policies into a technical policy using this tool. As a first step, you need to define your business security requirements or policies. Once you have that documented, you can use Microsoft SCW to create a policy template for different types of servers. In general, these business security requirements can be achieved by disabling unwanted services, blocking unused ports, modifying registry settings, and restricting network and server access. In other words, Microsoft SCW will help you to identify minimum functionality requirements for a server-based on an installed role or service on that particular server. Then this policy can be applied to a server or set of servers using Microsoft SCW, or any other mechanisms like **Group Policy Objects** (**GPOs**).

The following is a five-step process to get you to implement the policy in an efficient manner:

1. Define your business security policy.
2. Translate it into a technical policy.
3. Create a policy template using a tool.
4. Policy review and validation.
5. Policy implementation.

Security Configuration Wizard

The Microsoft Security Configuration Wizard tool has four major sections: Role-Based Service Configuration, Network Security, Registry Settings, and Auditing Policy. Each of these sections has sub-categories to address specific service requests, based on the top level category. The following table provides a high-level explanation of the available options inside Microsoft SCW:

Role-Based Service Configuration	
Server role	This section provides an option to select or deselect appropriate roles based on your requirements. SCW will automatically detect installed roles on the server. All the dependent roles will also be selected automatically.
Client features	In this section, you can select client features that are specific for the role you have chosen in the previous step.
Administration option	Provides an option to select different administration tools and options.
Additional services	By default, SCW will select all required service-based roles, features, and administrative options. This section will give you an option to review these configurations and to make changes if needed.
Handling unwanted services	In this section, you will have an option to select unidentified services. SCW will not display services if they are not present in the local system.
Network Security	
Network security rules	In this section, you can select firewall rules, traffic types, ports, and so on.
Registry Settings	
SMB security setting	Provides an option to enable or disable SMB security signing.
LDAP Signing requirement	If the Domain Controller role is selected, you will see an option to configure LDAP signing.
Outbound Authentication methods	This section provides an option to configure remote computer authentication methods. You will have an option to select either domain account or local account.
Auditing Policy	
System Audit Policy	This section provides an option to enable or disable auditing on a selected server.

Since creating a business security policy is beyond the scope of this book, my assumption would be that you have a business security policy already defined and in place. So we will be starting with the *Translating your policy into a technical policy* section.

Translating your policy into a technical policy

In this stage, as a security administrator, your job is to convert the existing business security policy into a technical policy. Since we are planning to use Microsoft SCW for this exercise, we can map our policy directly into an SCW policy.

I always use a worksheet to map these policies so as to make sure they align with existing options in the tool. The following is a sample worksheet. It helps an administrator identify the policies that are available in SCW and map them accordingly. On the left side of the worksheet, we have **Business Security Policy**. They directly come from the business or service owners. On the center of the worksheet, we have **Technical Policy**; in this case, I have included all available SCW roles and services in this section. The right column, **Comments**, is for mentioning any additional steps or comments required to complete the task.

As an example, you can see a sample internal portal server policy in the following worksheet where I have mapped a **Business Security Policy** to a **Technical Policy**:

Business Security Policy		**Technical Policy**	**Comments**
		Role-Based Service Configuration (SCW)	
It must be a dedicated server for the proposed application. All other non-dependent services must be disabled.		Server role	Review #4 and #5 as well.
Required client features must be running on the server to support the application.		Client features	
Administrators must be able to remotely administer the server, IIS task scheduler, WMI, and log files.		Administration option	
Custom monitoring service (InfraMon) must be enabled and running on all servers.		Additional services	
All unwanted and non-dependent services must be disabled.		Handling unwanted services	

Business Security Policy		Technical Policy	Comments
	Network Security (SCW)		
Only HTTP port 80 and 443 allowed to this server. All other non-dependent ports and services must be disabled.		Network security rules	
	Registry Settings (SCW)		
Client computers must be running Windows 7 or higher to access this application.		SMB security setting	
		LDAP Signing requirement	
Only domain users can access this application.		Outbound Authentication methods	
	Auditing Policy (SCW)		
Successful and failed login attempts must be audited and saved.		System Audit Policy	
	Testing (SCW)		
Solution must be tested and evaluated in the lab before implementing in production.			Test the security policy in the lab using SCW.
	Implementation (GPO)		
Solution must be deployed using an automated mechanism. It must be transparent to the application developers and owners.			Export security policy and GPO and implement it in the correct OU.
	Rollback Plan (GPO)		
Must be able to roll back to previous state if/as needed.			Use GPO.

In the preceding exercise, we had a perfect one-to-one matching between Security Business Policy and SCW options, but in the real world, it may be different. So you may need to modify the policy worksheet based on your requirements. If the options are not available in SCW, you may need to configure it manually using GPO or other mechanisms.

Creating a policy template

In order to generate a policy template, you must be a local administrator on the server. SCW can be run from a local server or from a remote server. If you are running SCW from a remote server, you need to make sure that the required ports and firewall rules are enabled on this remote server. By default, SCW tries to establish an `admin$` share connection to the remote server. Perform the following steps:

1. Open **Server Manager**. You can open **Server Manager** from the status bar, or by typing `Server Manager` in the **Windows Start** screen.
2. From the **Tools** menu, select the **Security Configuration Wizard** option.

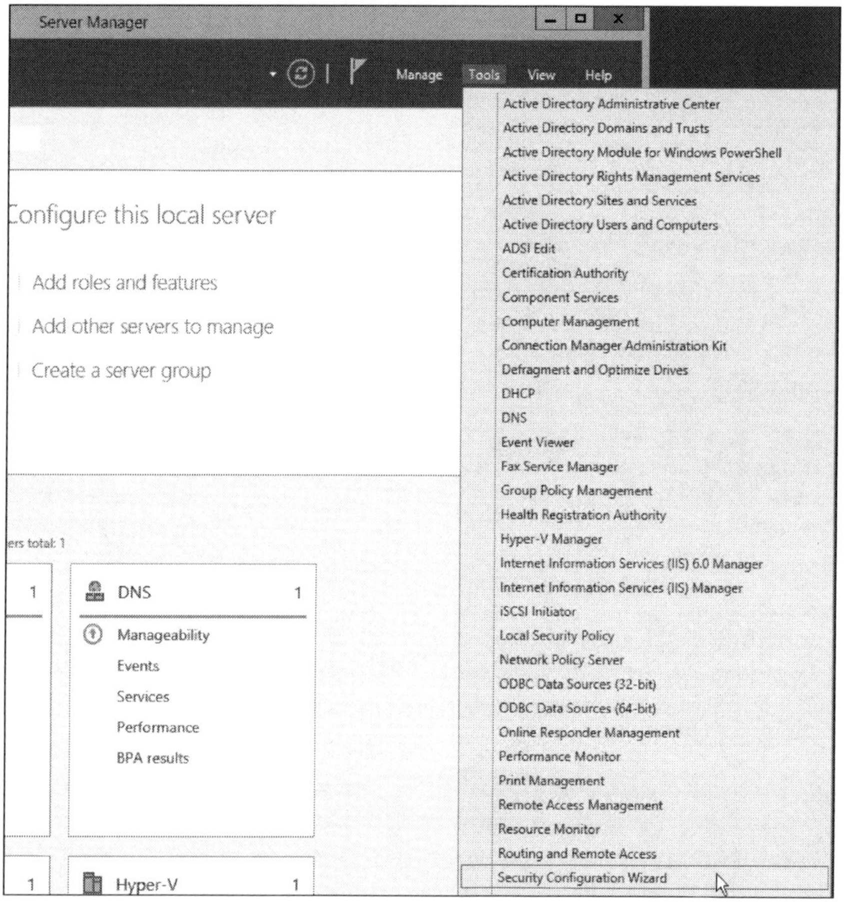

Selecting the Security Confguration Wizard option

3. Click on **Next** on the **Welcome to the Security Configuration Wizard** page.

4. Select the **Create a new security policy** option on the **Configuration Action** page. Click on **Next**.

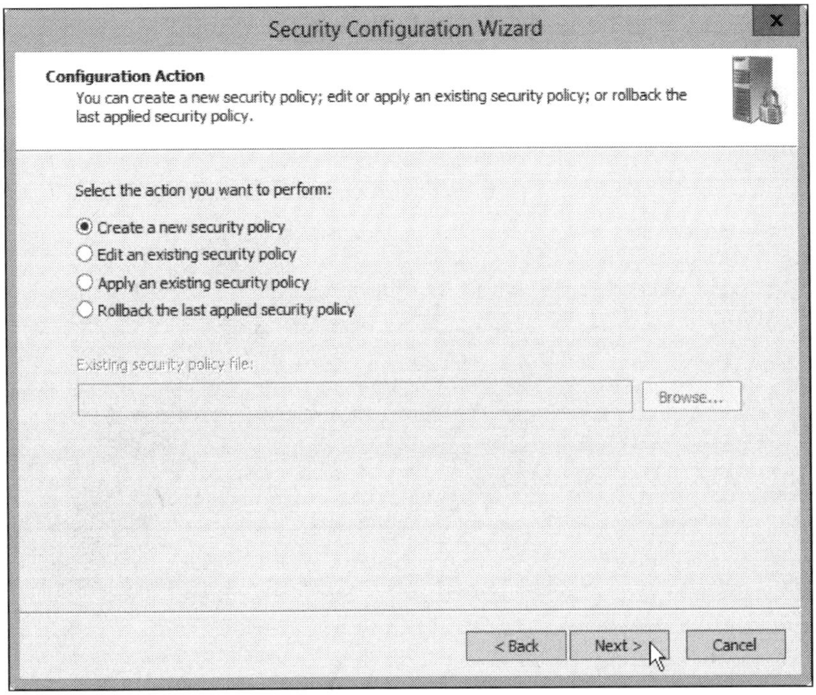

5. On the **Select Server** page, enter the server name in the **Server** textbox, or click on the **Browse** button to search for a server from the **Active Directory**. This server will be used to create a baseline policy based on the roles and features installed on this server.
6. If you specify a remote server, and the current logged-in user does not have local administrative permissions on the remote server, you can specify an alternate account using the **Specify User Account...** option. Click on **Next**.
7. SCW analyzes the remote server and updates the configuration database based on the installed role and features on the selected server. You can see the details by selecting the **View Configuration Database** option from the **Processing Security Configuration Database** page:
    - The **View Configuration Database** option opens the **SCW Viewer** window to display the configuration database.
    - If you see **Windows Security Warning** for the **ActiveX** control, select **Yes** to continue the operation.

- The **Security Configuration Database** option has five different sections—**Server Roles**, **Client Features**, **Administration and Other Options**, **Services**, and **Windows Firewall**. You will be evaluating and modifying these settings based on your business security policy requirement.
- You can safely close the **SCW Viewer** window without interrupting any other tasks.
- Click on **Next** to continue.

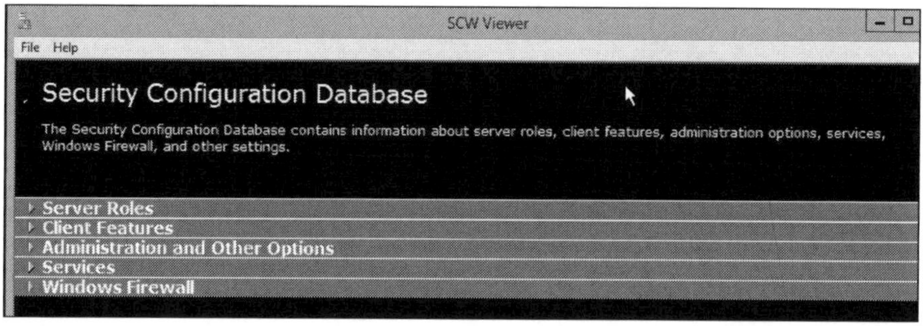

8. Click on **Next** on the **Role-Based Service Configuration** page.
9. In the **Select Server Roles** window:
    - From the **View** drop-down box, you can select **All roles**, **Installed Roles**, **Uninstalled Roles**, or **Select Roles**. Since we are creating a baseline policy based on an install role, we will select **Installed Roles**.

> If the required roles are not installed on the server, you can add these roles from **Server Manager** by selecting the **Add roles and features** option. All required roles must be installed prior to creating a baseline policy.

- You will notice that some of the roles are selected by default. These are some of the required or dependent components for successful creation, implementation, and rollback of these policies.

- Select the appropriate roles here. As an example, I am selecting the **Web Server** role here.
- Click on **Next** to continue.

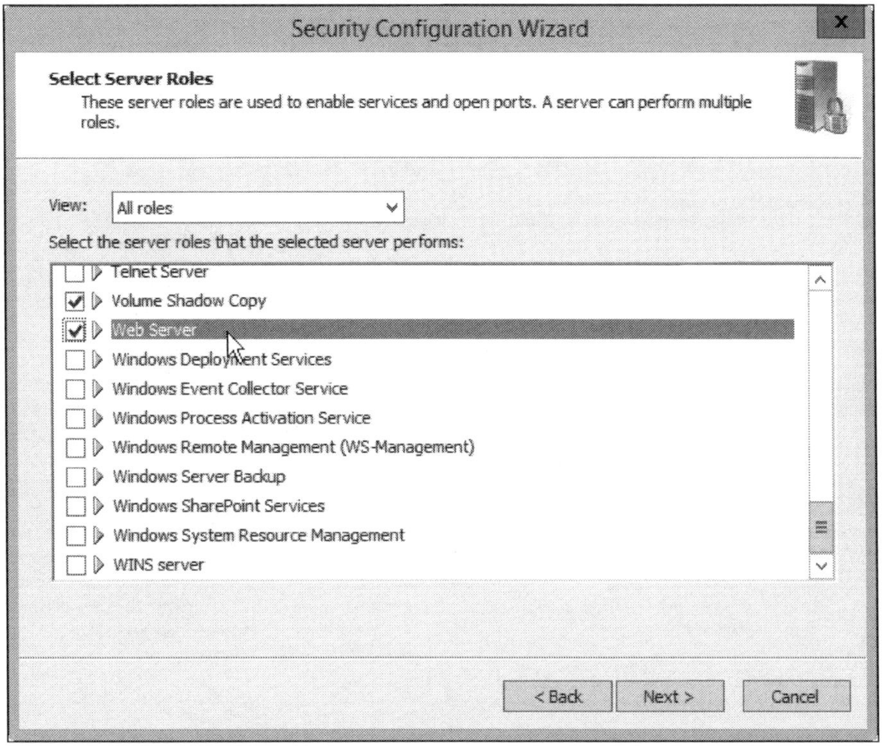

10. On the **Select Client Features** page, select the appropriate client features based on your security requirements. Click on **Next**.
11. On the **Select Administrative and Other Options** page, select the appropriate options based on your security policy requirement. Click on **Next**.

12. As an example, in this exercise, I will be selecting the following administrative options:
    - **Remote Windows Administration**.
    - Also, you will see a few new options based on the selected roles and features on the previous page.
    - Select **Web Server options** from the **View** drop-down menu.

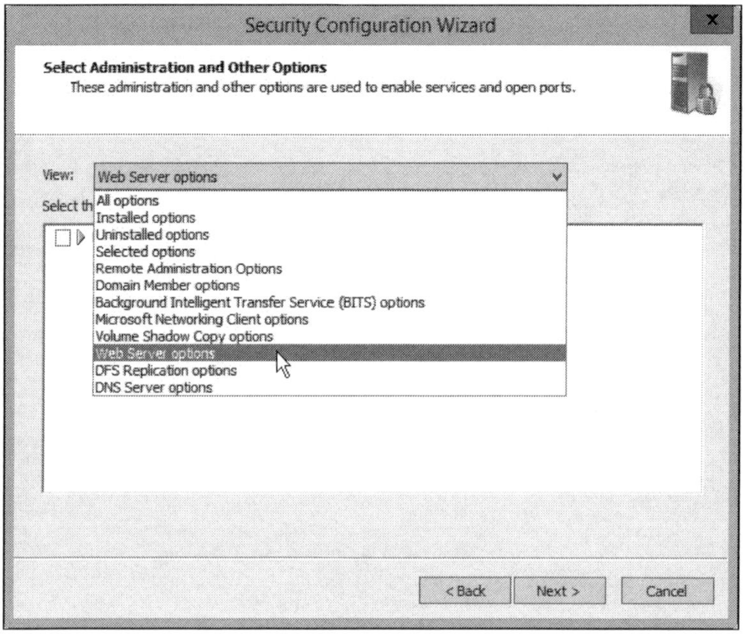

- Here, I am using my worksheet as an example. Based on the requirement, we need to have remote administration enabled. So, I will be selecting the **Remote Administration for Web Server (IIS)** option.

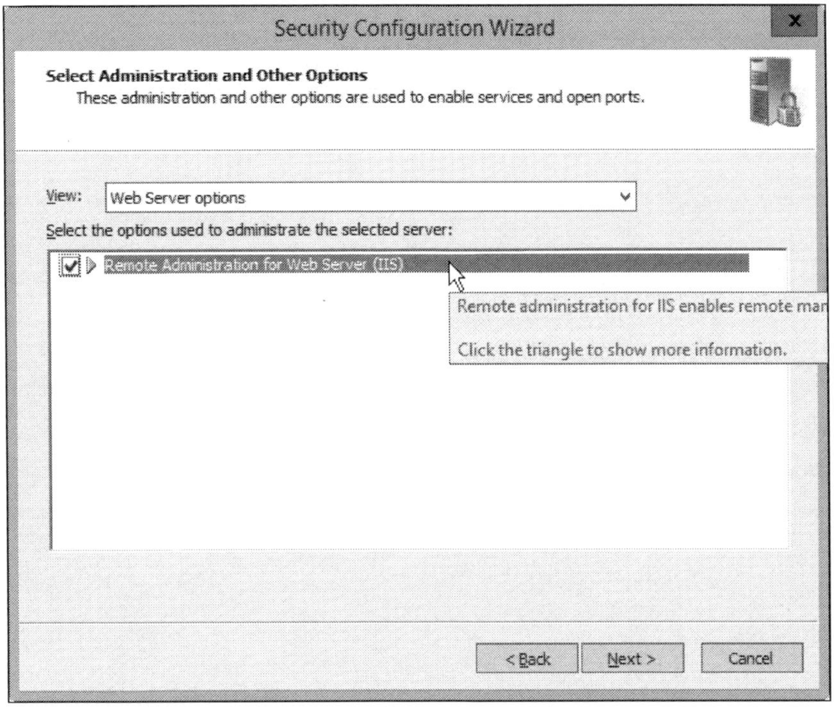
Security Configuration Wizard
Select Administration and Other Options
These administration and other options are used to enable services and open ports.
View:
Web Server options
Select the options used to administrate the selected server:
Remote Administration for Web Server (IIS)
Remote administration for IIS enables remote man
Click the triangle to show more information.
< Back
Next >
Cancel

- Click on **Next.**

13. On the **Select Additional Services** page, select the additional services based on your requirement. According to my security policy requirement, "*A custom monitoring service (InfraMon) must be enabled and running on all servers.*" As shown in the following screenshot, you will have an option to select or deselect additional services from this window. Click on **Next**.

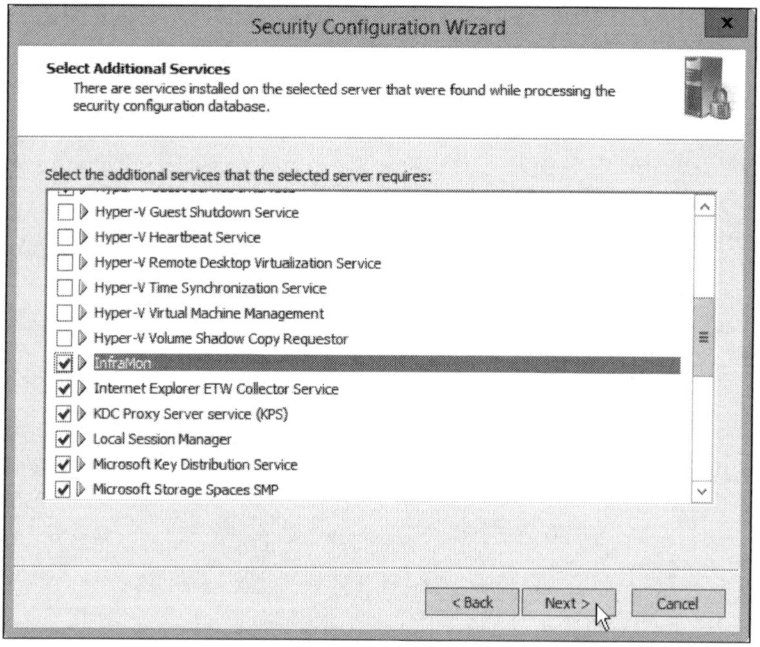

14. On the **Handling Unspecified Service** page, select the appropriate option based on your security policy requirement. Unspecified services are services that are not part of the default configuration database. Since they are unknown to the SCW application, and may be a security threat, you will be presented with the following two options:
    - **Do not change the startup mode of the service**: This will leave the existing startup mode (Automatic, Manual, and so on) of the services intact.
    - **Disable the service**: If you are not sure about the listed service, you can use the **Disable the service** option to disable these types of services at operating system startup.
    - Once you complete the configuration, you can click on **Next** to proceed to the next step in the process.

15. You can confirm these settings on the **Confirm Service Changes** window. Click on **Next.**
16. Click on **Next** to continue with network security configuration, from the **Network Security** window. If you do not have a network security requirement, you can skip this configuration using the **Skip this section** option.
17. In the **Network Security Rules** window, select the appropriate firewall rules. For example, if you need to modify the HTTP traffic rule, you can:
    - Select the **World Wide Web Services (HTTB Traffic-In)** rule.
    - Select **Edit** to edit an existing policy or **Add** to add a custom policy.

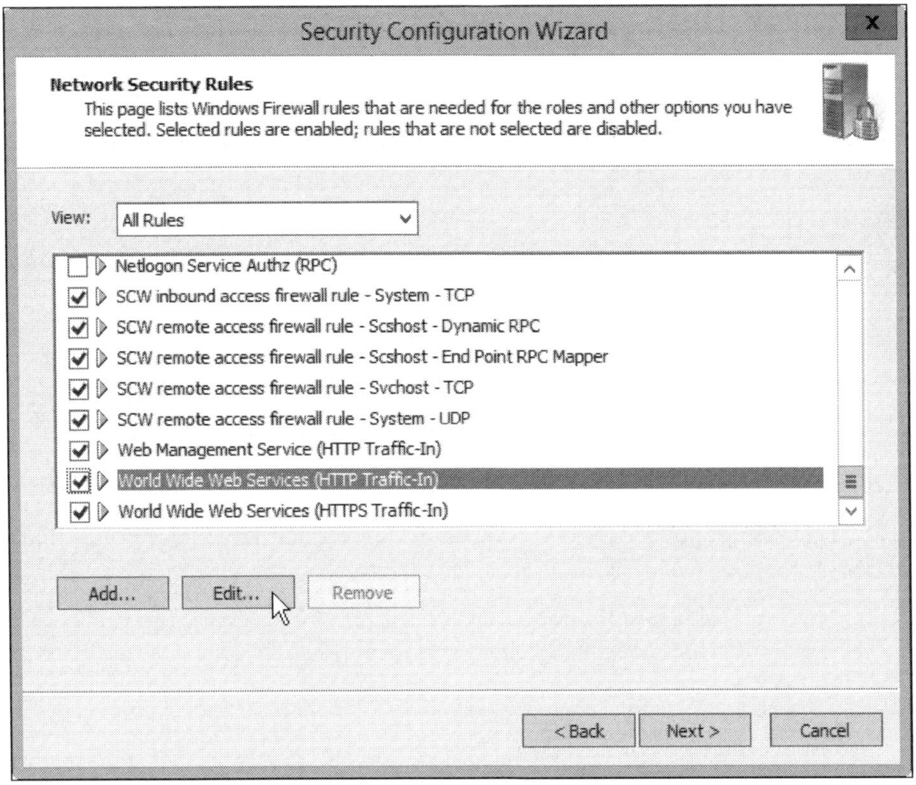

18. On the **Add** or **Edit** rule window, you have the following tabs:
    - **Program and Services**: Enable or disable services and programs
    - **Protocols and Ports**: Enable or disable ports and protocols
    - **Scope**: Restrict IP address traffic based on selected IP address range

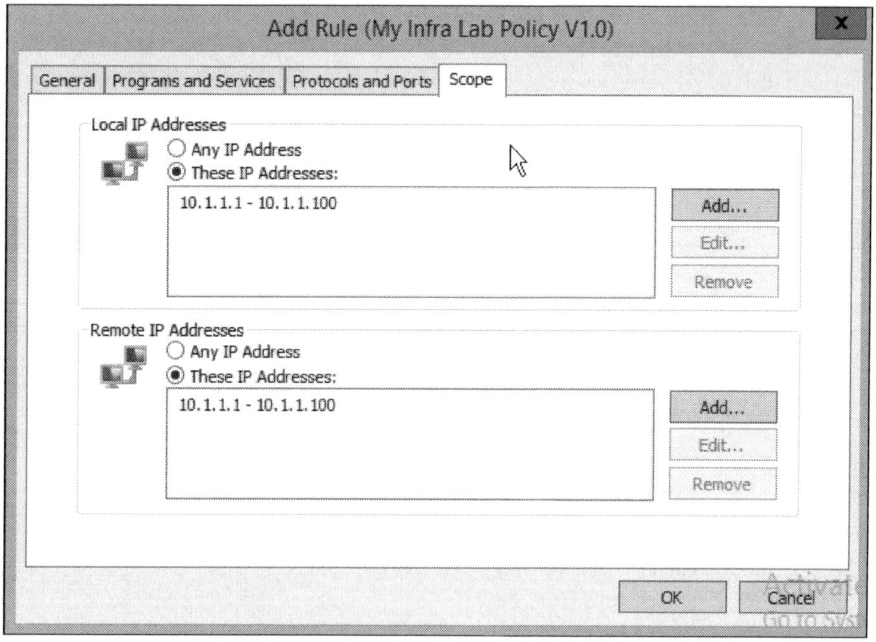

    - Click on **Next**.

19. Click on **Next** to continue with registry security configuration, from the **Registry Security** window.
20. If you don't have a registry security requirement, you can skip this configuration using the **Skip this section** option.

21. On the **Require SMB Security Signatures** page, select the appropriate options based on your security policy requirement.

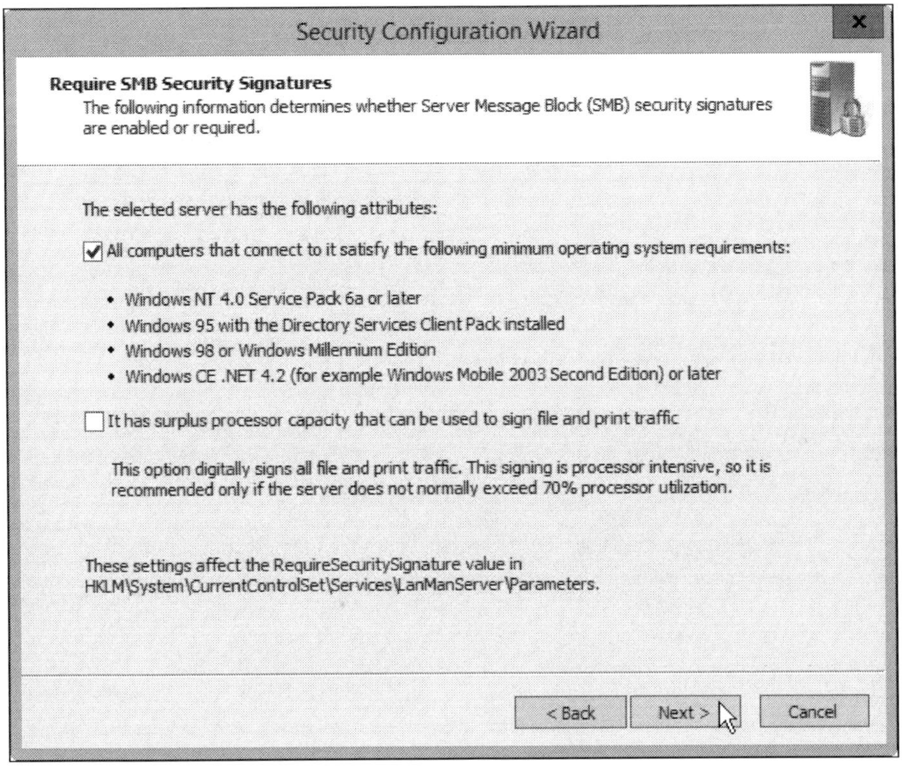
Security Configuration Wizard
Require SMB Security Signatures
The following information determines whether Server Message Block (SMB) security signatures are enabled or required.
The selected server has the following attributes:
All computers that connect to it satisfy the following minimum operating system requirements:
Windows NT 4.0 Service Pack 6a or later
Windows 95 with the Directory Services Client Pack installed
Windows 98 or Windows Millennium Edition
Windows CE .NET 4.2 (for example Windows Mobile 2003 Second Edition) or later
It has surplus processor capacity that can be used to sign file and print traffic
This option digitally signs all file and print traffic. This signing is processor intensive, so it is recommended only if the server does not normally exceed 70% processor utilization.
These settings affect the RequireSecuritySignature value in HKLM\System\CurrentControlSet\Services\LanManServer\Parameters.
< Back
Next >
Cancel

22. Click on **Next**

23. On the **Outbound Authentication Methods** page, select the appropriate options. Click on **Next**.

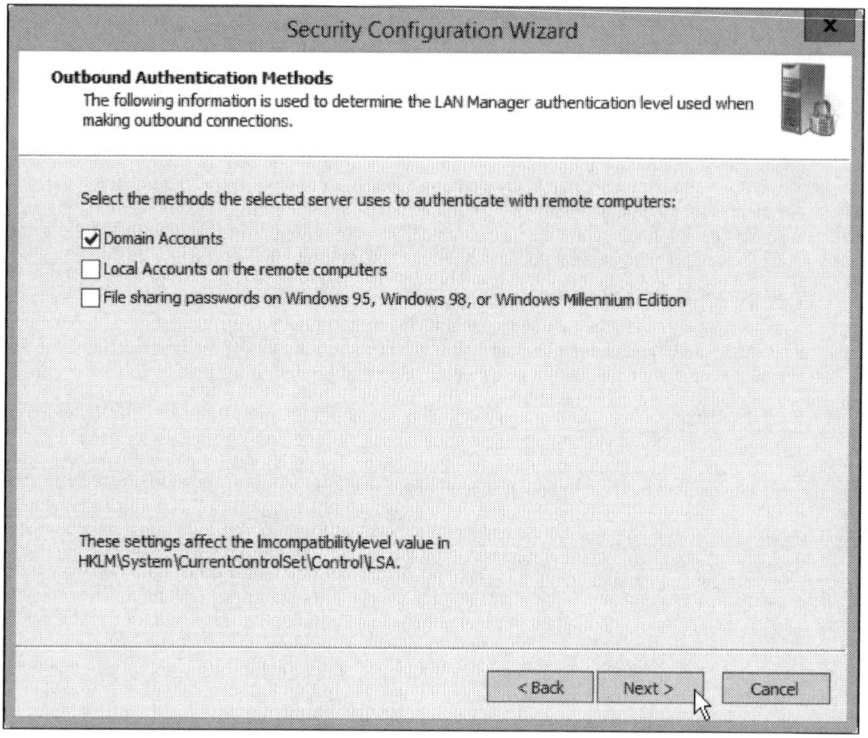
Security Configuration Wizard
Outbound Authentication Methods
The following information is used to determine the LAN Manager authentication level used when making outbound connections.
Select the methods the selected server uses to authenticate with remote computers:
Domain Accounts
Local Accounts on the remote computers
File sharing passwords on Windows 95, Windows 98, or Windows Millennium Edition
These settings affect the lmcompatibilitylevel value in HKLM\System\CurrentControlSet\Control\LSA.
< Back
Next >
Cancel

24. On the **Outbound Authentication using Domain Account** page, select the appropriate options based on your security requirement. The following are the available options:
    - **Windows NT 4.0 Service Pack 6a or later operating system**
    - **Clock that is synchronized with the select server's clock**

25. Click on **Next**.

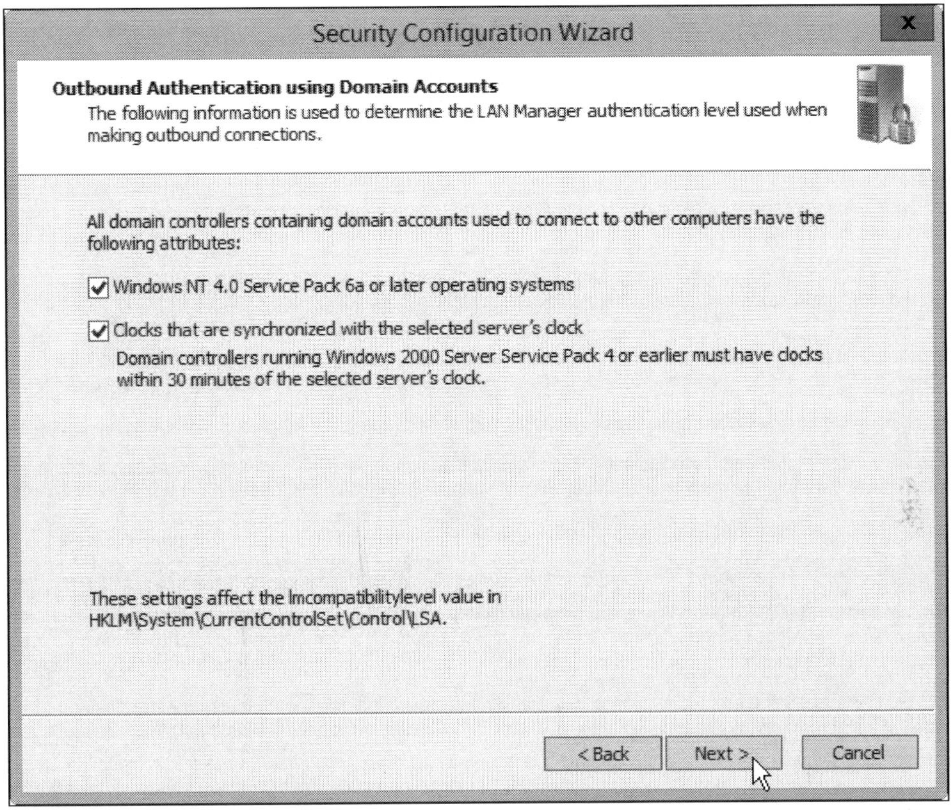
Security Configuration Wizard
Outbound Authentication using Domain Accounts
The following information is used to determine the LAN Manager authentication level used when making outbound connections.
All domain controllers containing domain accounts used to connect to other computers have the following attributes:
Windows NT 4.0 Service Pack 6a or later operating systems
Clocks that are synchronized with the selected server's clock
Domain controllers running Windows 2000 Server Service Pack 4 or earlier must have clocks within 30 minutes of the selected server's clock.
These settings affect the lmcompatibilitylevel value in HKLM\System\CurrentControlSet\Control\LSA.
< Back
Next >
Cancel

26. On the **Registry Setting Summary** page, review the selected settings and click on **Next** to continue.

27. Select **Next** to continue with audit policy configuration from the **Audit Policy** window:
    - If you don't have auditing requirements, you can skip this configuration using the **Skip this section** option, or you can configure the auditing by selecting the options from the **System Audit Policy** page. As an example, I will be selecting the **Audit successful and unsuccessful activities** option.
    - Click on **Next**.

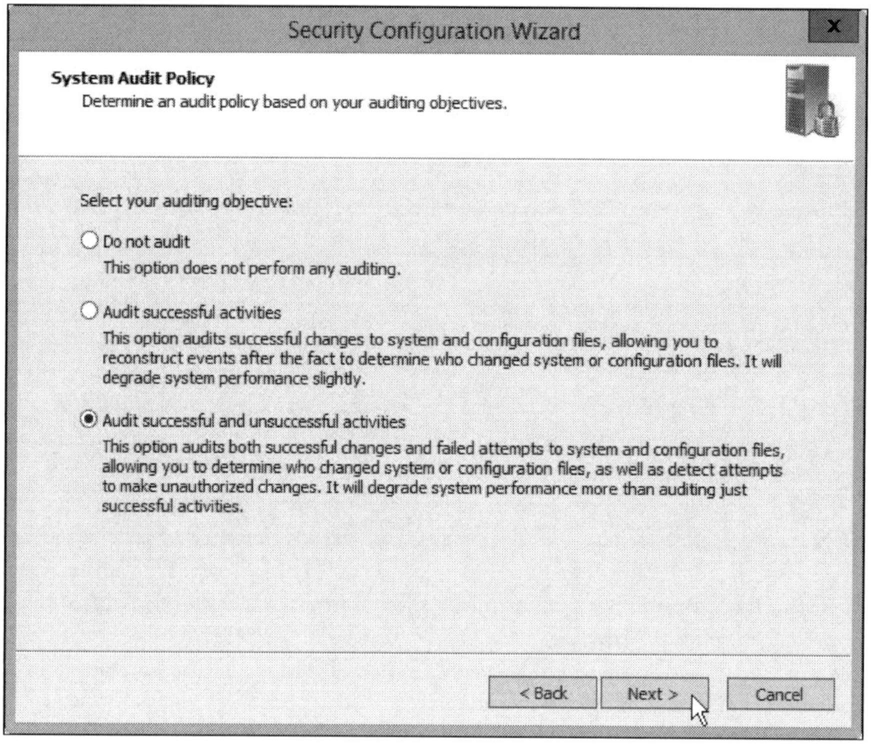
Security Configuration Wizard
System Audit Policy
Determine an audit policy based on your auditing objectives.
Select your auditing objective:
Do not audit
This option does not perform any auditing.
Audit successful activities
This option audits successful changes to system and configuration files, allowing you to reconstruct events after the fact to determine who changed system or configuration files. It will degrade system performance slightly.
Audit successful and unsuccessful activities
This option audits both successful changes and failed attempts to system and configuration files, allowing you to determine who changed system or configuration files, as well as detect attempts to make unauthorized changes. It will degrade system performance more than auditing just successful activities.
< Back
Next >
Cancel

28. On the **Audit Policy Summary** page, review the selected settings and click on **Next** to continue.
29. Click on **Next** on the **Save Security Policy** page.
30. On the **Security Policy File Name** page, enter the **Name** and **Description** values for the policy. Click on **Next**.

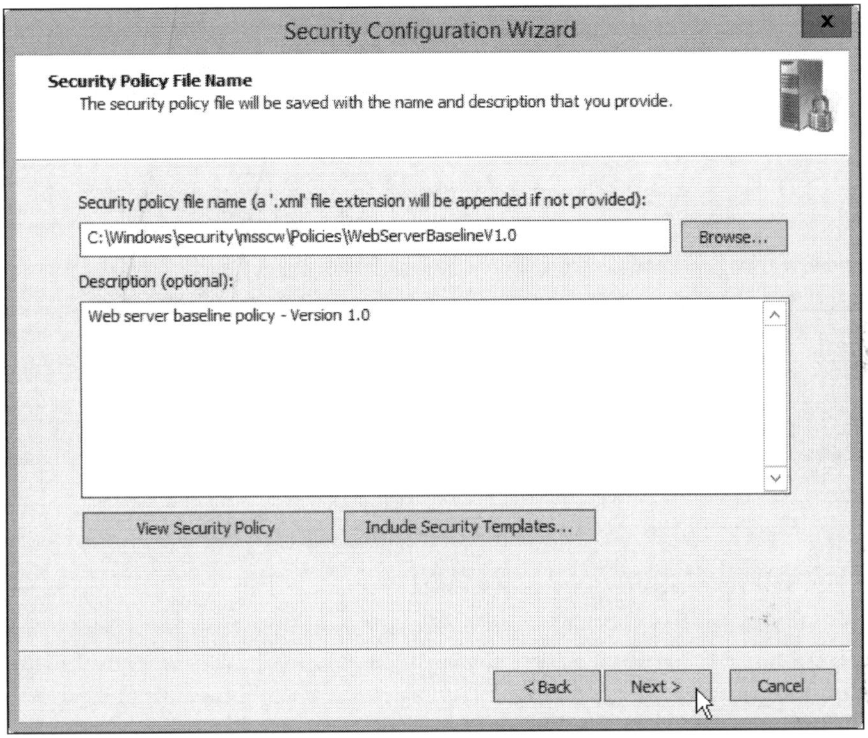

31. Select the **Apply Later** option on the **Apply Security Policy** page.

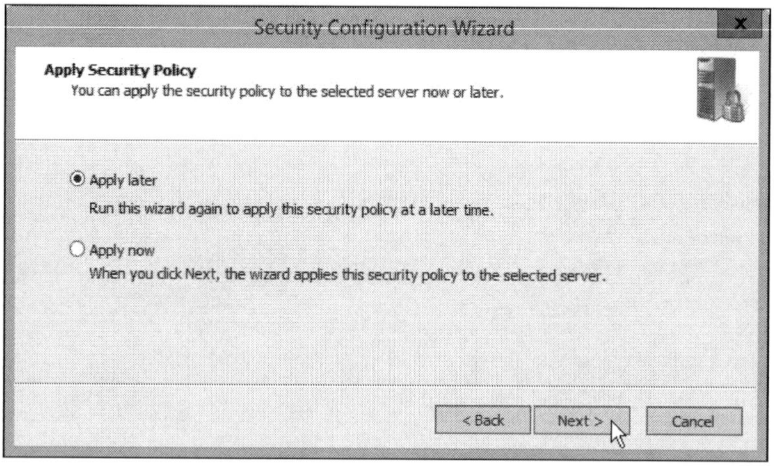
Security Configuration Wizard
Apply Security Policy
You can apply the security policy to the selected server now or later.
Apply later
Run this wizard again to apply this security policy at a later time.
Apply now
When you click Next, the wizard applies this security policy to the selected server.
< Back
Next >
Cancel

32. Click on **Finish** on the **Completing the Security Configuration Wizard** page.

> By default, all the polices will be saved in the `%Systemroot%\Security\MSSCW\Policies` folder.

Policy review and validation

At this point, you have created a baseline security template based on your business security requirement. As always, it is a best practice to evaluate these configurations in an isolated lab environment before it is implemented in the production environment.

Microsoft SCW creates an XML file as an output policy file, which can be reviewed by using any XML reader. Microsoft has provided a command-line supplement SCW tool called **SCWCMD** to accomplish this. SCWCMD is a powerful tool that can support the following actions:

- **SCWCMD analyze**: Analyzes the computer based on your security policy
- **SCWCMD configure**: Applies SCW security to a computer
- **SCWCMD register**: This updates the SCW database based on your custom roles and features

- **SCWCMD rollback**: This will roll back the policies from the previously applied computer
- **SCWCMD transform**: This converts an SCW-generated policy to a GPO-based policy
- **SCWCMD view**: This views the existing SCW policy

We will be using the SCWCMD tool with view option for our policy review and validation process:

- From the command prompt, enter the following command:

```
SCWCMD view /x:WebServerBaseLineV1.0.xml
```

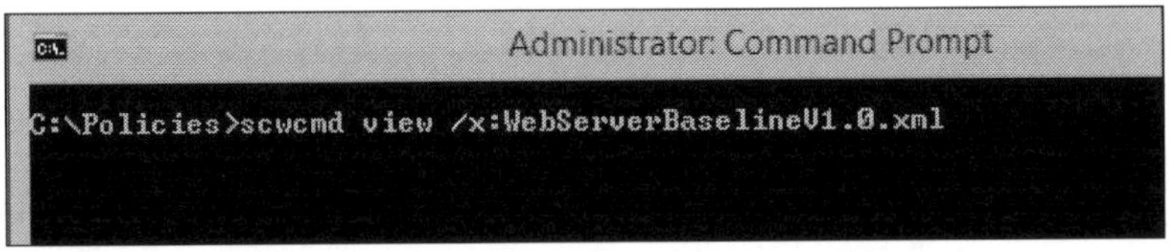

- It will open **SCW Viewer**. Click on **Yes** to access **Windows Security Warning**. You should be able to review the policy settings from **SCW Viewer**.

Once you have verified the settings, you can apply it to one server to evaluate the result. We will be using Security Configuration Wizard (**SCW**) to achieve this:

1. Open **Security Configuration Wizard (SCW)** from **Server Manager**.
2. Click on **Next** in the **Welcome** window.
3. In the **Configuration Action** window, select the **Apply an existing security policy** option.
4. In the **Existing security policy file** window, select the previously created policy file.

5. Click on **Next**.

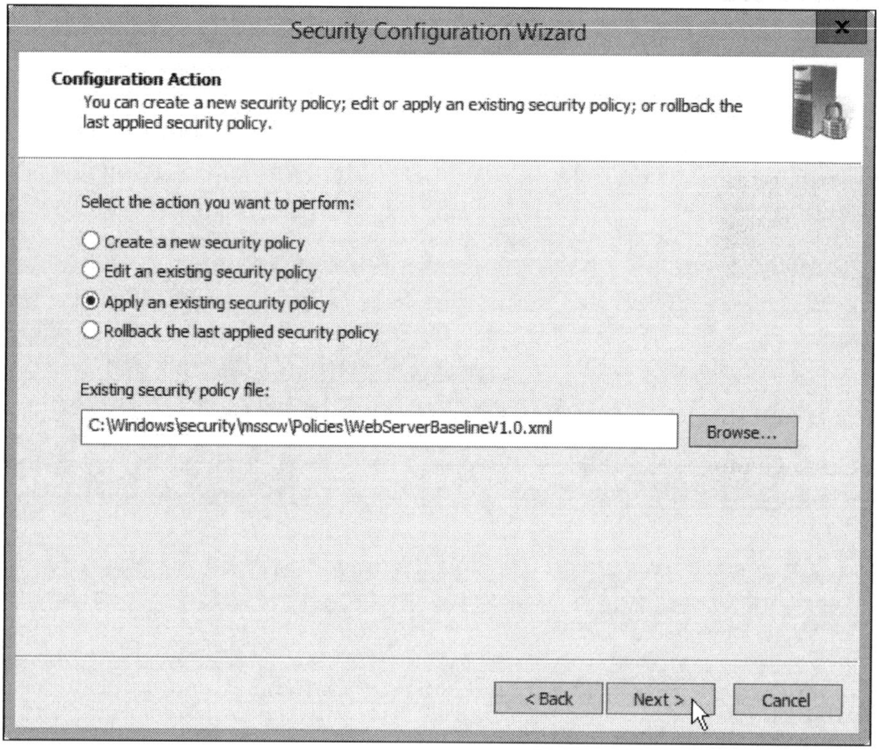

6. In the **Select Server** window, select the correct destination server. Click on **Next.**
7. You can view the policy detail in the **Apply Security Policy** window. Click on **Next** to continue.

At this point, as an administrator, your job is to validate and verify the result. Once you are satisfied with the result, you can move to the production implementation.

Policy implementation

Applying a policy using Microsoft SCW is suitable for a small environment or testing purposes. However, in an enterprise environment, it may not be sufficient. Some type of automated mechanism should be in place. Since Microsoft **Group Policy Object** (**GPO**) is a commonly used tool in any environment, we can use GPO to deploy these security configurations into the designated servers. Since Microsoft SCW and Microsoft GPO are not directly connected, the first step in the process is to export output of the SCW XML file into the GPO format, and then import this into Active Directory.

In our scenario, we will be using the **SCWCMD Transform** command with the syntax scwcmd transform /p:<SCWPolicy.xml> /g:<GPOName>:

1. Open the command line from your Windows Server 2012 server.
2. Type scwcmd transform /p:WebServerBaseLineV1.0.XML /g:WebServerBaselineV1.0 and press *Enter*.

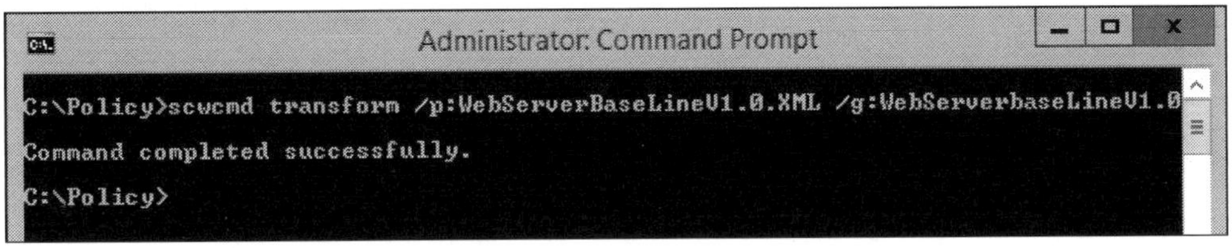

3. This will convert and export the policy into Active Directory.
4. Open **Group Policy Manager Console**. You can open it from **Server Manager** or type Group Policy Manager on the start screen.
5. Expand your **Domain**, **Domain Name**, and then **Group Policy Objects** nodes. The exported policy will be in the **Group Policy Objects** node.
6. The GPO configuration can be verified by evaluating the policies in the **Settings** tab.

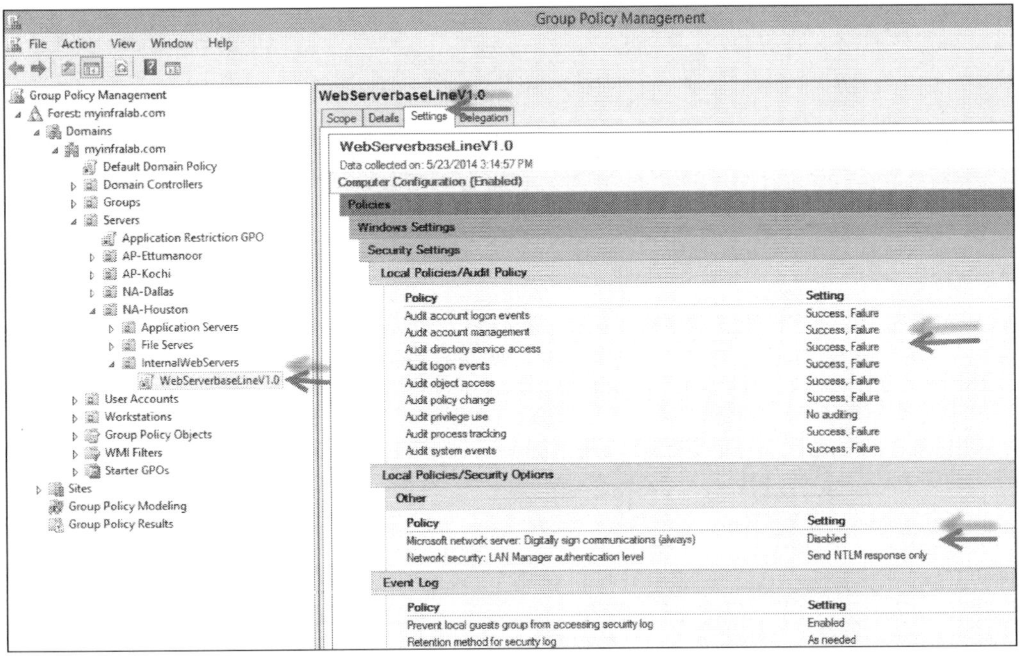

7. Once you are satisfied with the policy, it can be deployed (linked) to an existing **Organizational Unit** (**OU**). In this scenario, we will be linking it to an OU called **InternalWebServers**.

> Keep in mind that the `SCWCMD Trasnform` command will only export the polices into Active Directory. You need to manually link these GPO, using **Group Policy Administration** console.

8. Locate the correct OU by expanding the top level OU. In this scenario, I will be selecting the **InternalWebServers** OU.
9. Right-click on the **InternalWebServers** OU and select the **Link an Existing GPO** option.

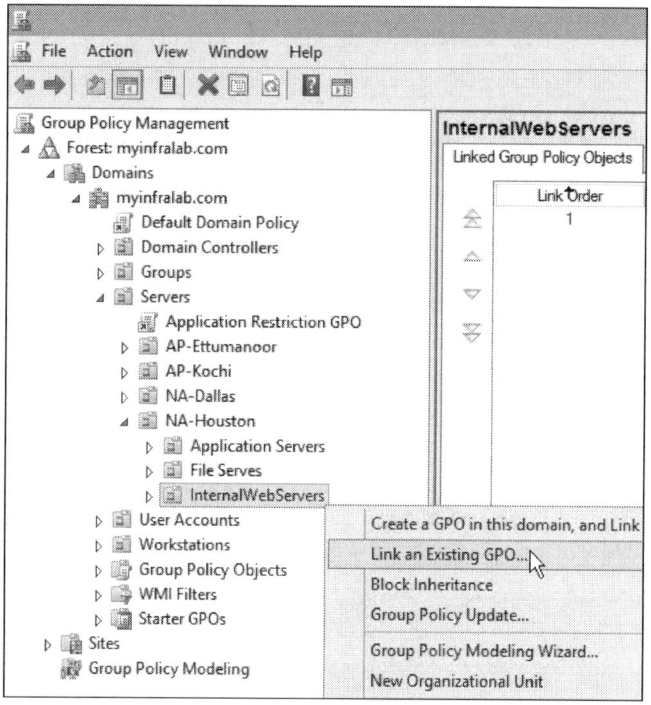

10. Select the **WebServerBaseLiveV1.0** GPO from the **Select GPO** window. Click on **OK**.
11. This will link the existing GPO to this OU and all severs inside this OU will automatically receive the policy.

> The GPO will get updated on to these computers during the default GPO interval. However, you can force the update manually by using the `GPUpdate/Force` command, or by selecting the **Group Policy Update** option from the GPMC console.

Analyzing the result and troubleshooting

The **SCWCMD** tool provides an option to troubleshoot the computers so as to ensure that these computers are in compliance with your security policy. We will be using the `SCWCMD Analyze` option to analyze a computer's existing policy against an implemented policy. We can use this command against any computer regardless of whether you have used SCW or GPO to implement these policies. The result will be saved in an XML file in the working directory, unless you have specified a different path. These files can be viewed using the `SCWCMD View` option.

Here, I am running the `SCWCMD Analyze` command against a non-hardening server to demonstrate the result:

1. From the command prompt, enter the `SCWCMD Analyze /m:Server02 /p:WebServerBaseLineV1.0.XML` command.

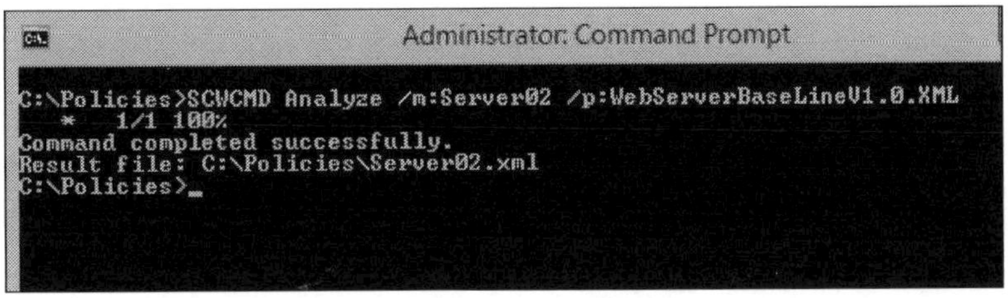

2. The output will be saved in the same directory and the default filename will be the server name. In this scenario, it will be called `Server02.XML`.
3. The `SCWCMD view` command can be used to view this file. This command will open the result file in **SCW Viewer**.
4. From the command prompt, enter `SCWCMD View /x:Server02.XML`.
5. If you receive an **Active X Windows Security Warning**, click on **Yes** to continue.

6. Depending on the policy and configuration of the server, you will see different listings such as **Misconfigured Services**, **Rules are not on the system**, and the like on the **Security Configuration Wizard Analysis Results** window.

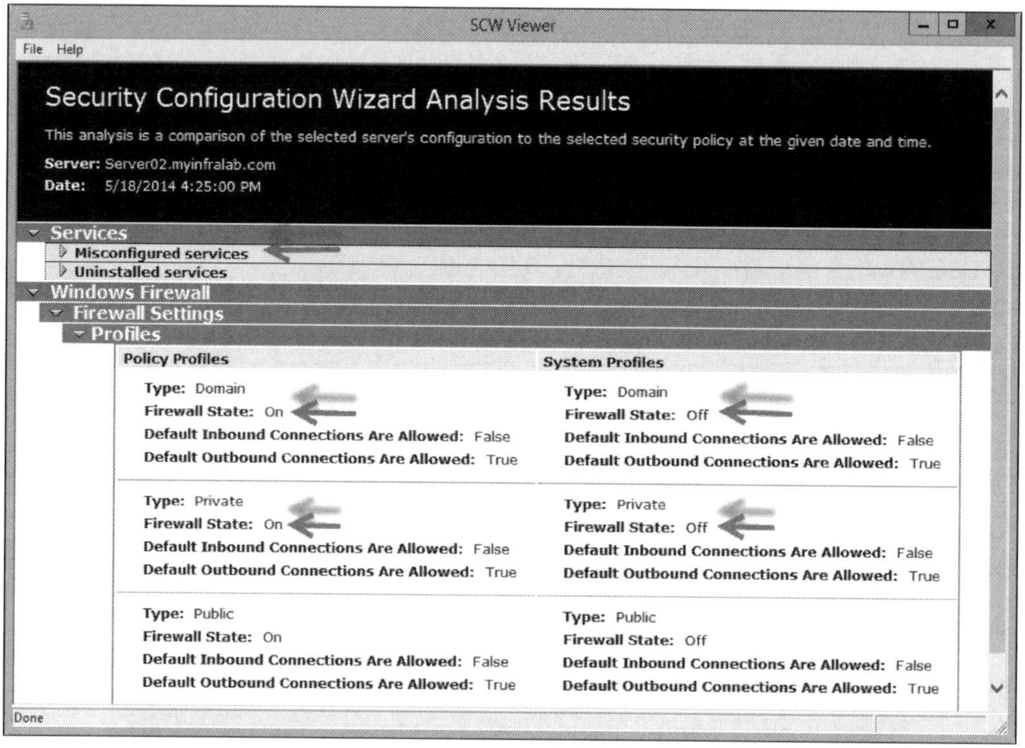

A backup or rollback plan

A backup or rollback plan is important for any business. Microsoft SCW provides an easy method to revert the changes to its previous state. During the policy implementation, SCW will create the rollback files on the local server with the current configuration. These are XML files and are located in `%systemdir%\security\msscw\rollbackfiles folder`.

> Rollback files are located on the local server itself.

If the rollback files are not available in the default folder, you will receive the following error message during the server selection:

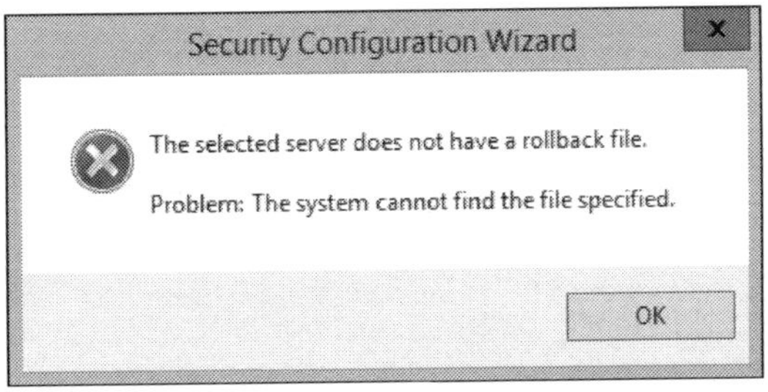
Security Configuration Wizard
The selected server does not have a rollback file.
Problem: The system cannot find the file specified.
OK

Once you perform the rollback operation, the XML files get deleted from the `rollbackfiles` folder. So, if you want to keep a record of these policies and settings, you will need to back up these files before performing the rollback operation.

> Microsoft SCW can only roll back the changes that have been applied by the SCW tool. If you use any other mechanisms like GPO, SCW won't be able to revert these changes.

If you use GPO to implement the policy, you can move these servers to a different OU to avoid applying these policies. Keep in mind that some policies are tattooed into the system. In that case, you need to create another GPO to revert these changes.

The following instructions provide the details of a rollback method using SCW"

1. Open **Security Configuration Wizard** from **Server Manager**.
2. Click on **Next** in the **Welcome** window.

3. From the **Configuration Action** window, select the **Rollback the last applied security policy** option. Click on **Next**.

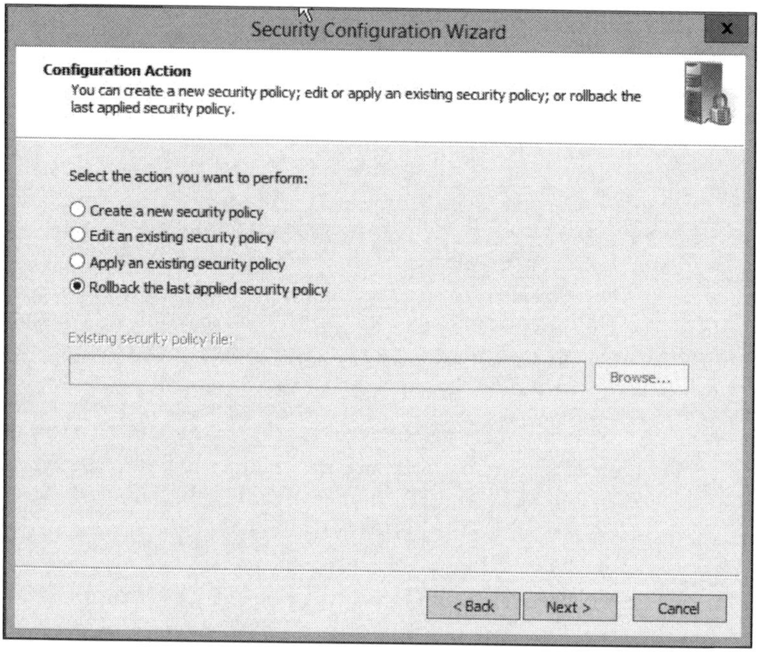

4. In the **Select Server** window, select the appropriate server name. Click on **Next.**

5. In the **Rollback Security Configuration** window, you can click on **View Rollback File** to verify the rollback details. It will open **SCW Viewer**. Click on **Next** to continue with the rollback operation.

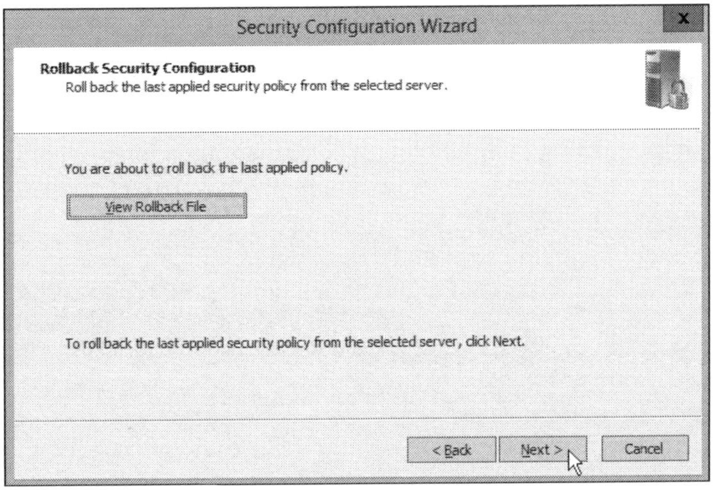
Security Configuration Wizard
Rollback Security Configuration
Roll back the last applied security policy from the selected server.
You are about to roll back the last applied policy.
View Rollback File
To roll back the last applied security policy from the selected server, click Next.
< Back
Next >
Cancel

6. You will see the status and progress in the next screen. Click on **Next**.
7. Click on **Finish** on the **Completing the Security Configuration Wizard** screen to complete the rollback operation.

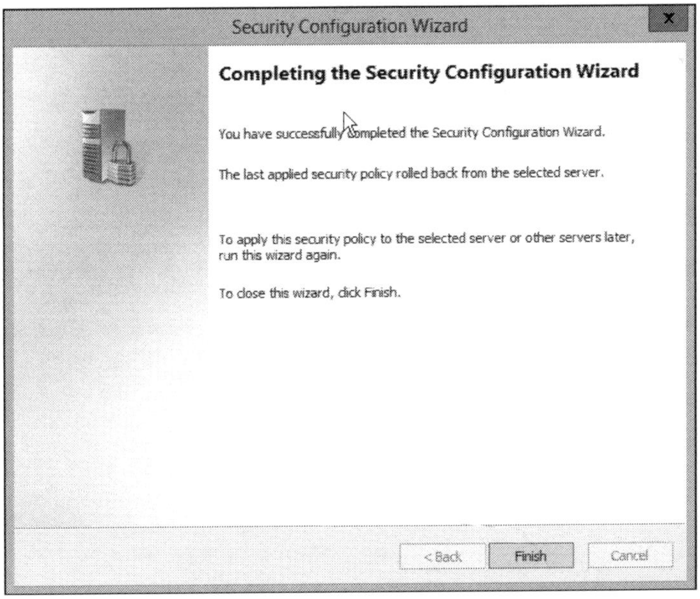
Security Configuration Wizard
Completing the Security Configuration Wizard
You have successfully completed the Security Configuration Wizard.
The last applied security policy rolled back from the selected server.
To apply this security policy to the selected server or other servers later, run this wizard again.
To close this wizard, click Finish.
< Back
Finish
Cancel

Summary

The focus of this chapter was to provide a method to implement a baseline server security policy based on your business requirement. I believe we have achieved this by using Microsoft Security Configuration Wizard (SCW). Once you have established a server platform security, you have to implement other aspects of security like application restriction, security to minimize server exploitation, and so on. Also, it is critical to have a management and administration method to maintain and monitor these polices. In the coming chapters, I will be explaining a few tools to accomplish these tasks.

2
Native MS Security Tools and Configuration

In *Chapter 1, Operating System and Baseline Security*, we talked about baseline security and creating a baseline security template using **Microsoft Security Configuration Wizard (SCW)**. In this chapter, I will introduce another powerful Microsoft tool called **Microsoft Security Compliance Manager (SCM)**. As its name suggests, it is a platform for managing and maintaining your security and compliance polices.

At this point, we have established baseline security based on your business requirement, using Microsoft SCW. These polices can be a pure reflection of your business requirements. However, in an enterprise world, you have to consider compliance, regulations, other industry standards, and best practices to maximize the effectiveness of the security policy. That's where Microsoft SCM can provide more business value. We will talk more about the included SCM baselines later in the chapter.

The goal of the chapter is to walk you through the configuration and administration process of Microsoft SCM and explain how it can be used in an enterprise environment to support your security needs. Then we will talk about a method to maintain the desired state of the server using a Microsoft tool called **Attack Surface Analyzer (ASA)**. At the end of the chapter, you will see an option to add more security restrictions using another Microsoft tool called **AppLocker**.

Microsoft SCM

Microsoft SCM is a centralized security and compliance policy manager product from Microsoft. It is a standalone application. Microsoft develops these baselines and best practice recommendations based on customer feedback and other agency's recommendations—I have mentioned a few of these in *Chapter 1, Operating System and Baseline Security*. These polices are consistently reviewed and updated. So, it is important that you are using the latest policy baseline. If there is a new policy, you will be able to download and update the baseline from the Microsoft SCM console itself. Since Microsoft SCM supports multiple input and output formats such as XML, **Group Policy Objects** (**GPO**), **Desired Configuration Management** (**DCM**), **Security Content Automation Protocol** (**SCAP**), and so on, it can be a centralized platform for your network infrastructure and other security and compliance products. It is also possible to integrate SCM with **Microsoft System Center 2012 Process Pack for IT GRC**. More details can be found at `http://technet.microsoft.com/en-us/library/dd206732.aspx`. Since the focus of this book is around Windows Server security, we will be focusing only on the security policies. We will not be covering the compliance portion of the Microsoft SCM tool.

Installing Microsoft SCM

We will start with the installation process. As mentioned earlier, it is a standalone product. It uses Microsoft SQL Server 2008 or higher as the database. If you don't have a SQL database already installed on your system, the SCM installation process will automatically install Microsoft SQL Server 2008 Express Edition. You can perform the following steps to install Microsoft SCM:

1. Download **Microsoft Security Compliance Manager** from `http://www.microsoft.com/en-us/download/details.aspx?id=16776`.
2. Double-click on **Security_Compliance_Manager_Setup.exe** to start the installation process.
3. Click on **Next** on the welcome window. Make sure to select the **Always check for SCM and baseline updates** option.
4. Accept the **License Agreement** option and click on **Next**.
5. Select the installation folder from the **Installation Folder** window by clicking on the **Browse** button. Click on **Next**.
6. On the **Microsoft SQL Server 2008 Express** window, click on **Next** to install Microsoft SQL Server 2008 Express Edition. If you have Microsoft SQL Server already installed on your system, you can select the correct server details from this window.

7. Accept the **License Agreement** option for SQL Server 2008 Express and click on **Next**.
8. Click on **Install** on the **Ready to Install** window to begin the installation.
9. You will see the progress in the **Installing the Microsoft Security Compliance Manager** window. If it asks you to restart the computer, click on **OK**.
10. Click on **Finish** to complete the installation.

This section provides a high level overview of the product before starting the administration and management process. The left pane of the SCM console provides the list of all available baselines. This is the baseline library inside SCM. The center pane displays more information based on your policy section from the baseline library. The right pane, also called the Actions pane, provides commands and options to manage your policies.

As you can see in the following screenshot, it provides a few options to export these policies into different formats. So, if you have a different compliance manager tool, you can use these files with your existing tool.

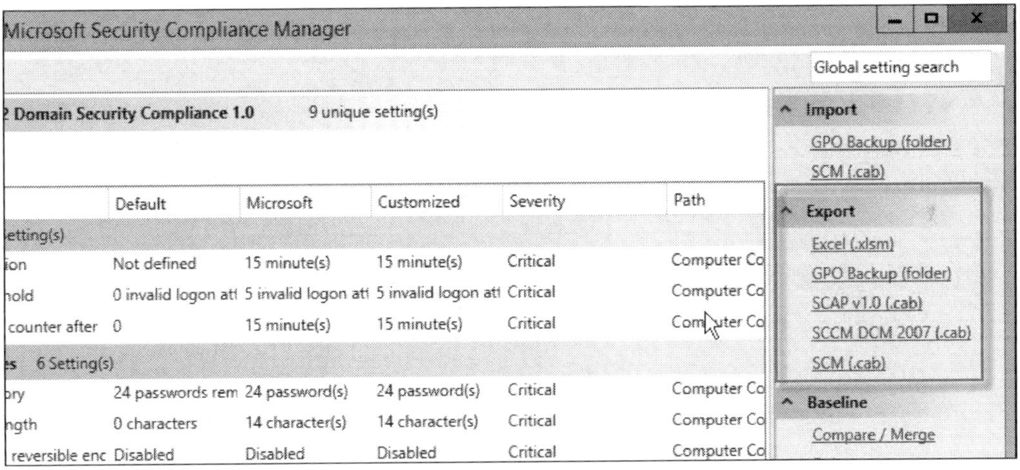

SCM – Export options

In compliance with other products, Microsoft SCM supports different severity levels—critical, optional, important, and none. As you can see in the following screenshot, on a custom policy, the severity levels can be changed to **None**, **Important**, **Optional**, or **Critical** based on your requirements:

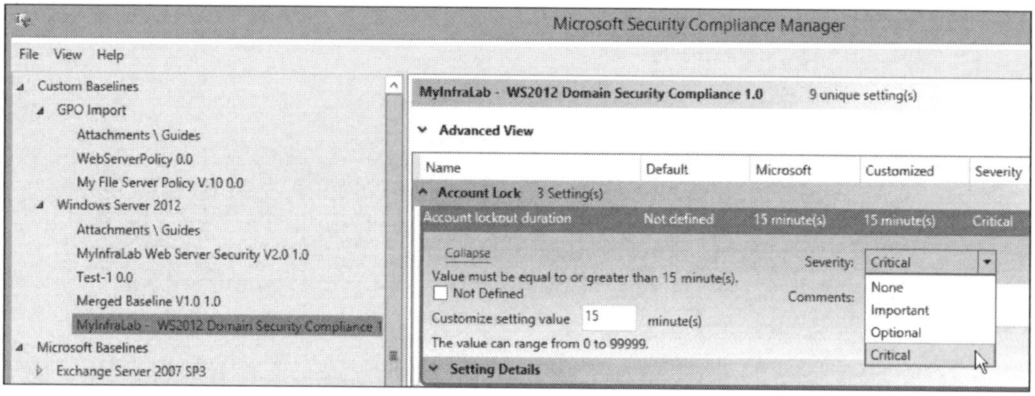

For each of these events, you will see additional details and reference articles (**CCE**, **OVAL**, and so on) in the **Setting Details** section.

Administering Microsoft SCM

This section provides you with an overview of Microsoft SCM and some administration procedures to create and manage policies. These tasks can be achieved by performing the following steps:

1. Open **Security Compliance Manager**. If you see a **Download Updates** popup window, click on the **Download** button to start the download and complete the database update process.
2. **Security Compliance Manager** consists of mainly two sections: **Custom Baselines** and **Microsoft Baselines**. We will go through the details later in this chapter.

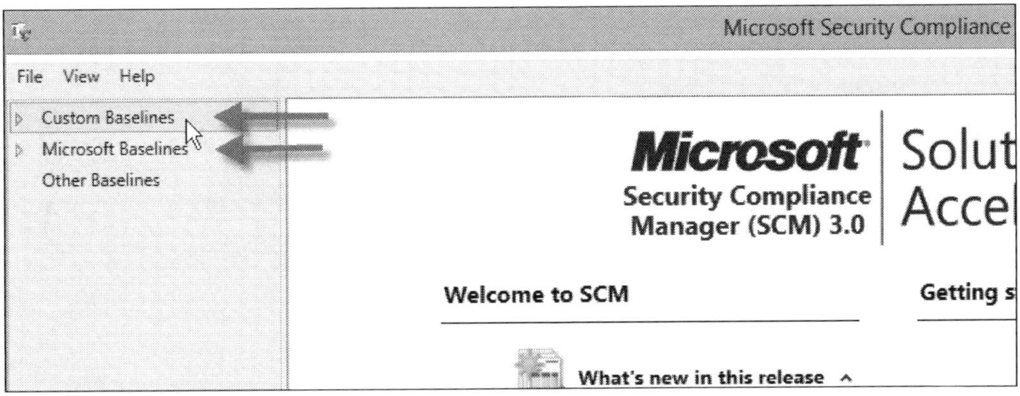

SCM - Baselines

3. Expand **Microsoft Baselines**. Since we are focusing more on Windows Server 2012, I will start with this section.
4. Select the **Windows Server 2012** node. This node contains predefined security polices based on Microsoft and industry best practices.

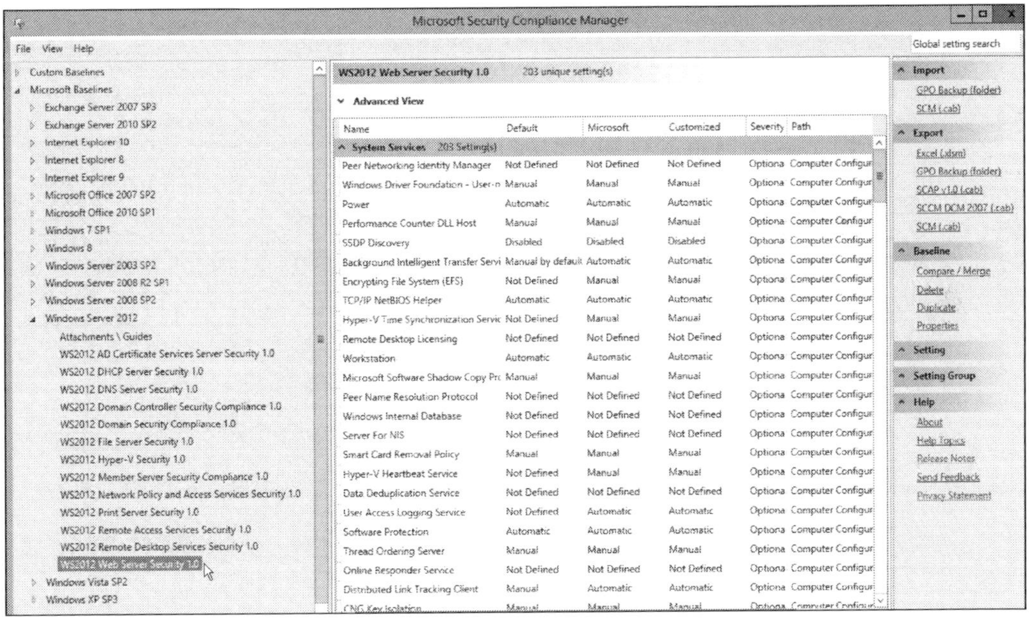

5. Since we worked on a web server policy in *Chapter 1*, *Operating System and Baseline Security*, I will use the predefined **WS2012 Web Server Security** template for this exercise.

> You will not be able to make changes to the settings in the default template. If you need to make changes, you can make a copy of the template and make changes there.

6. Select the **WS2012 Web Server Security** template. From the right pane, select the **Duplicate** option.

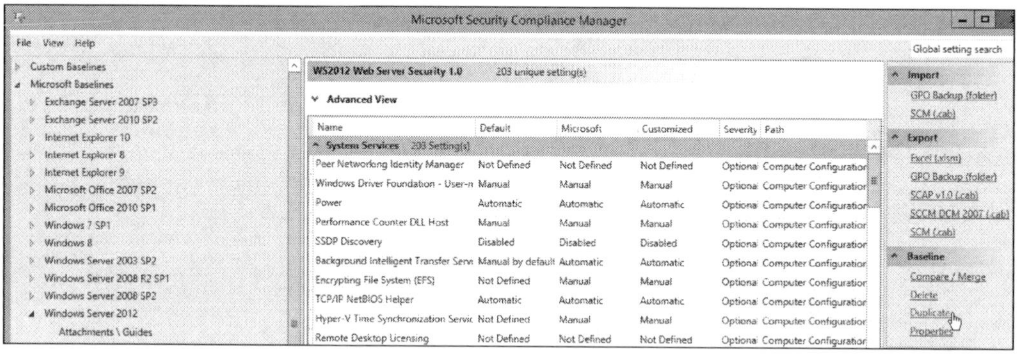

7. In the **Duplicate** window, enter the name for this new security policy. Click on **Save**. The new template will be saved under the **Custom Baselines** node.

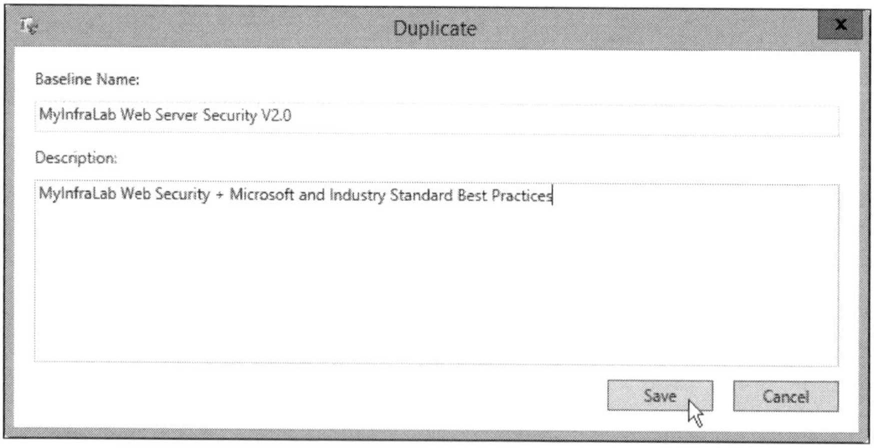

8. You can review the policy and make necessary changes in the newly created policy.

Creating and implementing security policies

At this point, you have installed SCM and are familiar with the basic administration tasks. From this section onwards, you will be working on a real-world scenario where you will be exporting a policy from Active Directory, importing into SCM, merging with an SCM baseline, and importing back into Active Directory. In *Chapter 1, Operating System and Baseline Security*, you created a web server policy using SCW and imported it into Active Directory. In this section, our goal is to export this web server policy and merge it with an SCM baseline and import it back into Active Directory.

Exporting GPO from Active Directory

We will start by exporting the existing web server policy from Active Directory. The following steps can be performed to export (backup) an Active Directory GPO-based policy:

1. Open the **Group Policy Manager** console.
2. Expand **Forest** | **Domain** | **Domain Name** | **Group Policy Objects**.
3. Right-click on the appropriate GPO and select **Back Up**.

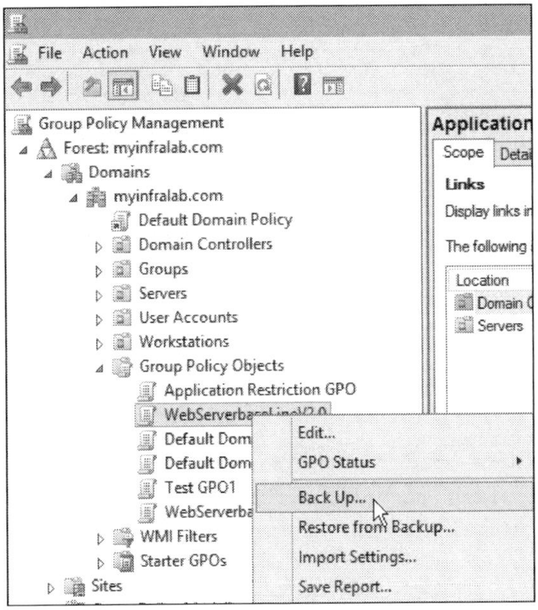

GPO - Back up

4. In the **Back Up Group Policy Object** window, enter the **Location** and **Description** details for the backup file. Click on the **Back Up** button to start the backup operation.
5. You will see the progress in the **Backup** window. Click on **OK** when it completes the backup operation.

> GPO can also be backed up using the `Backup-GPO PowerShell` cmdlet. The following is an example:
>
> `Backup-Gpo. Name- "WebServerbaselineV2.0". Path- D:\ Backup -Comment "Baseline Backup"`

The backup folder name will be the GUID of the GPO itself.

Importing GPO into SCM

An exported GPO-based policy can be imported directly into SCM. An administrator can perform the following steps to complete this task:

1. Open **Microsoft Compliance Security Manager**.
2. From the **Import** section on the right pane, select the **GPO Backup (Folder)** option.

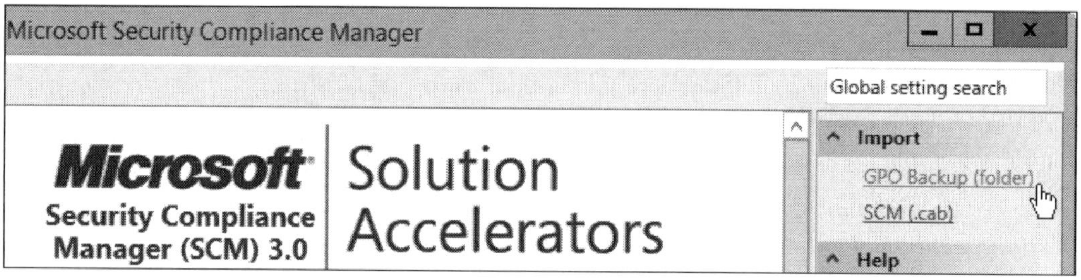

SCM – Import

3. In the **Browse For Folder** window, select the GPO backup folder. Click on **OK**.
4. In the **GPO Name** window, confirm or change the baseline name. Click on **OK**.

5. In the **SCM Log** window, you will see the status. Click on **OK** to close the window.

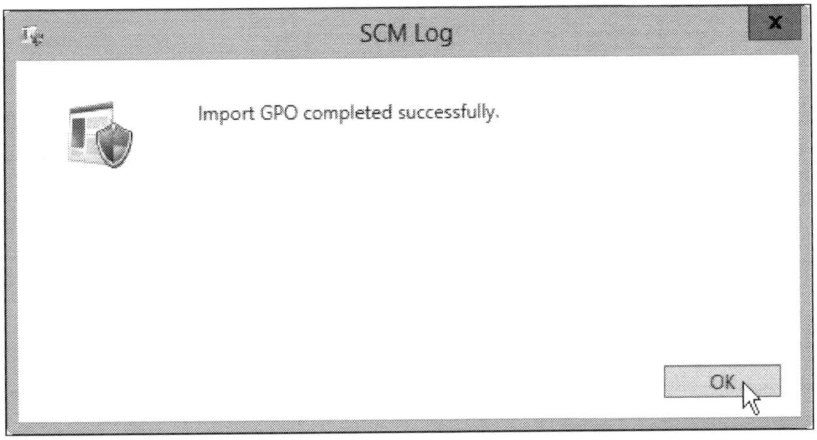

6. You will see the imported policy under **Custom Baselines** | **GPO Import** | **Policy Name**.

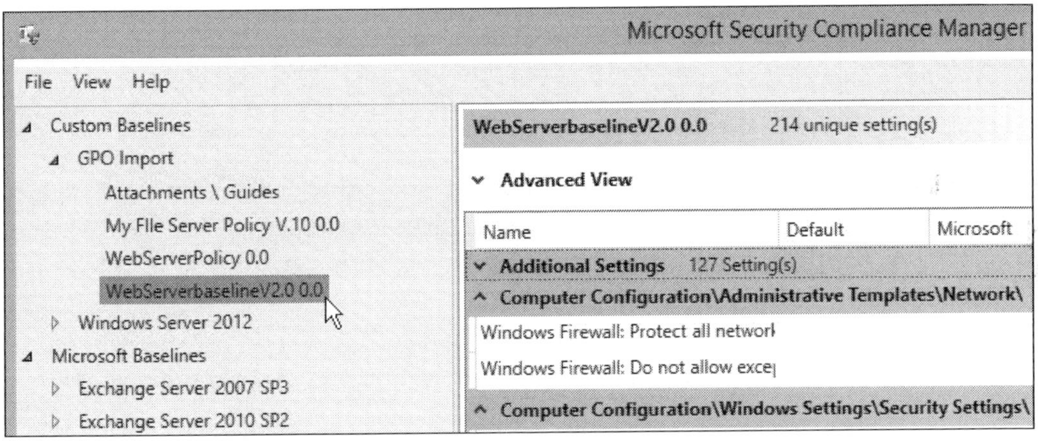

> Currently, SCM supports importing from GPO backup and SCM CAB files. If you have some other policy or baseline (for example, DISA STIGs) that you would like to import into SCM, you need to import these polices into Active Directory first, and then export/backup to GPO before you can import into SCM.

Merging imported GPO with the SCM baseline policy

The third step in this process is to merge the imported policy with the SCM baseline policy. Keep in mind that some configurations and settings will be lost when you merge an existing GPO with the SCM baseline policy. For example, service-related or ACL configurations may not be preserved when you associate and merge with an SCM baseline policy. If you have these types of configuration in your GPO and want to retain them, you may need to split the GPO and use two separate GPOs. Inside the SCM, the import process is to map these configurations with the SCM library to preserve these settings. If it doesn't match or map, these settings will be dropped from the new baseline policy. For this exercise, my assumption is that you don't have a custom configuration or settings in the imported policy. The following steps can be used to **Associate** and **Merge** a GPO-based policy into an SCM-based policy:

1. Select the imported policy in **Microsoft Compliance Security Manager**. From the right pane, select the **Associate** option from the **Baseline** section.

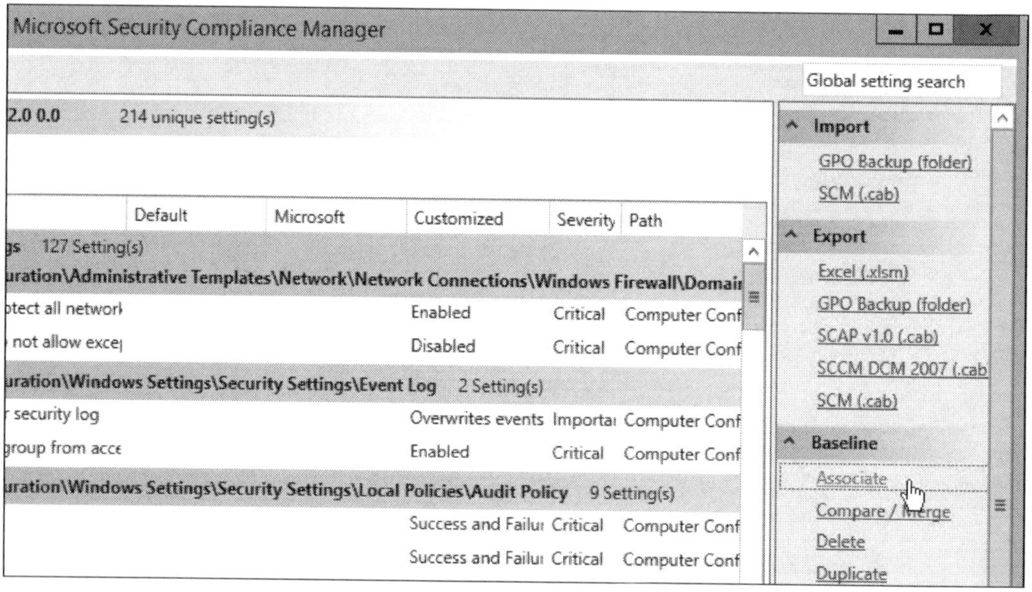

Selecting the Associate option

2. From the **Associate Product with GPO** window, select the appropriate baseline policy. Since we are working with a Windows Server 2012 policy, I will be selecting **Windows Server 2012** as the product. If you have a different operating system, select the correct policy from the product list. Click on **Associate**.

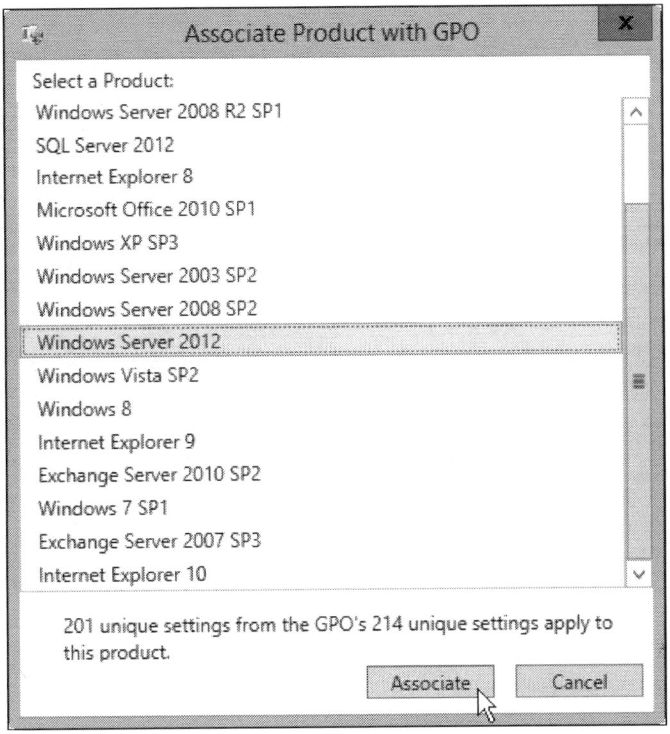

Your custom policy must have unique settings in the baseline policy in order to associate a custom policy with the SCM baseline policy; otherwise, the **Associate** button will be grayed out.

Enter a name for this policy in the **Baseline Policy** window.

1. You will see this policy in the **Custom Baselines | Windows Server 2012** section.
2. Select this policy. From the right pane, select the **Compare/Merge** option from the **Baseline** section.

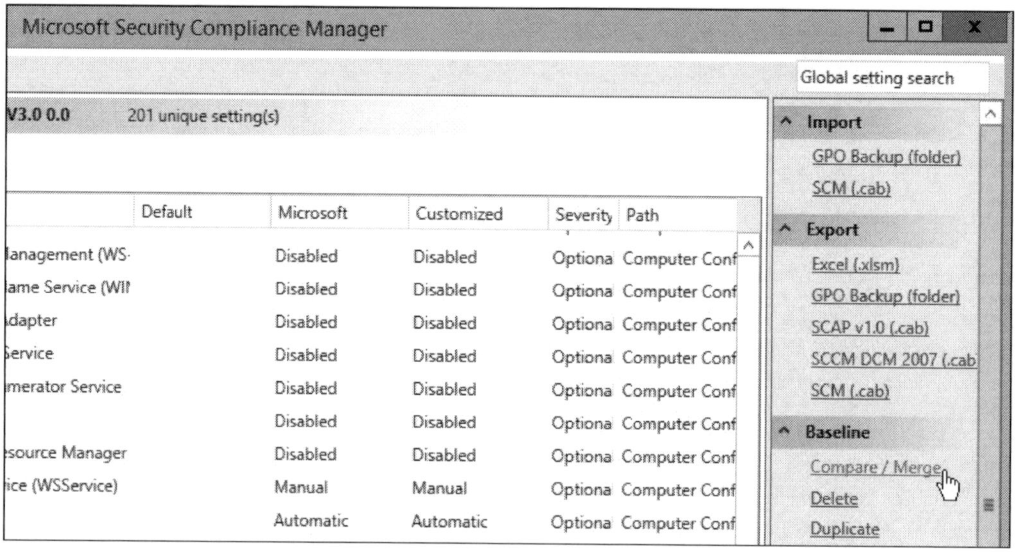

Selecting the Compare / Merge option

3. Now you have associated your policy with an SCM baseline policy. The next step is to compare and merge your policy with a baseline SCM policy. From the **Compare Baseline** window, select the appropriate baseline policy. Since we are working with a web server baseline, we will be selecting **WS2012 Web Server Security 1.0** as the policy. Click on **OK**.

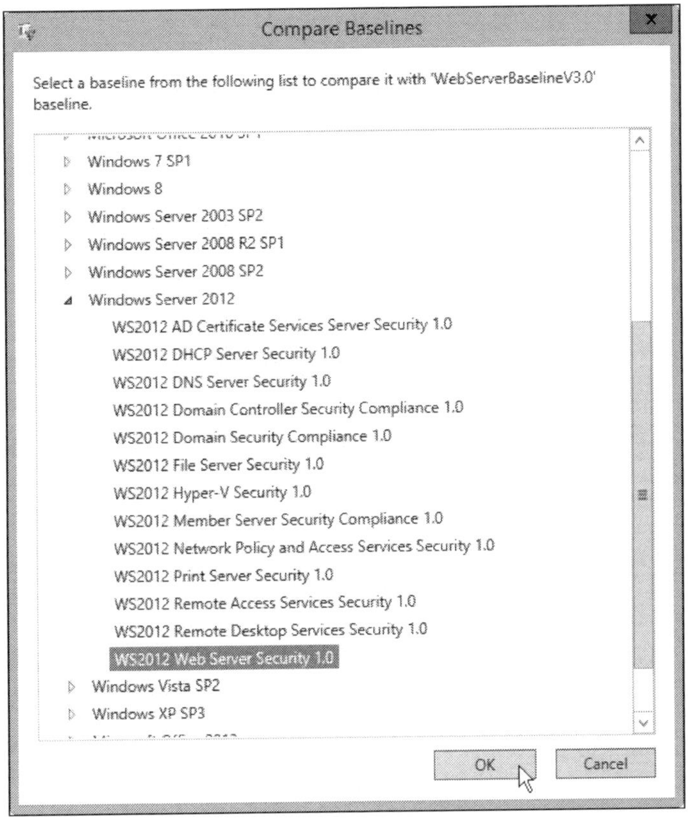

4. You will see the result in the **Compare Baselines** window. You can review the differ and match details here. Since we are planning to merge these two polices, we will be selecting the **Merge Baselines** option.

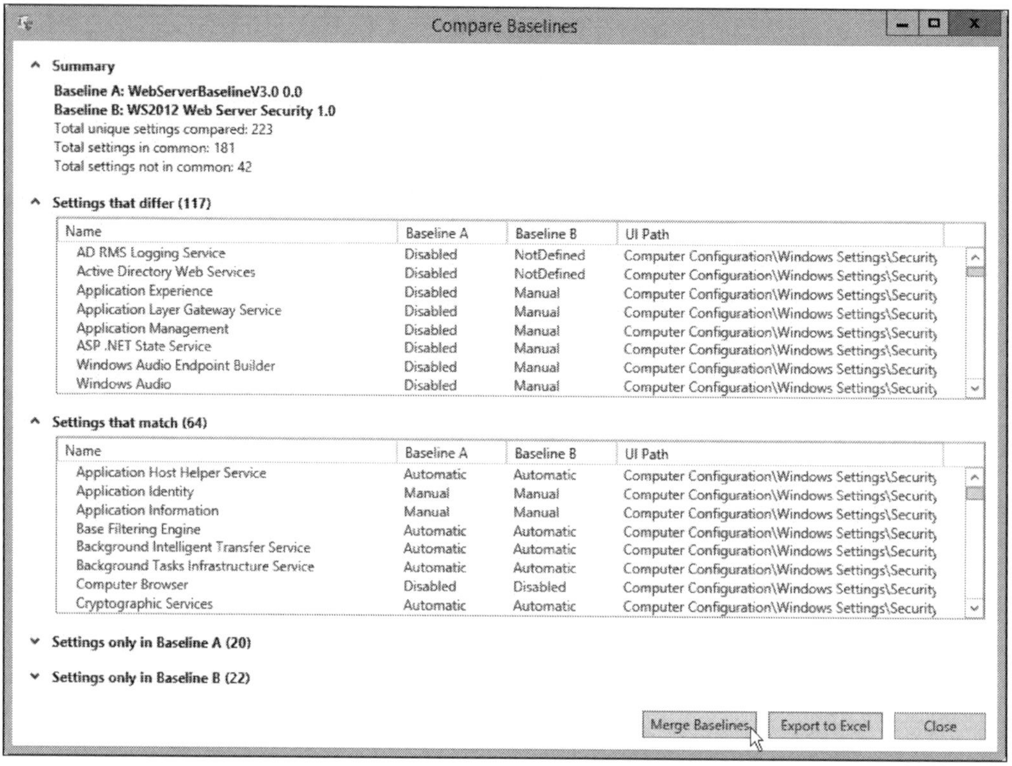

5. You will see the summary report in the **Merge Baselines** window. Click on **OK**.
6. In the **Specify a name for the merged baseline** window, enter a new name for this policy. Click on **OK**.
7. This merged policy will be stored in the **Custom Baselines- Windows Server 2012** section.

Exporting the SCM baseline policy

At this point, you have created a new policy that contains your custom policy and best practices provided by SCM. The next step is to export this policy to a supported format. Since we are dealing with Active Directory and GPO, we will be exporting it into a GPO-based policy. You can perform the following steps to export an SCM policy to a GPO-based backup policy:

1. Select the policy from **Microsoft Compliance Security Manager**. From the **Export** section, select the **GPO Backup (Folder)** option.

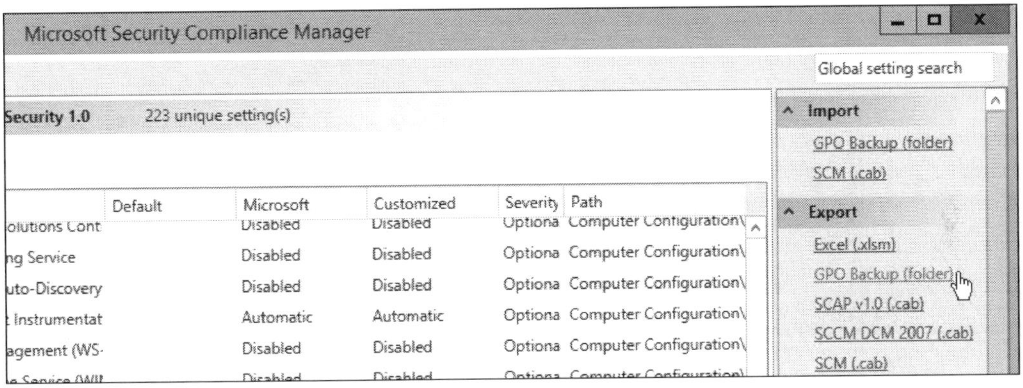

GPO Backup (Folder)

2. From the **Browse for Folder** window, select the folder to store this policy in. Click on **OK**.

Importing a policy into Active Directory

The final step in this process is to import these settings back to Active Directory. This can be achieved by using **Group Policy Management Console (GPMC).** The following steps can be used to import an SCM-based policy into Active Directory:

1. Open **Group Policy Manager Console**.
2. Expand **Forest** | **Domain** | **Domain Name** | **Group Policy Objects**.

3. Right-click on the appropriate policy. Select the **Import Settings** option.

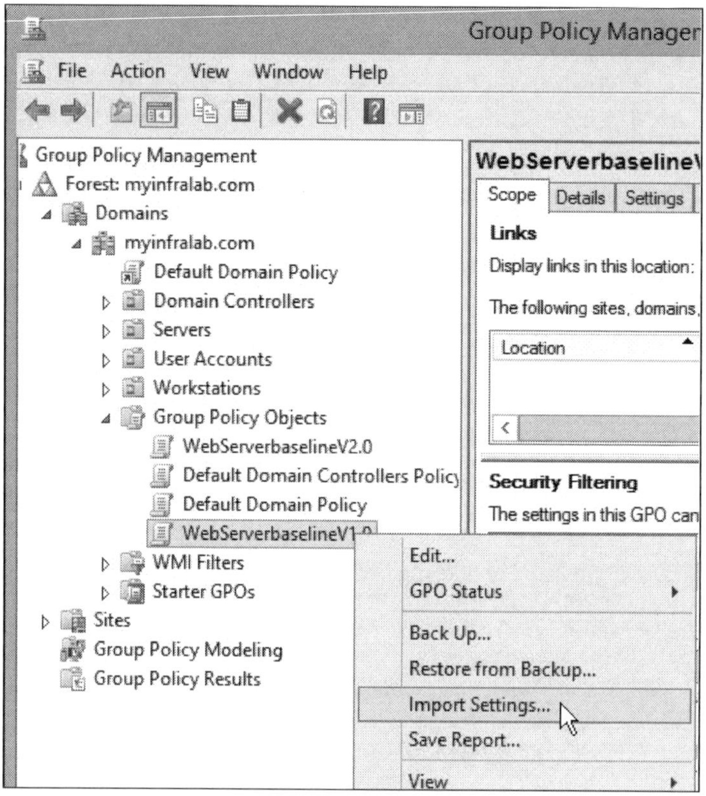

The Import Settings option

4. Click on **Next** in the **Welcome** window.
5. It is always a best practice to back up the existing settings. Click on **Backup** to continue with the backup operation. Once you have completed the backup, click on **Next** in the **Backup GPO** window.
6. In the **Backup Location** window, select the backup location folder. Click on **Next**.
7. Confirm the GPO name in the **Source GPO** window. Click on **Next**.

8. You will see the scanning settings in the **Scanning Backup** window. Click on **Next** to continue.
9. Click on **Finish** in the **Completing the Import Settings Wizard** window to complete the import operation.
10. Click on **OK** in the **Import** window.

Maintaining and monitoring the integrity of a baseline policy

Once you have baseline security in place, whether it is a true business policy or a combination of business and industry practices, you will need to maintain this state to ensure the security and integrity. The whole idea is to compare your baseline image with the current image in order to validate the settings. There are many ways to achieve this. Microsoft has a free tool called **Attack Surface Analyzer** (**ASA**) that can be used to compare the two states of the system. The details and capabilities of this tool can found at `http://www.microsoft.com/en-us/download/details.aspx?id=24487`.

Microsoft ASA

An administrator can perform the following steps to install, configure, and generate an Attack Surface Report using Microsoft ASA:

1. Download Attack Surface Analyzer from `http://www.microsoft.com/en-us/download/details.aspx?id=24487`.
2. Complete the installation. It is a standalone, simple MSI installation process.
3. Open the Attack Surface Analyzer tool.

4. The first step is to create the baseline state. Select the **Run New Scan** option and enter a name for the CAB file. Click on **Run Scan** to start the scanning process.

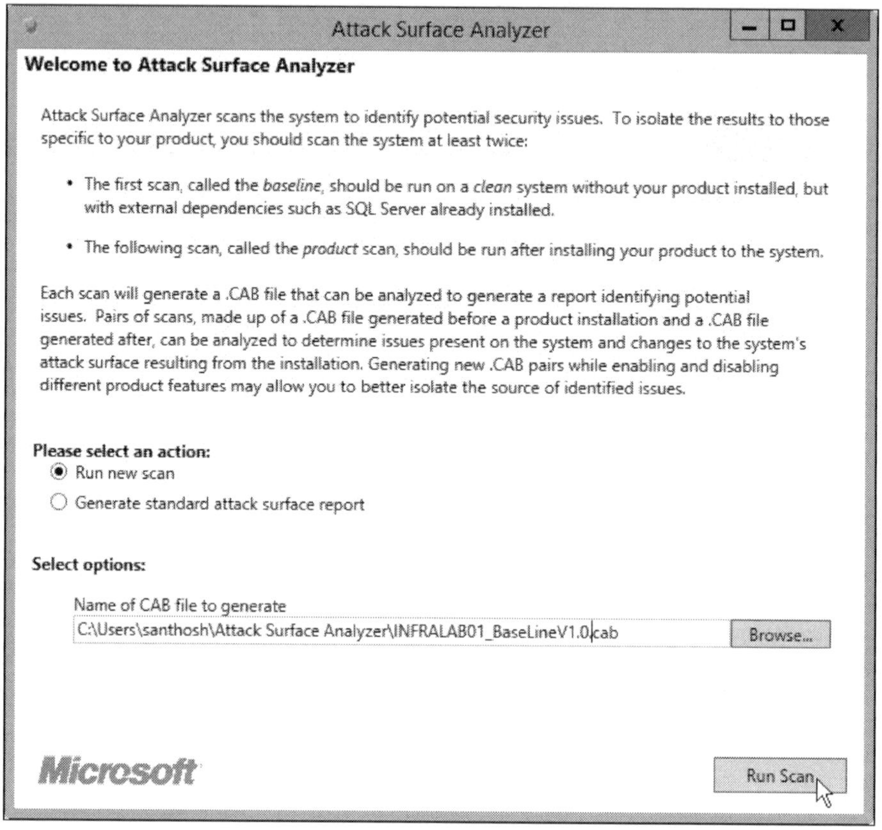
Attack Surface Analyzer
Welcome to Attack Surface Analyzer
Attack Surface Analyzer scans the system to identify potential security issues. To isolate the results to those specific to your product, you should scan the system at least twice:
• The first scan, called the baseline, should be run on a clean system without your product installed, but with external dependencies such as SQL Server already installed.
• The following scan, called the product scan, should be run after installing your product to the system.
Each scan will generate a .CAB file that can be analyzed to generate a report identifying potential issues. Pairs of scans, made up of a .CAB file generated before a product installation and a .CAB file generated after, can be analyzed to determine issues present on the system and changes to the system's attack surface resulting from the installation. Generating new .CAB pairs while enabling and disabling different product features may allow you to better isolate the source of identified issues.
Please select an action:
Run new scan
Generate standard attack surface report
Select options:
Name of CAB file to generate
C:\Users\santhosh\Attack Surface Analyzer\INFRALAB01_BaseLineV1.0.cab
Browse...
Microsoft
Run Scan

5. You will see the status and progress in the **Collecting Data** window. When it completes, it will create a CAB file with the result.

6. The second step in this process is to analyze the baseline state against the existing server so as to identify the differences. You will need to create another report (**Product CAB**) to compare the CAB file with the baseline CAB.
7. Select the **Run New Scan** option again and enter a name for the product CAB file. Click on **Run Scan** to start the scanning process. Complete the CAB creation process.

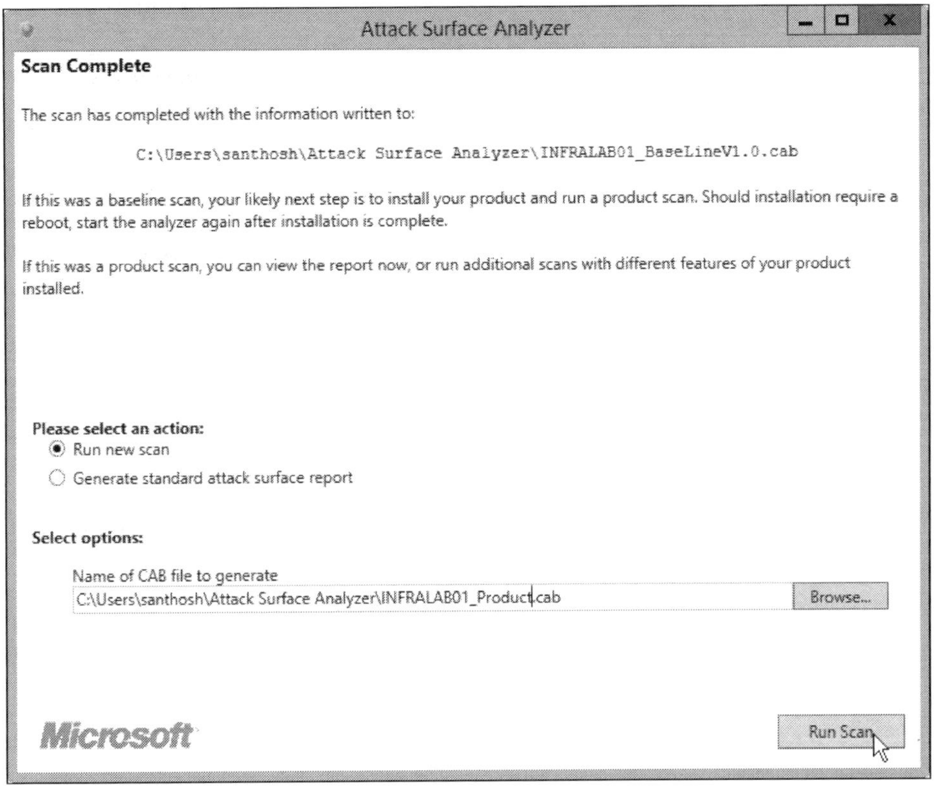
Attack Surface Analyzer
Scan Complete
The scan has completed with the information written to:
C:\Users\santhosh\Attack Surface Analyzer\INFRALAB01_BaseLineV1.0.cab
If this was a baseline scan, your likely next step is to install your product and run a product scan. Should installation require a reboot, start the analyzer again after installation is complete.
If this was a product scan, you can view the report now, or run additional scans with different features of your product installed.
Please select an action:
Run new scan
Generate standard attack surface report
Select options:
Name of CAB file to generate
C:\Users\santhosh\Attack Surface Analyzer\INFRALAB01_Product.cab
Browse...
Microsoft
Run Scan

8. The third step in the process is to compare the baseline CAB with the product CAB to get the delta. Select the **Generate Standard Attack Surface Report** option. In the **Select Options** section, select the baseline CAB name, select the product CAB name, and enter a name for the attack report. Click on **Generate** to start the process. You will see the status in the **Running Analysis** window.

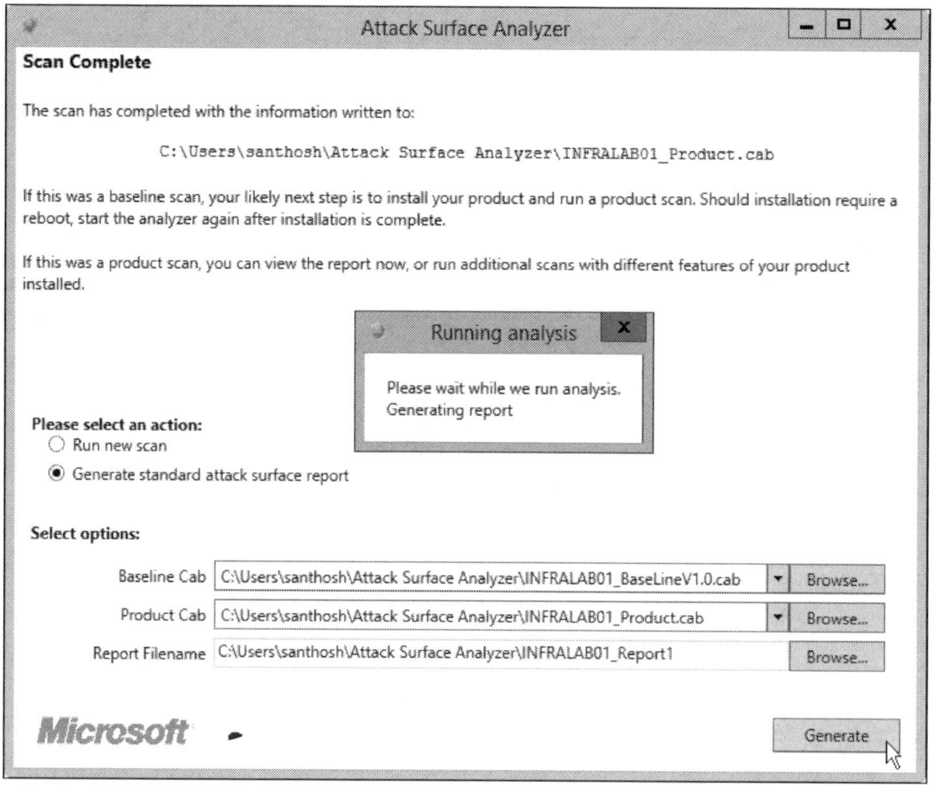
Attack Surface Analyzer
Scan Complete
The scan has completed with the information written to:
C:\Users\santhosh\Attack Surface Analyzer\INFRALAB01_Product.cab
If this was a baseline scan, your likely next step is to install your product and run a product scan. Should installation require a reboot, start the analyzer again after installation is complete.
If this was a product scan, you can view the report now, or run additional scans with different features of your product installed.
Running analysis
Please wait while we run analysis.
Generating report
Please select an action:
Run new scan
Generate standard attack surface report
Select options:
Baseline Cab
C:\Users\santhosh\Attack Surface Analyzer\INFRALAB01_BaseLineV1.0.cab
Product Cab
C:\Users\santhosh\Attack Surface Analyzer\INFRALAB01_Product.cab
Report Filename
C:\Users\santhosh\Attack Surface Analyzer\INFRALAB01_Report1
Browse...
Microsoft
Generate

9. The report will be opened automatically in the web browser. This report has three sections: **Report Summary**, **Security Issues**, and **Attack Surface**.

10. The following is an example of a **Security Issues** report:

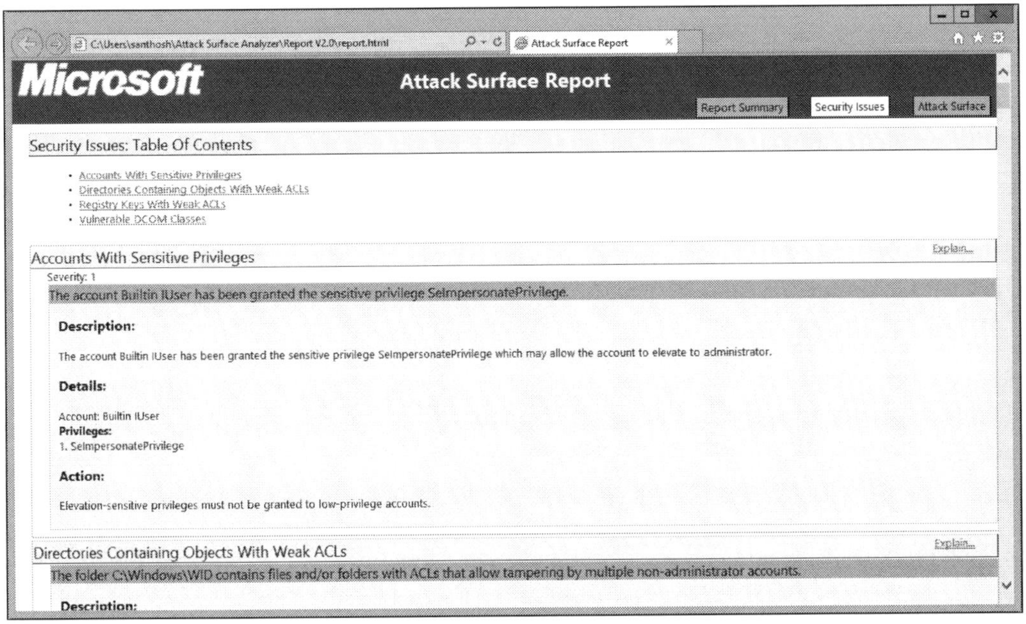

Microsoft
Attack Surface Report
Report Summary
Security Issues
Attack Surface
Security Issues: Table Of Contents
Accounts With Sensitive Privileges
Directories Containing Objects With Weak ACLs
Registry Keys With Weak ACLs
Vulnerable DCOM Classes
Accounts With Sensitive Privileges
Severity: 1
The account Builtin IUser has been granted the sensitive privilege SeImpersonatePrivilege.
Description:
The account Builtin IUser has been granted the sensitive privilege SeImpersonatePrivilege which may allow the account to elevate to administrator.
Details:
Account: Builtin IUser
Privileges:
1. SeImpersonatePrivilege
Action:
Elevation-sensitive privileges must not be granted to low-privilege accounts.
Directories Containing Objects With Weak ACLs
The folder C:\Windows\WID contains files and/or folders with ACLs that allow tampering by multiple non-administrator accounts.

Application control and management

At this point, you have a baseline policy for your server platform. Now we can add more restrictions based on your requirements to provide a more secure environment. In the following section, my plan is to introduce an option to "blacklist" and "whitelist" some of the applications using a built-in native option called AppLocker. The details of the AppLocker application can be found at `http://technet.microsoft.com/en-us/library/hh831409.aspx`.

AppLocker

AppLocker polices are part of **Application Control Policies** in GPOs. There are four types of built-in rules: Executable, Windows Installable, Script, and Packed App rules. Before you create or enforce a policy, you need to perform an inventory check to identify the current usage of these applications in your environment. AppLocker has an inventory process called **Auditing** that helps you to achieve this.

In this scenario, our goal is to block unauthorized access of the **NLTEST** application from all servers.

Creating a policy

As the first step, you need to identify the current usage of the application in your environment. The following steps can be performed to create a new **AppLocker** policy in an Active Directory environment:

1. Open **Group Policy Manager Console**.
2. Expand **Forest** | **Domain** | **Domain Name**.
3. Right-click on the **Group Policy Object** node and select **New**.
4. Enter a name for the GPO in the **New GPO** window. Leave **Source Starter GPO** as **(none)**. Click on **OK**. This will create a new blank GPO in the **Group Policy Object** node. We will be using this GPO to configure the **AppLocker** settings.
5. Right-click on the newly created GPO and select **Edit**. This will open the **Group Policy Management Editor** window.
6. Expand **Policies** | **Windows Settings** | **Security Settings** | **AppLocker**. Right-click on **Executable Polices** and select **Create Default Rules**. These default rules allow users and built-in administrators to run default programs and administrators to run files and applications. Based on your requirements, you can modify and delete these rules.

> The default AppLocker rule allows *everyone* to run files located only in the Windows folder, and the administrator can run all files.
>
> 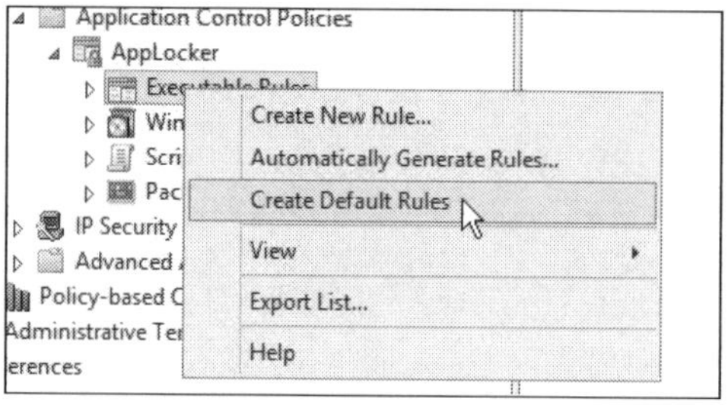
>
>
> The default AppLocker rule

7. Expand **Policies** | **Windows Settings** | **Security Settings** | **AppLocker**. Right-click on **Executable Polices** and select **Create New Rules**.
8. Click on **Next** in the **Create Executable Rules** window.
9. In the **Permission** window, select **Deny**. In the **User or Group** section, click on **Select** and select the **Server Admins** group. Here, I have created a security group with all server administrators in that group.

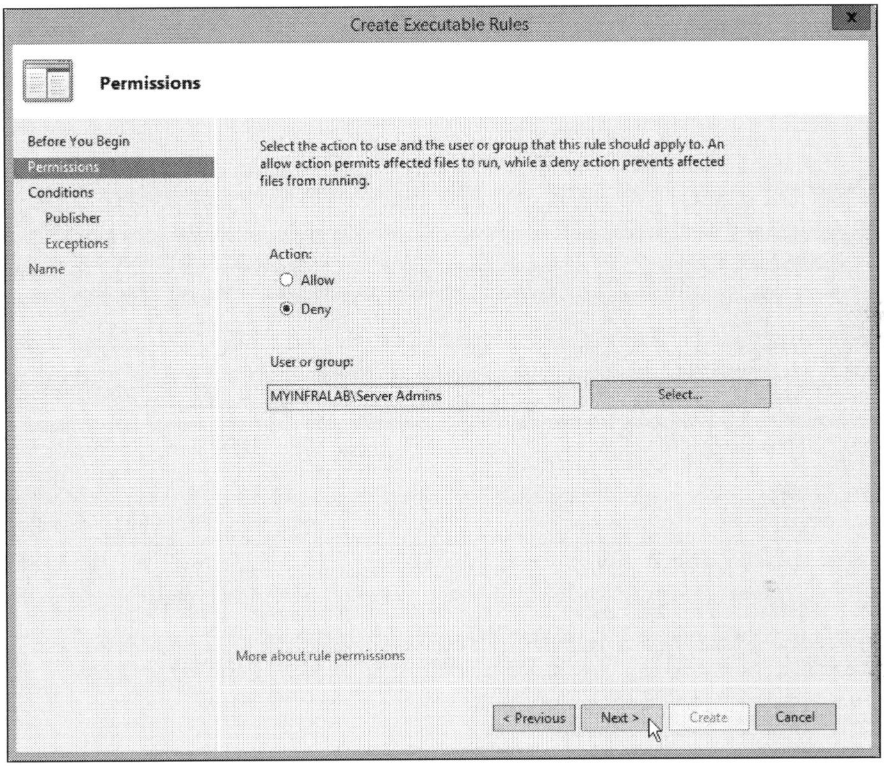

10. In the **Conditions** window, select the **File Hash** option. Click on **Next**.

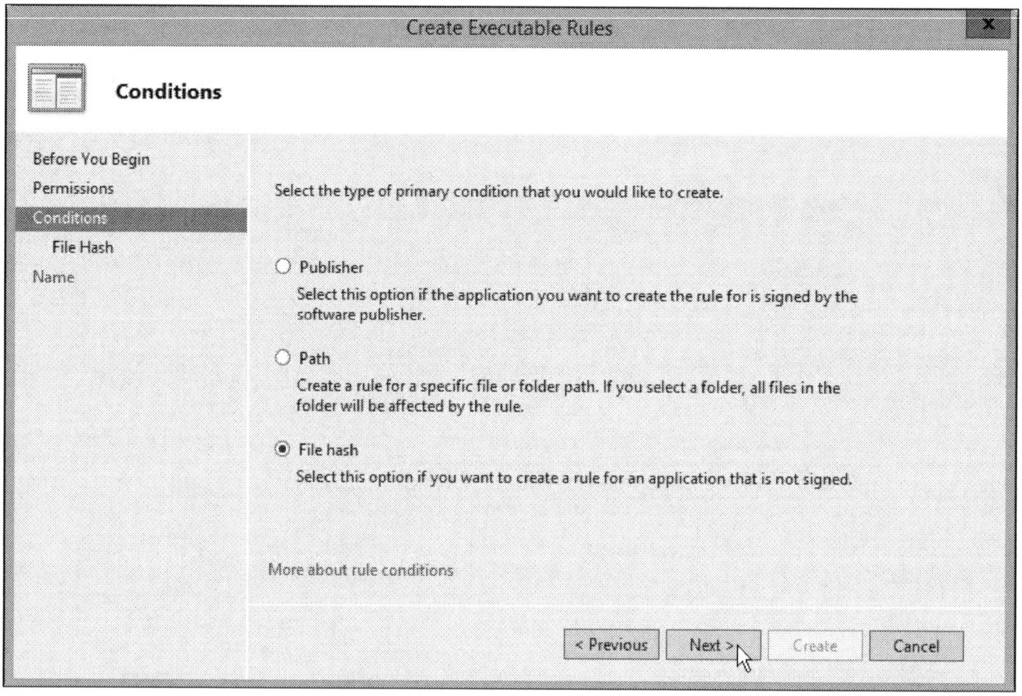
Create Executable Rules
Conditions
Before You Begin
Permissions
Conditions
File Hash
Name
Select the type of primary condition that you would like to create.
Publisher
Select this option if the application you want to create the rule for is signed by the software publisher.
Path
Create a rule for a specific file or folder path. If you select a folder, all files in the folder will be affected by the rule.
File hash
Select this option if you want to create a rule for an application that is not signed.
More about rule conditions
< Previous
Next >
Create
Cancel

11. In the **File Hash** window, select the correct file name using the **Browse File** option. In this scenario, I will be selecting the `NLTEST.exe` file. Click on **Next**.

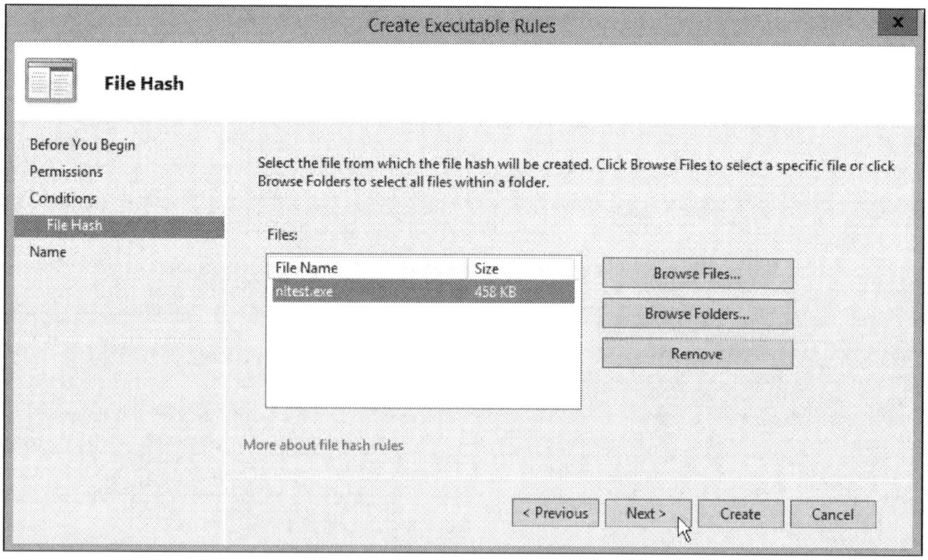
Create Executable Rules
File Hash
Before You Begin
Permissions
Conditions
File Hash
Name
Select the file from which the file hash will be created. Click Browse Files to select a specific file or click Browse Folders to select all files within a folder.
Files:
File Name
Size
nltest.exe
458 KB
Browse Files...
Browse Folders...
Remove
More about file hash rules
< Previous
Next >
Create
Cancel

12. In the **Name and Description** window, select or enter an appropriate name for this rule. Click on **Create**.

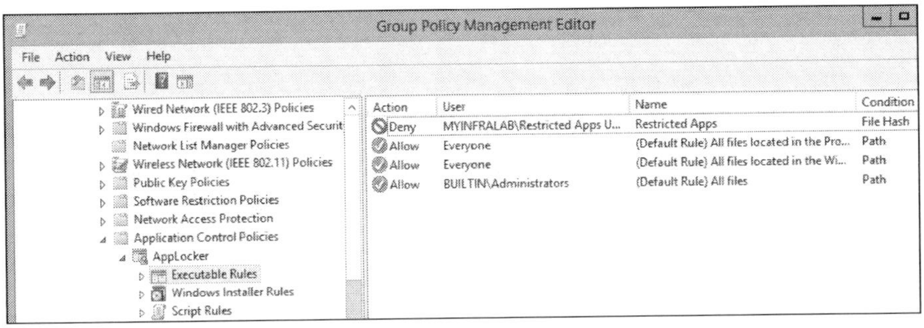

Auditing a policy

The next step in this process is to audit the previously created polices to ensure that there will not be any adverse effects to your environment. An administrator can perform the following steps to audit an existing policy in an Active Directory environment:

1. Right-click on **AppLocker (Policies | Windows Settings | Security Settings)** and go to **Properties**.

2. On the **Enforcement** tab, select appropriate rule types as **Configured**. From the drop-down list, select the rule as **Audit only**. Click on **OK**.

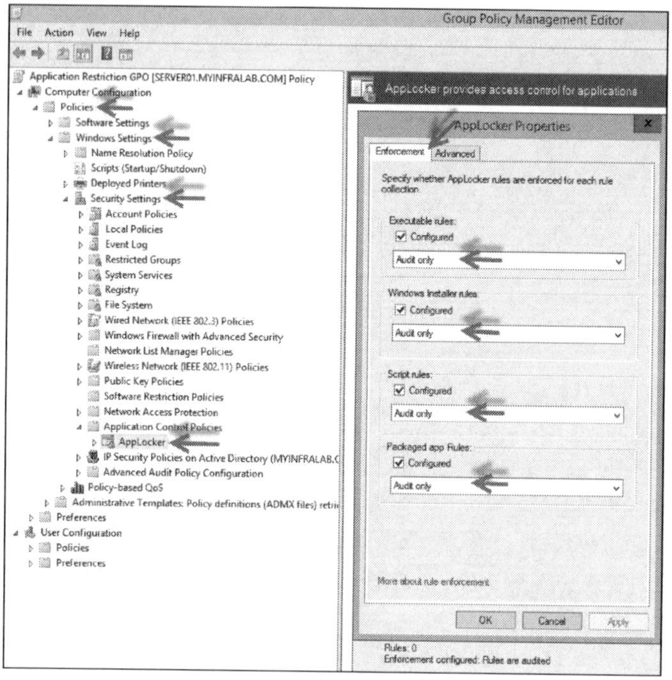

GPO – AppLocker policy

> The **Application Identity** service is responsible for tracking the application usage. This must be set to **Automatic** to be able to collect the application usage report.

3. You can see the application usage and history in the **Event** log. Open **Event Viewer**.

4. Navigate to **Applications and Services Logs** | **Microsoft** | **Windows** | **AppLocker**.

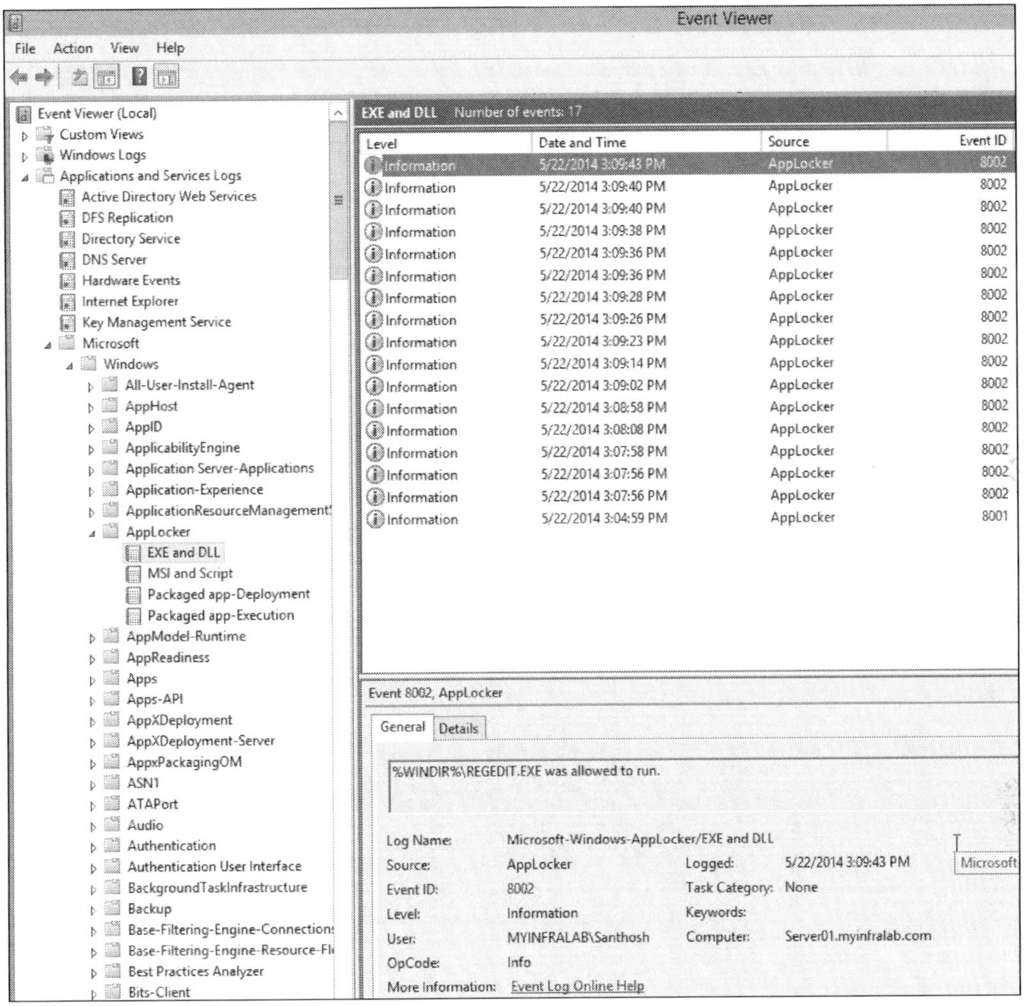

5. Based on your policy configuration, you will see the appropriate event information in the **AppLocker** section.

In an enterprise world, manually checking the items in an event log is not going to be a viable option. You have a few options available to automate this process. You can forward the event log to a central server (Event Forwarding) and verify from that single console, or you can use the `Get-WinEvent` PowerShell cmdlet to collect these events remotely.

The following section provides an option to evaluate these logs using the `Get-WinEvent` PowerShell cmdlet. By default, AppLocker events are located in the **Applications and Services Logs | Microsoft | Windows | AppLocker** section of the **Event Viewer**.

The `Get-WinEvent -ComputerName "SERVER01.MYINFRALAB.COM" -LogName *AppLocker* | fl | out-file Server01.txt` cmdlet filters all AppLocker-related events from `Server01` and puts them in the output file `Server01.txt`.

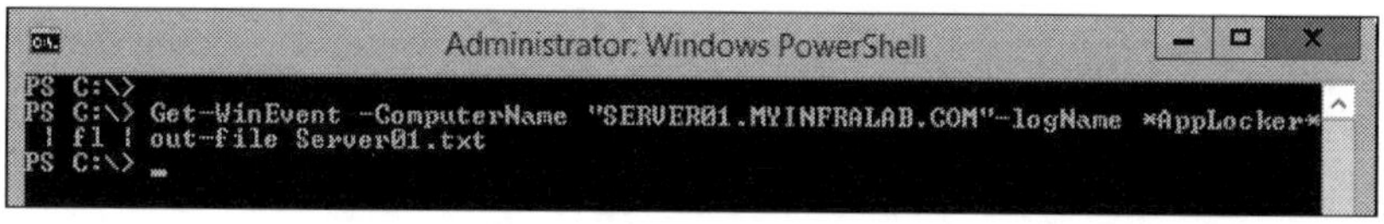

Here are some of the events that you will see in the event log:

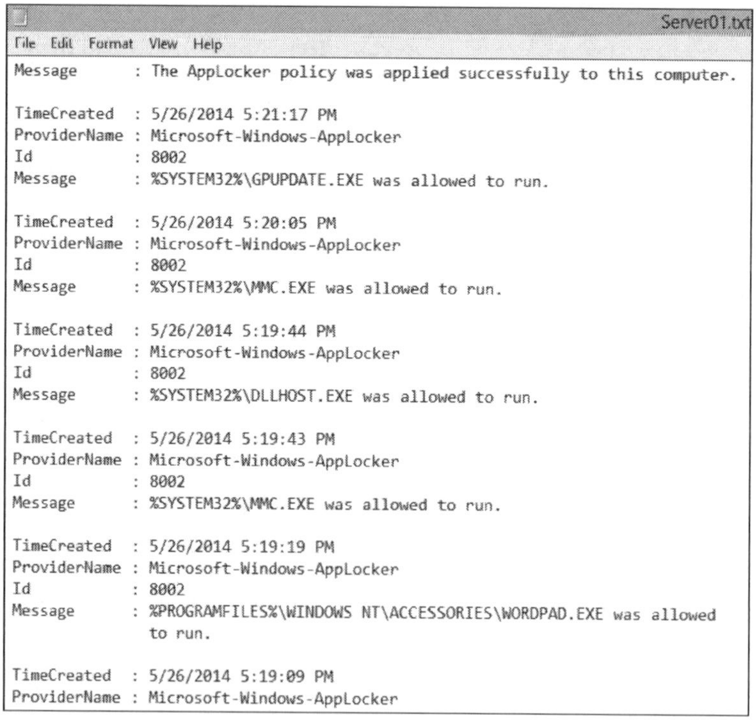

```
Message      : The AppLocker policy was applied successfully to this computer.

TimeCreated  : 5/26/2014 5:21:17 PM
ProviderName : Microsoft-Windows-AppLocker
Id           : 8002
Message      : %SYSTEM32%\GPUPDATE.EXE was allowed to run.

TimeCreated  : 5/26/2014 5:20:05 PM
ProviderName : Microsoft-Windows-AppLocker
Id           : 8002
Message      : %SYSTEM32%\MMC.EXE was allowed to run.

TimeCreated  : 5/26/2014 5:19:44 PM
ProviderName : Microsoft-Windows-AppLocker
Id           : 8002
Message      : %SYSTEM32%\DLLHOST.EXE was allowed to run.

TimeCreated  : 5/26/2014 5:19:43 PM
ProviderName : Microsoft-Windows-AppLocker
Id           : 8002
Message      : %SYSTEM32%\MMC.EXE was allowed to run.

TimeCreated  : 5/26/2014 5:19:19 PM
ProviderName : Microsoft-Windows-AppLocker
Id           : 8002
Message      : %PROGRAMFILES%\WINDOWS NT\ACCESSORIES\WORDPAD.EXE was allowed
               to run.

TimeCreated  : 5/26/2014 5:19:09 PM
ProviderName : Microsoft-Windows-AppLocker
```

If you have multiple computers to evaluate, you can create a simple PowerShell script to automatically input the computer names. The following is a sample PowerShell script. The `Servers.txt` file will be your input file that contains all of the server names:

```
$OutPut = "C:\Input\Output.txt"

Get-Content "C:\Input\Servers.txt" | Foreach-Object {

$_| out-file $OutPut -Append -Encoding ascii

Get-WinEvent -ComputerName "Infralab01.MYINFRALAB.COM" -LogName
*AppLocker* | fl | out-file $OutPut -Append -Encoding ascii

}
```

Implementing the policy

Once you have verified the audit result, you can enforce the policy using the AppLocker GPO. The following steps can be used to implement the AppLocker GPO in an Active Directory environment:

1. Open **Group Policy Manager Console**.
2. Expand the **Forest** | **Domain** | **Domain Name** | **Group Policy Object** node.
3. Right-click on the **Server Application Restriction** GPO and select **Edit**. This will open a **Group Policy Management Editor MMC** window.

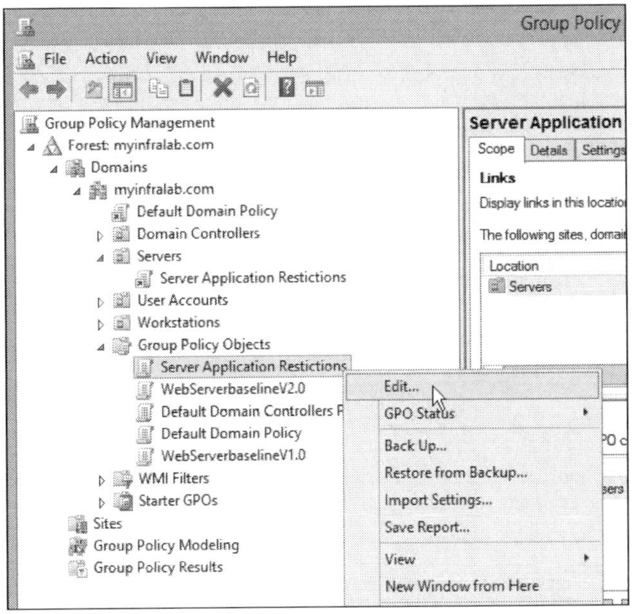

Opening the Group Policy Management Editor MMC window

4. From **Group Policy Management Editor**, expand **Policies | Windows Settings | Security Settings**. Right-click on **AppLocker** and select **Properties**.
5. In the **AppLocker Properties** window, change **Executable rules** to **Enforce rules**. Click on **OK**:

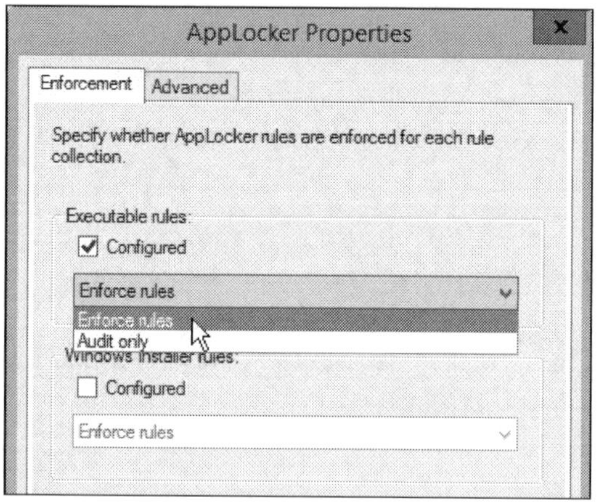

6. Close the **Group Policy Management Editor MMC** window.

The new policy will apply to the server based on your Active Directory replication interval and GPO refresh cycle. You can use the `GPUPDATE/Force` command to force the GPO on to a local server. Two different results are shown in the following screenshots.

As you can see in the following screenshot, the user `Johndoe` was denied the execution of the `NLTEST.exe` application:

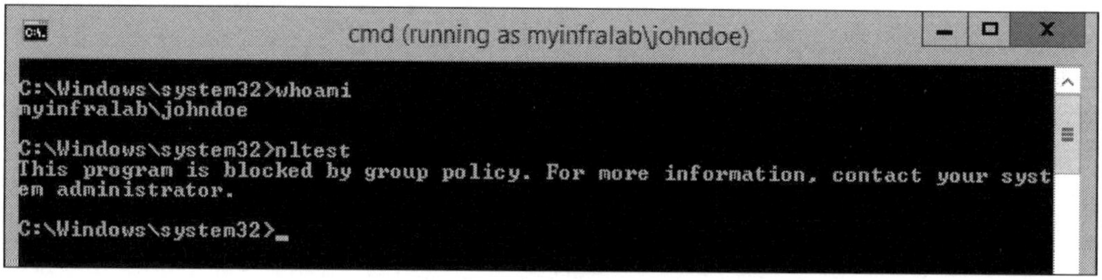

Since the following user was part of the **Server Admins** group, the user was allowed to execute the NLTEST.exe application:

```
Administrator: Command Prompt - cmd                    _ □ X

C:\Windows\System32>whoami
myinfralab\santhosh

C:\Windows\System32>nltest /?
Usage: nltest [/OPTIONS]

   /SERVER:<ServerName> - Specify <ServerName>

   /QUERY - Query <ServerName> netlogon service
   /REPL - Force partial sync on <ServerName> BDC
   /SYNC - Force full sync on <ServerName> BDC
   /PDC_REPL - Force UAS change message from <ServerName> PDC

   /SC_QUERY:<DomainName> - Query secure channel for <Domain> on <ServerName>
   /SC_RESET:<DomainName>[\<DcName>] - Reset secure channel for <Domain> on <Se
rverName> to <DcName>
   /SC_VERIFY:<DomainName> - Verify secure channel for <Domain> on <ServerName>
```

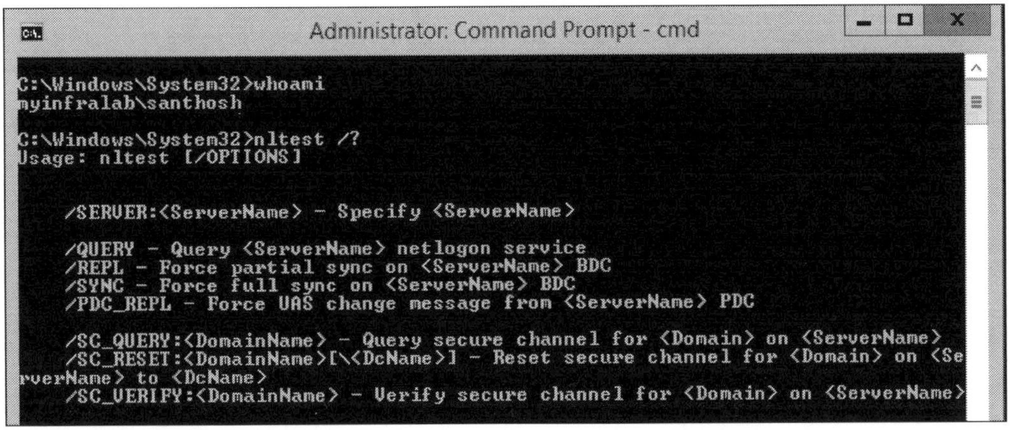

Some additional security recommendations to consider when installing and configuring AppLocker are included at http://technet.microsoft.com/en-us/library/ee844118(WS.10).aspx.

AppLocker and PowerShell

AppLocker supports PowerShell, and it has a PowerShell module called AppLocker. An administrator can create, test, and troubleshoot the AppLocker policies using these cmdlets. You need to import the AppLocker module before these cmdlets can be used. The following are the supported cmdlets in the module:

```
Administrator: Windows PowerShell                      _ □

PS C:\Users\santhosh> Get-Command *AppLocker*

CommandType      Name                                  ModuleName
-----------      ----                                  ----------
Cmdlet           Get-AppLockerFileInformation          AppLocker
Cmdlet           Get-AppLockerPolicy                   AppLocker
Cmdlet           New-AppLockerPolicy                   AppLocker
Cmdlet           Set-AppLockerPolicy                   AppLocker
Cmdlet           Test-AppLockerPolicy                  AppLocker

PS C:\Users\santhosh> _
```

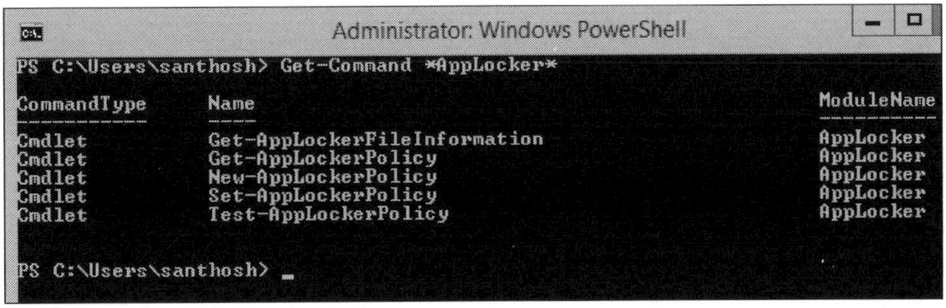

Summary

We started this chapter with baseline security for your server platform, which was originally created using Microsoft SCW. In this chapter, you learned how to incorporate this policy with the baseline and best practice recommendations using Microsoft SCM. Then you used AppLocker to enforce more application-based security. We also learned how to monitor the state of the server and compare it with the baseline to identify the security vulnerabilities and issues using Microsoft ASA. We will continue this journey in the next chapter in the same phase and provide more security options for your server infrastructure.

3

Server Roles and Protocols

The vulnerabilities of a server can be minimized by controlling the installed application, type of operating system you are using, opened ports, services, and so on. It is generally referred to as **Server Hardening**. The details and principles can be found at `http://en.wikipedia.org/wiki/Hardening_(computing)`. Microsoft has introduced the server roles concept to address some of these security concerns. To ensure that you can achieve maximum security and minimize the security breaches, the first step should be the selection of correct server type and server roles for your application. Then, you can apply baseline policies and templates to these servers, as mentioned in *Chapter 1, Operating System and Baseline Security*, and *Chapter 2, Native MS Security Tools and Configuration*, of this book, to ensure maximum security.

If you remember our conversation from *Chapter 1, Operating System and Baseline Security*, we started creating the security polices based on the installed roles on a server. Maintaining the consistent and baseline state of a server is the key to ensuring the integrity and security of the server platform. If there is a change in the initial state of the server, you must apply the updated baseline policy based on your business and technical requirements. This process can be an ongoing task.

In this chapter, you will learn the following:

- Monitoring and securing server roles
- Creating and maintaining the baseline state of the server
- Encrypting data using **Server Message Block** (**SMB**)

Server types and roles

If you are thinking about a secure server platform for your applications, you need to start with the type of server you are planning to use for your application; for example, the Server Core installation of Windows. The concept of **Server Core** is not new. It was introduced as part of Windows Server 2008. It helps to reduce the attack surface by minimizing the services running on the server, and by eliminating the need for the binary installation files to reside on the server. The general principles of attack surface can be found in the `http://en.wikipedia.org/wiki/Attack_surface` article. If your application can run on the Server Core installation of Windows, from a security standpoint, it is recommended to use Server Core as the installation type.

Once you have identified the correct server type for your application, you can start working on the role and feature required for this server. An administrator who has proper rights on a server can add or remove roles on a server. A Server Core installation can also be converted to a full server installation. The Windows Server 2012 operating system installation, configuration, and conversion details can be found in the book *Instant Migration from Windows Server 2008 and 2008 R2 to 2012 How-to, Packt Publishing*. This can be intentional or it can be a mistake. An unexpected change in the state of a server can lead to a major security issue in an organization. From a server security perspective, anyone with proper administrative rights is an authorized user to make changes on the server. This is the reason the Least Privilege concept plays a vital role in computer security. The details of the Least Privilege principle can be found at `http://en.wikipedia.org/wiki/Principle_of_least_privilege` article. As a security administrator, your job is to ensure that these servers are in alignment with your baseline policy that you created and implemented in *Chapter 1, Operating System and Baseline Security*, and *Chapter 2, Native MS Security Tools and Configuration*. If there is a change in the state of the server, the applied baseline security will become obsolete and inadequate. In the following section, my goal is to walk you through an option to monitor the current state of the server by comparing the baseline information against a production server.

> Windows Server 2012 operating system installation, configuration, and conversion details can be found in *Instant Migration from Windows Server 2008 and 2008 R2 to 2012 How-to, Packt Publishing.*

Managing servers using Server Manager

The new server manager for Windows Server 2012 provides a consolidated centralized view to monitor the servers by installed roles, service, and types. As you can see in the following screenshot, you can select the server type by roles or service from the left pane and the result will be displayed in the middle pane of the **Server Manager** window:

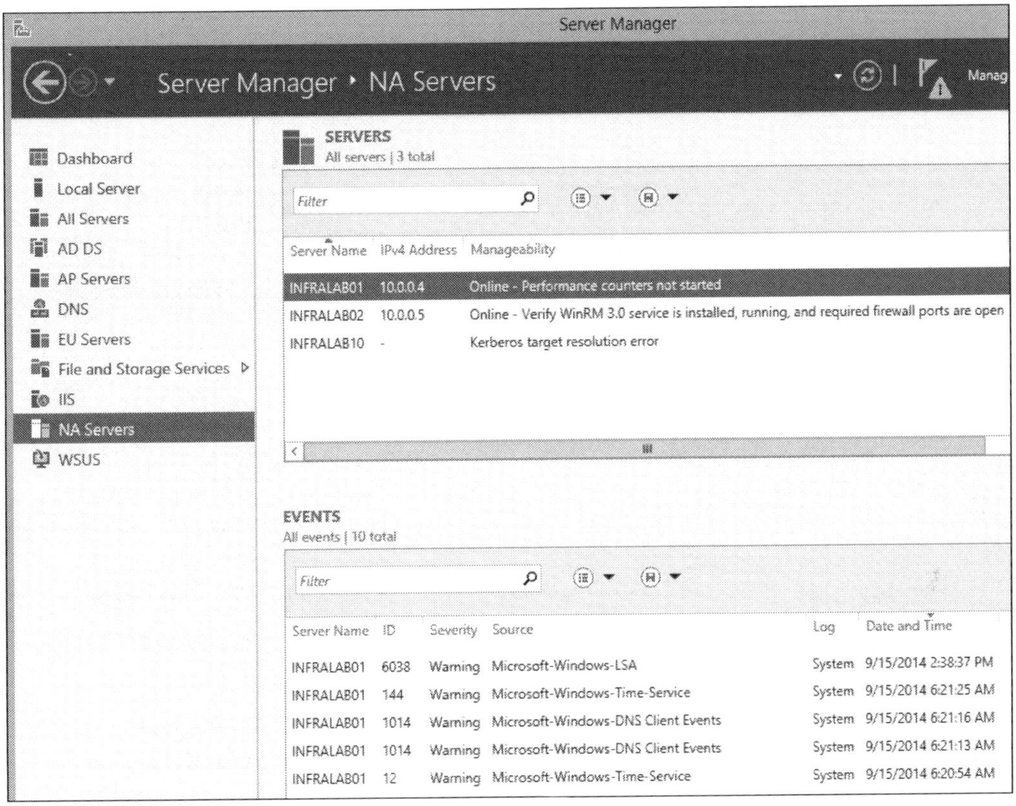

This management capability is good for a small to medium size environment. However, it may not be a viable option in an enterprise environment. Managing and monitoring thousands of servers using **Windows Server Manager** can be a challenge for an administrator. For a large enterprise environment, Microsoft System Center products may be the best option for managing large number of servers. The Microsoft System Center product details can be found at `http://www.microsoft.com/sam/en/us/systemcenter.aspx`. Since the Microsoft System Center configuration details are beyond the scope of this book, we will focus only on Windows Server Manager.

You can add or remove server roles using Server Manger and these new roles will appear in the **Server Manager** window. However, it has to be monitored in a proactive fashion to avoid any types of security threats to your organization. In order to identify the current state of a server, you need to compare the current state against a baseline server. You will be able to achieve this by running the Microsoft **Attack Surface Analyzer** (**ASA**) tool mentioned in *Chapter 2, Native MS Security Tools and Configuration*, of this book. What we are doing here is adding another layer to validation from a server administrator level. In an enterprise environment, all server administrators may not have access to all security tools. As an administrator, it is your responsibility to monitor and protect your servers.

Monitoring and securing server roles

Since **PowerShell** is a common administration tool for most administrators these days, I will be explaining a method using PowerShell cmdlet and script to manage and monitor the server roles. The first step in this process is to create a baseline for your server. This can be achieved by using the `Get-WindowsFeature` PowerShell cmdlet.

Creating a server role baseline report

You can follow the instructions in this section to create a report based on the installed role on servers. This report can be used as a server role baseline when comparing against production servers:

1. Identify a server as the baseline server. Since we were working with the web server from *Chapter 1, Operating System and Baseline Security*, you can select the same server for this exercise also.
2. Open the PowerShell command window using the administrator account. Run the `Get-WindowsFeature | Where-Object Installed | Select-Object -Property Name` cmdlet. The following screenshot displays the installed roles and features from the local server:

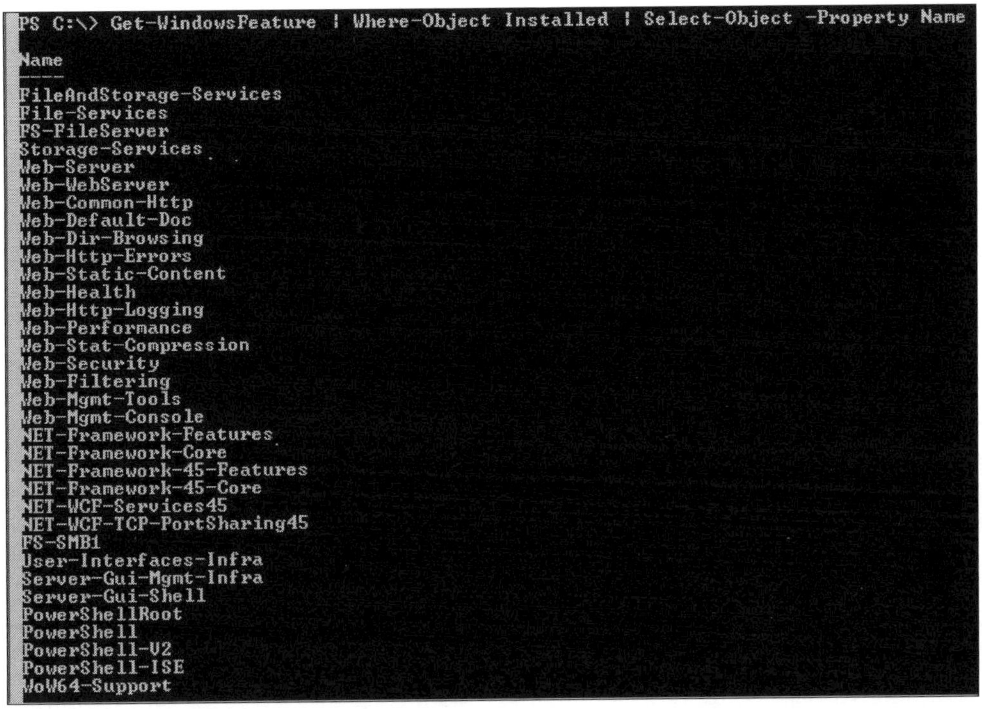
PS C:\> Get-WindowsFeature | Where-Object Installed | Select-Object -Property Name
Name

FileAndStorage-Services
File-Services
FS-FileServer
Storage-Services
Web-Server
Web-WebServer
Web-Common-Http
Web-Default-Doc
Web-Dir-Browsing
Web-Http-Errors
Web-Static-Content
Web-Health
Web-Http-Logging
Web-Performance
Web-Stat-Compression
Web-Security
Web-Filtering
Web-Mgmt-Tools
Web-Mgmt-Console
NET-Framework-Features
NET-Framework-Core
NET-Framework-45-Features
NET-Framework-45-Core
NET-WCF-Services45
NET-WCF-TCP-PortSharing45
FS-SMB1
User-Interfaces-Infra
Server-Gui-Mgmt-Infra
Server-Gui-Shell
PowerShellRoot
PowerShell
PowerShell-V2
PowerShell-ISE
WoW64-Support

> You can execute this command remotely by adding the `-ComputerName <Name of the remote computer>` parameter at the end of the `Get-WindowsFeature` cmdlet.

3. You can redirect this output to a file using the `Out-file` cmdlet in the following format:

```
Get-WindowsFeature | Where-Object Installed | Select-Object
-Property Name | Out-file "C:\BaseLines\WebServer_Role_
BaseLineV1.0.txt"
```

This will be your baseline report for the web server. Follow the same instructions to create the baseline report for other types of servers in your organization.

Analyzing production servers

The next step in this process is to compare this baseline against production servers so as to identify the current state of the server. If your baseline server is available and online, you can compare these two servers using the `Compare-Object` cmdlet. If the server is not available or online, you can use the previously created baseline file as an input for the script.

The following script assumes that the baseline server is available and online. The baseline server name is statically configured using the `$BaseLineServer` variable in the script. The input for this script is your production server names. It can be in the form of NetBIOS names, FQDNs, or IP address. The `Servers.txt` file must contain all your production server names that are compared against the baseline server or policy. There are two outputs for this script. You will see the real-time output on the console during the script execution. This report will be saved in the `Server_Role_Result.txt` file for future reference. An administrator can use the following instructions to proactively monitor their server environment for any changes:

1. Create a text file called `Servers.txt` with all your computer names. If you are using a different input name, make sure to update the `Get-Content` section with the new name of your input file.
2. Copy and paste the following PowerShell code into a text file and rename the file with the `.PS1` extension.

```
Clear
#Baseline Server (ReferenceObject)
$BaseLineServer = "InfraLab02.myinfralab.com"
#Output File
$OutPutFile = New-Item -ItemType File -Name "C:\Scripts\Server_
Role_Result.txt" -Force
#Servers.txt contains all server names (DifferenceObject)
Get-Content "C:\Scripts\Servers.txt" | Foreach-Object {
$ServerName = $_
$ServerName | out-file $OutPutFile -Append -Encoding ascii
#Current State of the server
$CurrentState = Get-WindowsFeature -ComputerName $ServerName |
Where-Object Installed | Select-Object -Property Name
#Baseline state
$BaseLine = Get-WindowsFeature -ComputerName $BaseLineServer |
Where-Object Installed | Select-Object -Property Name
#Difference will be stored in $Result variable
$Result = Compare-Object  -ReferenceObject $BaseLine
-DifferenceObject $CurrentState

    if ($Result)
```

```
        {
        Write-Host "$ServerName -> NOT in compliance with
Baseline" -ForegroundColor Red
        $Result.InputObject
        $Result.InputObject | out-file $OutPutFile -Append
-Encoding ascii
        }
    else
        {
         Write-Host "$ServerName-> In compliance with Baseline"
-ForegroundColor Green
        }

}
```

3. Open the PowerShell file using Notepad or any PowerShell editor.
4. Update the `$BaseLineServer` variable with your baseline server name. Save the file.
5. Open the PowerShell console and run the updated PowerShell script. Based on the number of servers you have in the input file, the available bandwidth, server availability, and so on, the script may take a few minutes to complete. You will see the following output on the PowerShell console during the script execution:

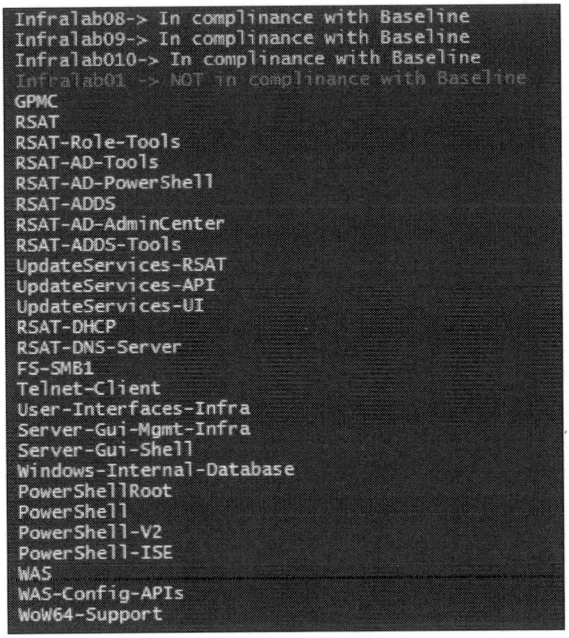
Infralab08-> In complinance with Baseline
Infralab09-> In complinance with Baseline
Infralab010-> In complinance with Baseline
Infralab01 -> NOT in complinance with Baseline
GPMC
RSAT
RSAT-Role-Tools
RSAT-AD-Tools
RSAT-AD-PowerShell
RSAT-ADDS
RSAT-AD-AdminCenter
RSAT-ADDS-Tools
UpdateServices-RSAT
UpdateServices-API
UpdateServices-UI
RSAT-DHCP
RSAT-DNS-Server
FS-SMB1
Telnet-Client
User-Interfaces-Infra
Server-Gui-Mgmt-Infra
Server-Gui-Shell
Windows-Internal-Database
PowerShellRoot
PowerShell
PowerShell-V2
PowerShell-ISE
WAS
WAS-Config-APIs
WoW64-Support

If the servers are in compliance with your baseline server role, you will see the server name and result in the green letters. If the servers are not in compliance with the baseline, you will see the server name in red and the additional server role will be displayed, as shown in the preceding screenshot.

The output will be saved in the output file `Server_Role_Result.txt` for future reference and analysis. The following is an example of this output file:

```
Name
----
GPMC
RSAT
RSAT-Role-Tools
RSAT-AD-Tools
RSAT-AD-PowerShell
RSAT-ADDS
RSAT-AD-AdminCenter
RSAT-ADDS-Tools
UpdateServices-RSAT
UpdateServices-API
UpdateServices-UI
RSAT-DHCP
RSAT-DNS-Server
FS-SMB1
Telnet-Client
User-Interfaces-Infra
Server-Gui-Mgmt-Infra
Server-Gui-Shell
Windows-Internal-Database
PowerShellRoot
PowerShell
PowerShell-V2
PowerShell-ISE
WAS
WAS-Config-APIs
```

The purpose of the script is to demonstrate a simple and easy method to generate a server report and compare it with the production server to identify the differences. In the real world, your scenario or requirement may be a little different, but this will provide you with a good starting point. To achieve your business and technical goals, you can extend this script based on your requirements. If you want to create an HTML-based result, you can use the `ConvertTo-HTML` cmdlet to achieve this. Also, you can automate the scanning and reporting process by configuring this script as a scheduled task.

After careful evaluation of the report, the identified unauthorized roles and features can be removed using the `Uninstall-WindowsFeature` PowerShell cmdlet. For example, the web server roles can be removed using the `Uninstall-WindowsFeature -Name Web-Server` command. This process can also be automated by using a scheduled task.

Server Message Block

Server Message Block (**SMB**) is a protocol that is mainly used by Windows. It allows computers to access or share files, printers, and other network resources remotely. The SMB protocol version 3.0 is a new introduction in Windows Server 2012. The version 3.0 uses the **Advanced Encryption Standard** (**AES**) method for encryption and signing.

Configuring and implementing SMB

The use or concept of encryption is not new. However, prior to Windows Server 2012, **Internet Protocol Security** (**IPSEC** or **IPsec**) was the only available option for transferring an encrypted data in Windows. Since the implementation of IPSEC required more administrative effort, configuration changes, and so on, it wasn't widely adopted in the industry. In Windows 2012 server, Microsoft introduced SMB version 3.0, which supports encrypting file, folder, or server. Unlike other encryption mechanisms, the SMB encryption can be enabled without any major implementation or configuration changes.

> SMB only encrypts data that is transferred using SMB Protocol. The IPSec will encrypt any protocol that is in transit using IP.

At a high level, the SMB configuration and implementation task can be divided into the following four step process:

1. Identify the server and client operating system to determine the best version of SMB for your organization.
2. Verify the current SMB configuration on file server and share.
3. Enable or disable the SMB configuration based on your business and technical requirements.
4. Verify and confirm the SMB communication between server and client.

Identifying the client and server operating system

In order to take advantage of SMB encryption, the client and server must support SMB version 3.0. By default, SMB 3.0 is included as part of Windows Server 2012 and Windows 8. If you have a mismatched SMB protocol during the communication, the lowest version of the protocol dialects will be used. So prior to enforcing SMB 3.0 in your environment, it is a good practice to identify and verify the existing operating details in your environment. A report on the operating system in an Active Directory environment can easily be generated by using the `Get-ADComputer` PowerShell cmdlet, as shown here:

```
Get-ADComputer -Filter * -Properties * |  Select Name, OperatingSystem
```

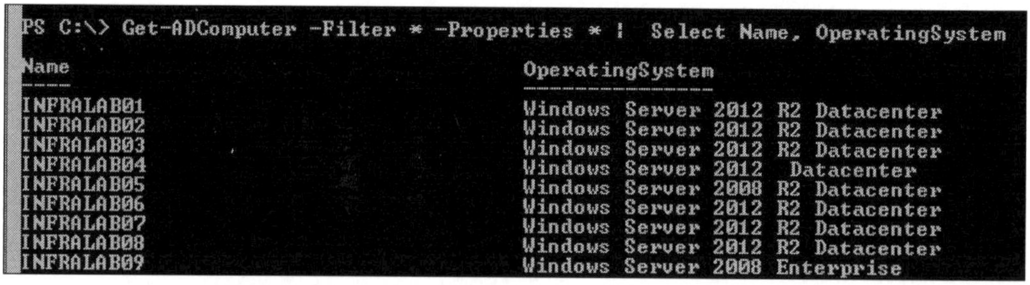

```
PS C:\> Get-ADComputer -Filter * -Properties * |  Select Name, OperatingSystem

Name                                OperatingSystem
----                                ---------------
INFRALAB01                          Windows Server 2012 R2 Datacenter
INFRALAB02                          Windows Server 2012 R2 Datacenter
INFRALAB03                          Windows Server 2012 R2 Datacenter
INFRALAB04                          Windows Server 2012  Datacenter
INFRALAB05                          Windows Server 2008 R2 Datacenter
INFRALAB06                          Windows Server 2012 R2 Datacenter
INFRALAB07                          Windows Server 2012 R2 Datacenter
INFRALAB08                          Windows Server 2012 R2 Datacenter
INFRALAB09                          Windows Server 2008 Enterprise
```

You can redirect the output of the preceding command to a file by using the `out-file` cmdlet, as shown in the following example:

```
Get-ADComputer -Filter * -Properties * |  Select Name, OperatingSystem
|out-file C:\Reports\ServerInfo.txt
```

> The SMB 3 is an open standard created by Microsoft. Other vendors will also announce the support of SMB3. For example, SAMBA 4 already supports SMB 3 Signing. The details can be found at `http://blog.fosketts.net/2012/12/12/samba-40-released-active-directory-smb-support/`.

Keep in mind that if a client doesn't support the configured SMB version, the user will get an **Access is Denied** error even if the user has permissions to access the file/folder. So it is important to verify the server and client version prior to enabling or enforcing the SMB version.

Verifying the current SMB configuration

On a Windows Server 2012, SMB V1, SMB V2, and SMB V3 are enabled by default. You can verify these configurations on a server by executing the `Get-SmbServerConfiguration` PowerShell cmdlet. The `True` or `False` value of the `EnableSMB1Protocol` and `EnableSMB2Protocol` attributes represents the current state of your server's SMB configuration.

> You won't see an SMB3 name on the list because Microsoft has renamed this service in Windows Server 2012.

```
PS C:\> Get-SmbServerConfiguration


AnnounceServer                  : False
AsynchronousCredits             : 64
AutoShareServer                 : True
AutoShareWorkstation            : True
CachedOpenLimit                 : 5
AnnounceComment                 :
EnableDownlevelTimewarp         : False
EnableLeasing                   : True
EnableMultiChannel              : True
EnableStrictNameChecking        : True
AutoDisconnectTimeout           : 0
DurableHandleV2TimeoutInSeconds : 30
EnableAuthenticateUserSharing   : False
EnableForcedLogoff              : True
EnableOplocks                   : True
EnableSecuritySignature         : False
ServerHidden                    : True
IrpStackSize                    : 15
KeepAliveTime                   : 2
MaxChannelPerSession            : 32
MaxMpxCount                     : 50
MaxSessionPerConnection         : 16384
MaxThreadsPerQueue              : 20
MaxWorkItems                    : 1
NullSessionPipes                :
NullSessionShares               :
OplockBreakWait                 : 35
PendingClientTimeoutInSeconds   : 120
RequireSecuritySignature        : False
EnableSMB1Protocol              : True
EnableSMB2Protocol              : True
Smb2CreditsMax                  : 2048
Smb2CreditsMin                  : 128
SmbServerNameHardeningLevel     : 0
TreatHostAsStableStorage        : False
ValidateAliasNotCircular        : True
ValidateShareScope              : True
ValidateShareScopeNotAliased    : True
ValidateTargetName              : True
EncryptData                     : False
RejectUnencryptedAccess         : True
```

> Keep in mind that in Windows Server 2012, if you enable or disable SMB V2, it will also enable or disable SMB V3.

Also, you can use the `Get-SmbShare` PowerShell cmdlet to verify the current encryption configuration on a file share. The `EncryptData` attribute will have a `True` or `False` value based on your encryption configuration.

```
PS C:\> Get-SmbShare | FL -Property Name,Path,EncryptData

Name        : ADMIN$
Path        : C:\Windows
EncryptData : False

Name        : C$
Path        : C:\
EncryptData : False

Name        : D$
Path        : D:\
EncryptData : False

Name        : IPC$
Path        :
EncryptData : False

Name        : SecureData1
Path        : C:\SecureData1
EncryptData : True

Name        : SecureData2
Path        : C:\Shares\SecureData2
EncryptData : True

Name        : SecureData3
Path        : C:\SecureData3
EncryptData : False

Name        : SecureData4
Path        : C:\SecureData4
EncryptData : False
```

Enabling or disabling the SMB encryption

The SMB encryption can be configured on an existing or a new share. The following step-by-step instructions can be used to enable or disable SMB encryption on an existing share:

1. Open **Server Manager** and navigate to **File and Storage Services** | **Shares**. You will see the existing shares in the middle pane.

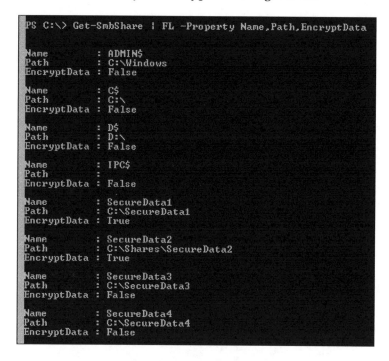

2. If you are enabling an encryption on an existing share, select the share name option and click on **Properties**, as shown in the following screenshot:

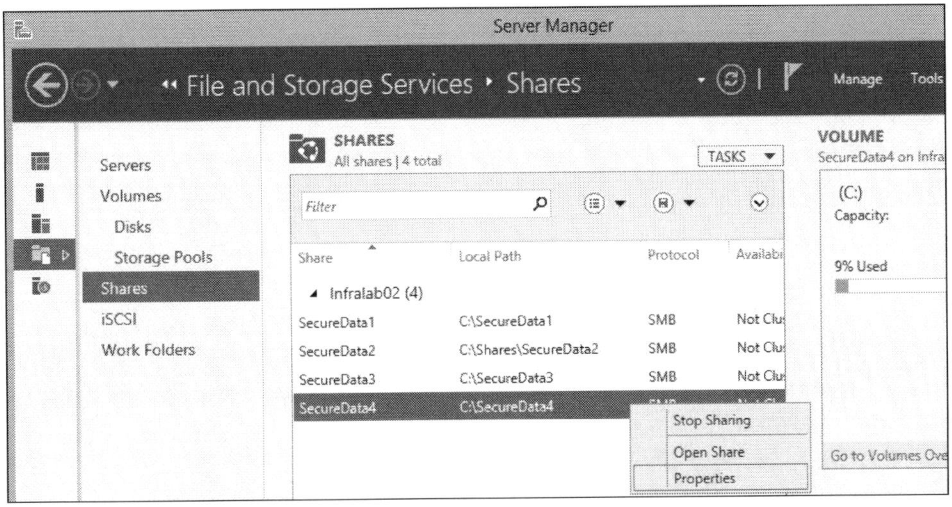
Server Manager
File and Storage Services ▸ Shares
Manage
Tools
Servers
Volumes
Disks
Storage Pools
Shares
iSCSI
Work Folders
SHARES
All shares | 4 total
TASKS
Filter
Share
Local Path
Protocol
Infralab02 (4)
SecureData1
C:\SecureData1
SMB
SecureData2
C:\Shares\SecureData2
SMB
SecureData3
C:\SecureData3
SMB
SecureData4
C:\SecureData4
Stop Sharing
Open Share
Properties
VOLUME
(C:)
Capacity:
9% Used

3. Select the **Settings** option and select the **Encrypt data access** checkbox. Click on **Apply** and **OK**.

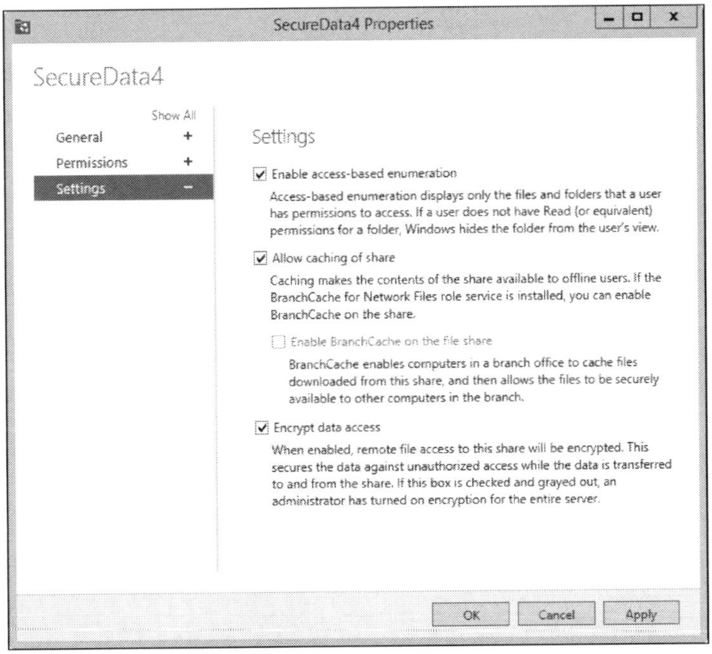
SecureData4 Properties
SecureData4
Show All
General
Permissions
Settings
Settings
Enable access-based enumeration
Access-based enumeration displays only the files and folders that a user has permissions to access. If a user does not have Read (or equivalent) permissions for a folder, Windows hides the folder from the user's view.
Allow caching of share
Caching makes the contents of the share available to offline users. If the BranchCache for Network Files role service is installed, you can enable BranchCache on the share.
Enable BranchCache on the file share
BranchCache enables computers in a branch office to cache files downloaded from this share, and then allows the files to be securely available to other computers in the branch.
Encrypt data access
When enabled, remote file access to this share will be encrypted. This secures the data against unauthorized access while the data is transferred to and from the share. If this box is checked and grayed out, an administrator has turned on encryption for the entire server.
OK
Cancel
Apply

4. If **Enable access-based enumeration** is selected, Windows displays the folder only if the user has the read permission. The **Allow caching of share** option provides a cashing mechanism for faster and offline access. If encryption is already enabled, you can uncheck the **Encrypt data access** checkbox to disable the encrypting on the share.

If you are creating a new share, you can complete both the processes in the same set of steps using **Server Manager**.

1. From the **Shares** tab inside **Server Manager**, navigate to **Task | New Share** as shown in the following screenshot:

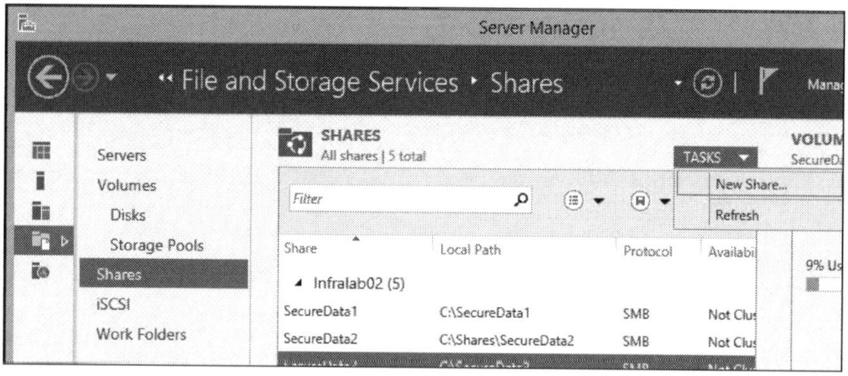

Creating a new share

2. On the **Select the profile for this share** window, select **SMB Share - Quick**. Click on **Next**.

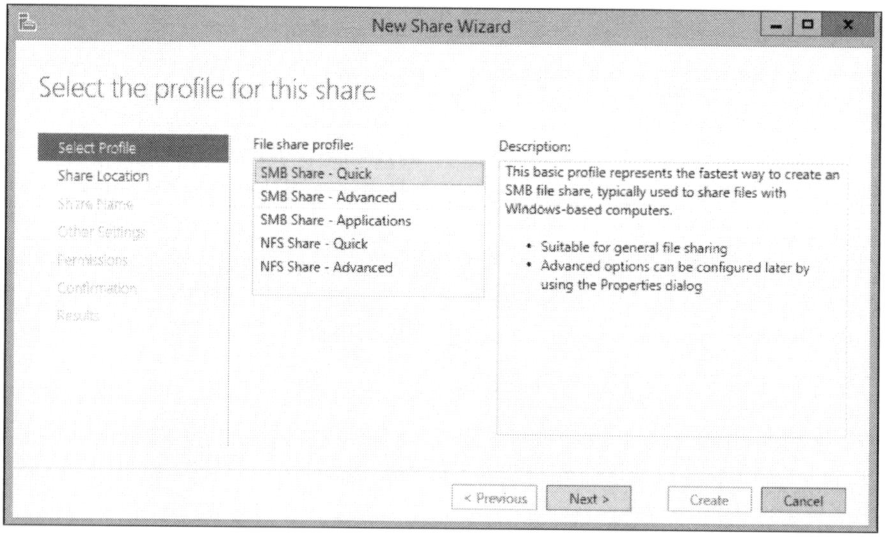

3. On the **Select the server and path for this share** window, select **Server name** and **Drive**, and click on **Next**.
4. Enter a new name for this share on the **Specify Share Name** window and click on **Next**.
5. On the **Configure share settings** window, enable the **Encrypt data access** option and click on **Next**, as shown in the following screenshot:

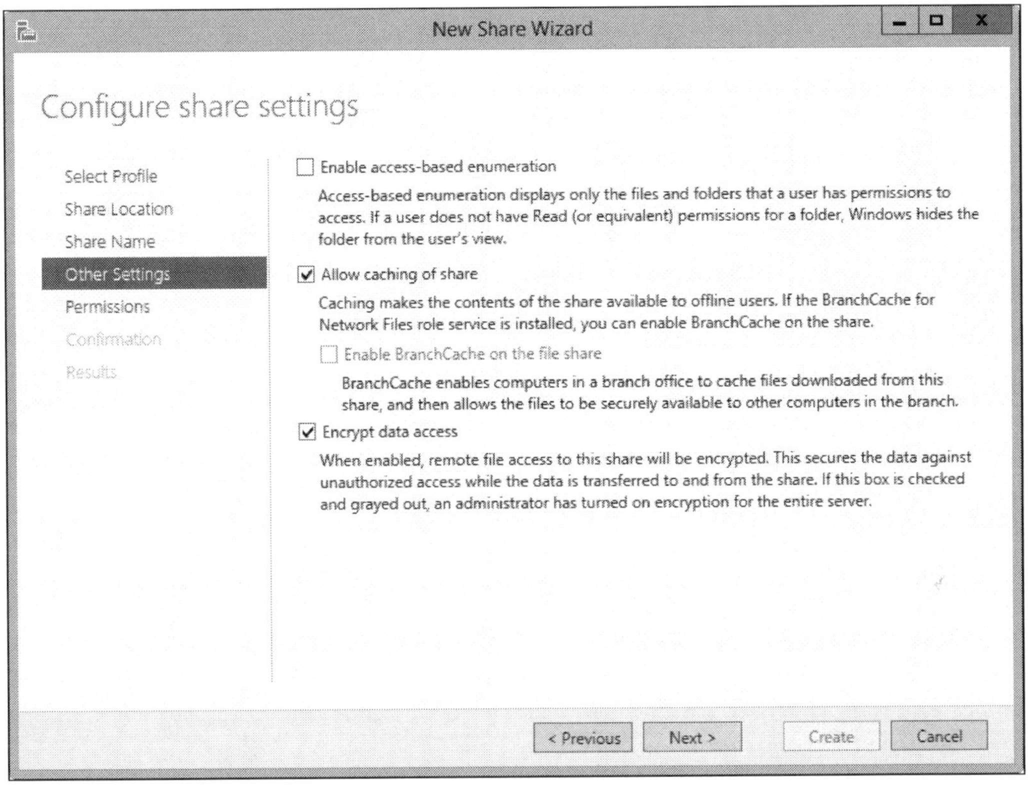
New Share Wizard
Configure share settings
Select Profile
Share Location
Share Name
Other Settings
Permissions
Confirmation
Results
Enable access-based enumeration
Access-based enumeration displays only the files and folders that a user has permissions to access. If a user does not have Read (or equivalent) permissions for a folder, Windows hides the folder from the user's view.
Allow caching of share
Caching makes the contents of the share available to offline users. If the BranchCache for Network Files role service is installed, you can enable BranchCache on the share.
Enable BranchCache on the file share
BranchCache enables computers in a branch office to cache files downloaded from this share, and then allows the files to be securely available to other computers in the branch.
Encrypt data access
When enabled, remote file access to this share will be encrypted. This secures the data against unauthorized access while the data is transferred to and from the share. If this box is checked and grayed out, an administrator has turned on encryption for the entire server.
< Previous
Next >
Create
Cancel

6. Update the appropriate permission based on your requirements in the **Specify permission to control access** window, and click on **Next**.
7. Click on the **Create** button on the **Confirm Selections** page to start the share creation and configuration process.

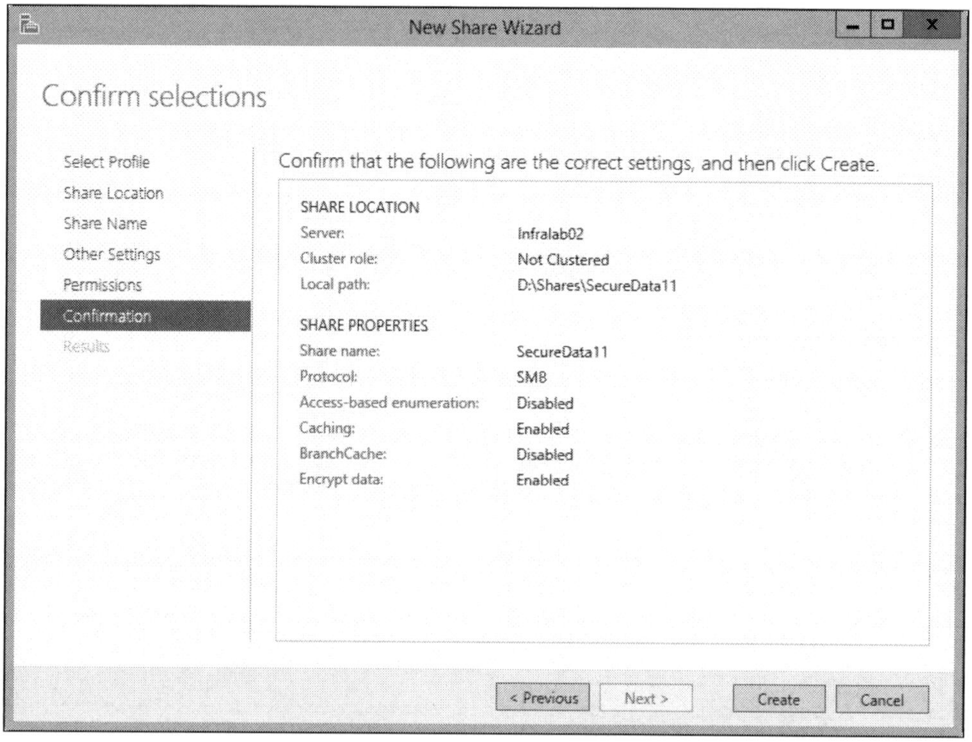

8. You will see the status and progress in the **View results** window. Click on **Close** to complete the process.

The encryption can also be configured with the `Set-SmbShare` PowerShell cmdlet using the syntax as shown in the following screenshot:

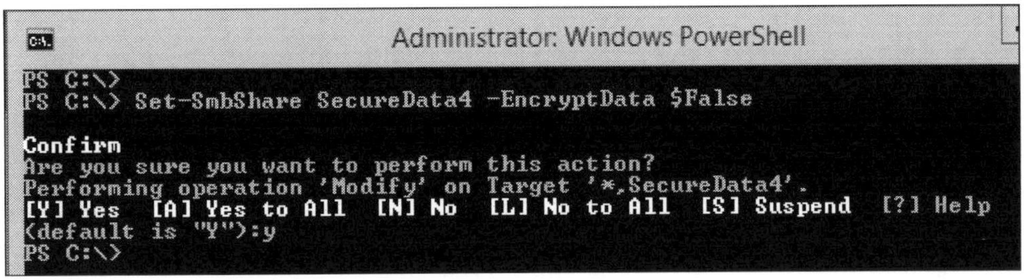

```
Administrator: Windows PowerShell
PS C:\>
PS C:\> Set-SmbShare SecureData4 -EncryptData $False

Confirm
Are you sure you want to perform this action?
Performing operation 'Modify' on Target '*,SecureData4'.
[Y] Yes  [A] Yes to All  [N] No  [L] No to All  [S] Suspend  [?] Help
(default is "Y"):y
PS C:\>
```

> Based on the `EncryptionData` value (`$True` for enabling and `$False` for disabling), you can enable or disable the encryption on a file share. Keep in mind that `Set-SmbShare` doesn't verify the existing encryption status during the execution of the cmdlet. So, if you are not sure about the current status of the encryption, you may want to run the `Get-SmbShare` cmdlet to verify this. The cmdlet details and syntax are provided in the previous section in this chapter. SMB encryption can be enabled per server as well, using the `Set-SmbServerConfiguration -EncryptData $true` PowerShell cmdlet.

Verifying SMB communication

Now you have configured the encryption on the share. The next step is to ensure that the communication between a client and server is done using SMB 3.0, instead of a legacy version of SMB. This can be achieved by executing the `Get-SmbConnection` PowerShell cmdlet from the remote computer. You can verify the value of the dialect number from the result to ensure these communications between server and client are using the correct version of SMB.

```
PS C:\> Get-SmbConnection

ServerName    ShareName     UserName       Credential     Dialect    NumOpens
----------    ---------     --------       ----------     -------    --------
infralab02    IPC$          MYINFRALA...   MYINFRALA...   3.02       0
infralab02    SecureData4   MYINFRALA...   MYINFRALA...   3.02       1
infralab02    SecureData6   MYINFRALA...   MYINFRALA...   3.02       1
```

As you can see in the preceding screenshot, the SMB dialect is listed as 3.X. This means both server and client were able to negotiate and are able to use the highest available version of the SMB protocol.

Summary

Implementing policies as well as maintaining the desired state are important in ensuring the integrity of a secure server platform. We started this chapter by evaluating the server types, role, and generating a baseline report based on your requirements. In this chapter, I explained a method using a PowerShell script to monitor the installed roles on a server by comparing them with a baseline server. The latter part of the chapter introduced SMB 3.0 and an encryption method to ensure the data integrity in your environment.

We will be using SMB encryption in the next chapter for virtualization and file server data security. You should be able to leverage information provided in the previous chapters to implement and maintain a secure server infrastructure in your business environment. Now it is time for us to work on securing other application-related components and roles of Windows Server 2012. You will see these details in the coming chapters.

4
Application Security

In this chapter, my goal is to provide you with an option to secure your application server platform using native Microsoft tools and technologies. Since applications run on a Windows Server platform, all baseline security and concepts that are introduced in the previous chapters are applicable to any application server.

On a high level, you can divide application server components into four major parts—server type, operating system, access mechanism, and data. If you apply security in these four major areas, you can protect your servers from security vulnerabilities. The baseline policies can be applied to the server type and operating system. However, the access mechanism and data protection will be based on your application and application data:

- **Server type**: The foundation of security starts from the selection of the server type. If there are no other business or technical requirements, it is a best practice to start with Windows Server Core as the server type. The list of supported roles on a Windows Server Core server is available on the Microsoft website. The details of supported roles can be found at `http://msdn.microsoft.com/en-us/library/hh846323(v=vs.85).aspx`.
- **Operating system**: The next level of security can be applied to the operating system itself. The operating system can be secured by applying appropriate baseline security policies. The details of creating and implementing baseline security using Microsoft **Security Configuration Wizard** (**SCW**) and Microsoft SCM are explained in *Chapter 1, Operating System and Baseline Security*, and *Chapter 2, Native MS Security Tools and Configuration*.
- **Access mechanism**: At this point, you have a secure server platform for your application. The next step is to control the server access method based on your application to maintain the security and integrity of the server. This can be achieved by using a proper **Access Control List** (**ACL**), a dynamic access control mechanism, delegation, firewall rules, and so on.

- **Data**: Once you have the secure platform for your application, you have to protect the actual application data on this server. The data can be secured by using proper a ACL, encryption, and so on.

In this chapter, I have selected four of the most widely used application scenarios, namely data print, web server, and virtualization, in order to demonstrate how we can apply security in these four levels. Even though demonstrating all application scenarios is beyond the scope of this book, you can apply these four levels of security on to any application or application server.

File or data server

Protecting proprietary and confidential information are key security considerations for any organization these days. In this section, you will learn how we can secure the data residing on Microsoft Windows Server 2012 using native and built-in Microsoft tools.

Applying baseline security

Based on your business and technical requirements, baseline polices can be created and implemented using Microsoft SCW and Microsoft SCM. I have discussed the importance of baseline security in *Chapter 1, Operating System and Baseline Security*, and *Chapter 2, Native MS Security Tools and Configuration*. Since our application is running on Microsoft Windows Server, as a security administrator, your job must start from a platform level. So let's start our journey with the implementation of baseline security for your application server.

From Microsoft SCM, you can select the correct baseline policy based on the role of the server. Since you are working with a file server, you can select the **File Server Security V1.0** policy from the list, as shown in the following screenshot:

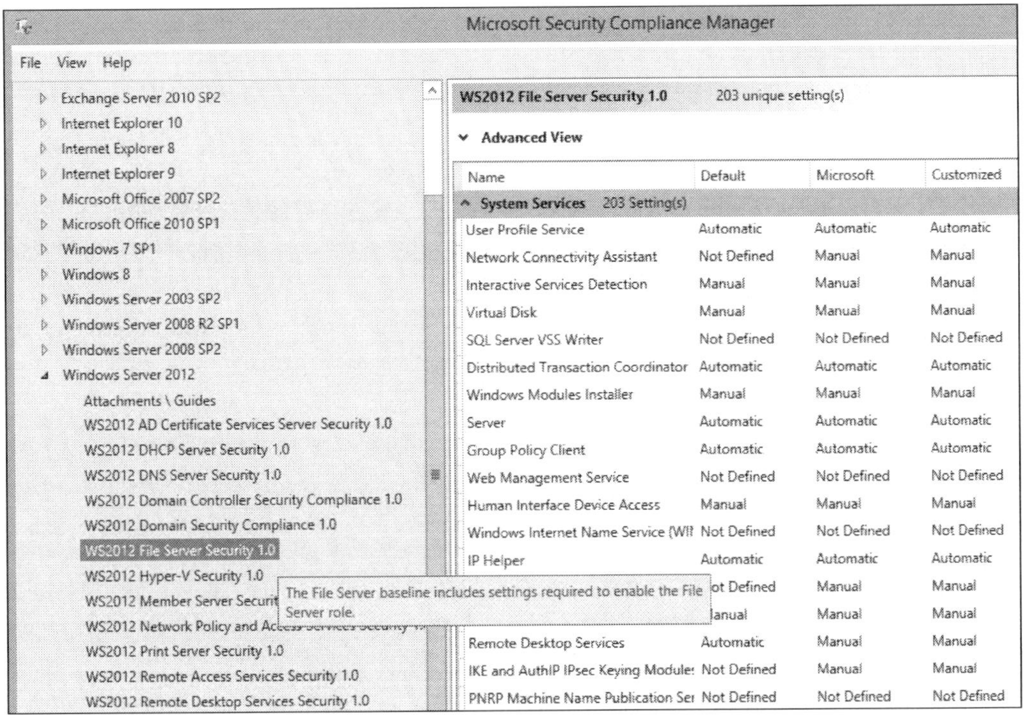

The next step in the process is to apply these polices onto your application servers. This can be achieved by manually applying this template onto a server, or by using GPO or some other automated mechanism. This configuration and step-by-step implementation details are explained in *Chapter 1, Operating System and Baseline Security*, and *Chapter 2, Native MS Security Tools and Configuration*.

The access mechanism

We have discussed **Server Message Block** (**SMB**) encryption and details in *Chapter 3, Server Roles and Protocols*. To secure your data on a file server and to harden the access mechanism, you enforce a certain SMB protocol version in your environment. The first step in this process is to disable the legacy SMB version protocol in your environment. The `Set-SmbServerConfiguration` PowerShell cmdlet can be used to disable or enable the SMB protocol version on Windows Server 2012.

To disable SMB version 1.0 on Windows Server, you can execute the `Set-SmbServerConfiguration -EnableSMB1Protocol $false` command from a PowerShell window, as shown in the following screenshot:

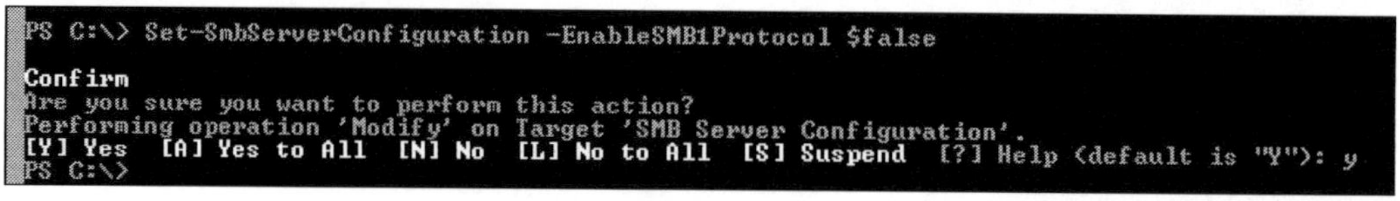
PS C:\> Set-SmbServerConfiguration -EnableSMB1Protocol $false
Confirm
Are you sure you want to perform this action?
Performing operation 'Modify' on Target 'SMB Server Configuration'.
[Y] Yes [A] Yes to All [N] No [L] No to All [S] Suspend [?] Help (default is "Y"): y
PS C:\>

It will prompt you for a confirmation. You can validate the configuration using the `Get-SmbServerConfiguration` cmdlet.

> The SMB protocol can also be disabled using a Group Policy Object. These configurations are available in the **Configuration** | **Windows Settings** | **Security Settings** | **Local Policies** | **Security Options** node.

Data protection

The next step in the process is to protect the actual data on the server. As mentioned previously, this can be achieved by using many methods. In the following sections, you will find the details of removing or protecting unwanted shares and enabling data encryption using Microsoft BitLocker.

Removing unwanted shares

An unused or unidentified data share can be a security challenge for any organization. So, it is important that you should continuously monitor and manage available shares and usage on the server in your organization. This can be accomplished by using a Microsoft tool or other third-party monitoring tools. In this section, my goal is to give you a solution using built-in commands and tools. Since PowerShell is the command administrator medium for most administrators these days, I will provide solutions using appropriate PowerShell cmdlets and functions.

The `Get-smbshare` PowerShell cmdlet can be used to list all the existing SMB shares from a server, as shown in the following screenshot:

```
PS C:\> Get-SmbShare

Name                ScopeName          Path                      Description
----                ---------          ----                      -----------
ADMIN$              *                  C:\Windows                Remote Admin
C$                  *                  C:\                       Default share
D$                  *                  D:\                       Default share
IPC$                *                                            Remote IPC
SecureData1         *                  C:\SecureData1
SecureData11        *                  D:\Shares\SecureData11
SecureData2         *                  C:\Shares\SecureData2
SecureData3         *                  C:\SecureData3
SecureData4         *                  C:\SecureData4
SecureData6         *                  C:\Shares\SecureData6
```

You can also get the share details and information by using the WMI commands; for example, `Gwmi -class Win32_Share`.

This can be a good starting point for identifying shares on a server. If you suspect an unidentified and unauthorized share on a server, you can use the `Remove-smbshare` cmdlet to forcibly disconnect all the connections to this share and remove the share from the server.

It is always a good practice to confirm the usage of the share before you disconnect them. So, if you are not sure about the usage, you can use `get-smbsession` to identify the usage before applying this command.

The following is the syntax of the `Remove-smbshare` cmdlet:

`Remove-smbshare -Name <ShareName>`

As you can see in the following screenshot, it will prompt you to confirm the delete process. You can use the `-Force` switch to override this default behavior.

```
PS C:\> Remove-SmbShare -Name "SecureData6"

Confirm
Are you sure you want to perform this action?
Performing operation 'Remove-Share' on Target '*,SecureData6'.
[Y] Yes  [A] Yes to All  [N] No  [L] No to All  [S] Suspend  [?] Help (default is "Y"): y
PS C:\> Get-SmbShare
```

By default, Windows Server creates a few default shares called Administrative Shares on a Windows server. Since administrative shares are different, the process of managing and controlling these shares is also different. You need to disable the automatic creation process by modifying the registry. If you have a valid business or technical requirement, the default behavior of the administrative shares creation process can be controlled by creating `AutoShareServerREG_DWORD` with a value of zero in the `HKEY_LOCAL_MACHINE\SYSTEM\CurrentControlSet\Services\LanmanServer\Parameters` registry. The server will have to be restarted to apply the changes on to the server.

Data encryption using BitLocker encryption

The management of a threat to confidential information and data from inside and outside of an organization can be a challenge. Encrypting the data using a strong algorithm can minimize data leakage even if someone hacks the data. Microsoft BitLocker is a built-in tool and mechanism that provides an encryption option to address these issues.

In the following section, I will explain a method on how to protect sensitive data using Microsoft BitLocker. For this exercise, you will be protecting human resources data using an Active Directory security group.

Installing BitLocker

Depending on which method of Microsoft BitLocker encryption you use, the first step in this process is to install the Microsoft BitLocker software on the server. This can be achieved by adding the **Bit locker Drive Encryption** feature as described in the following section:

1. Open **Server Manager**.
2. From the **Manage** menu, select the **Add Roles and Features** option.
3. Click on **Next** in the **Before you begin** window.
4. In the **Select installation type** window, select the **Role-based or feature-based installation** option. Click on **Next**.

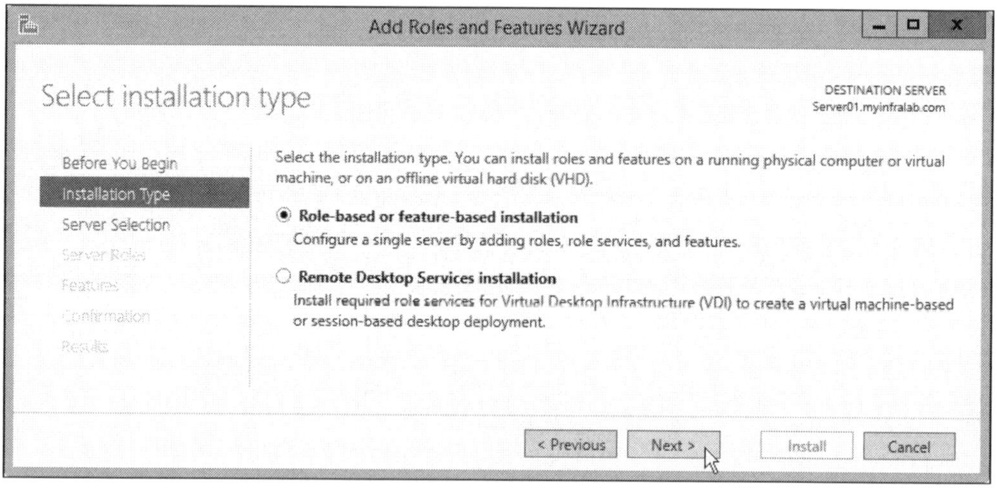
Add Roles and Features Wizard
Select installation type
DESTINATION SERVER
Server01.myinfralab.com
Before You Begin
Installation Type
Server Selection
Select the installation type. You can install roles and features on a running physical computer or virtual machine, or on an offline virtual hard disk (VHD).
Role-based or feature-based installation
Configure a single server by adding roles, role services, and features.
Remote Desktop Services installation
Install required role services for Virtual Desktop Infrastructure (VDI) to create a virtual machine-based or session-based desktop deployment.
< Previous
Next >
Install
Cancel

5. From the **Select destination server** window, select the appropriate server. Click on **Next**.

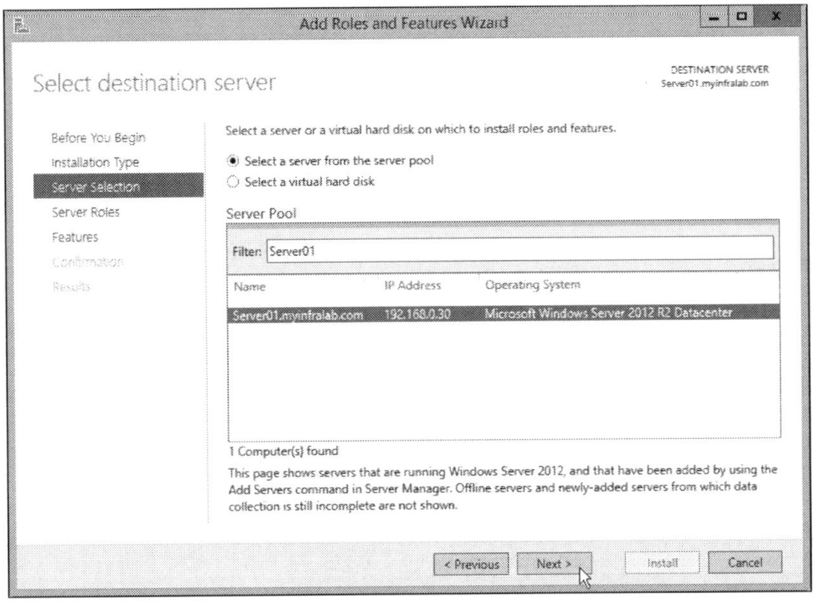

6. Click on **Next** in the **Select server roles** window.
7. From the **Select features** window, select the **Bit locker Drive Encryption** feature. If you receive the **Add features that are required for BitLocker Drive Encryption?** question, accept the default values and click on the **Add Features** option.

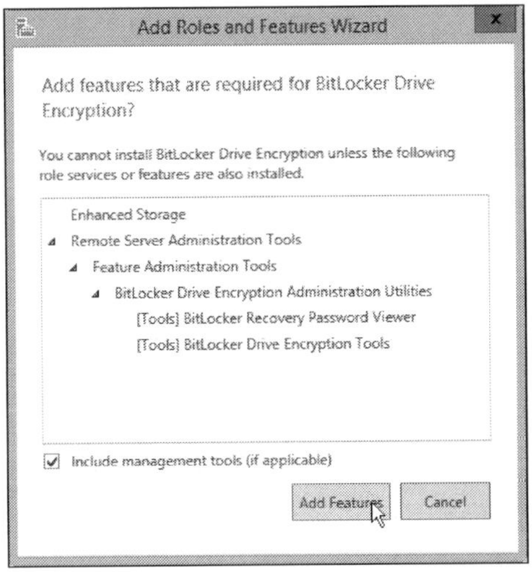

8. Click on **Next** in the **Select features** window to continue.

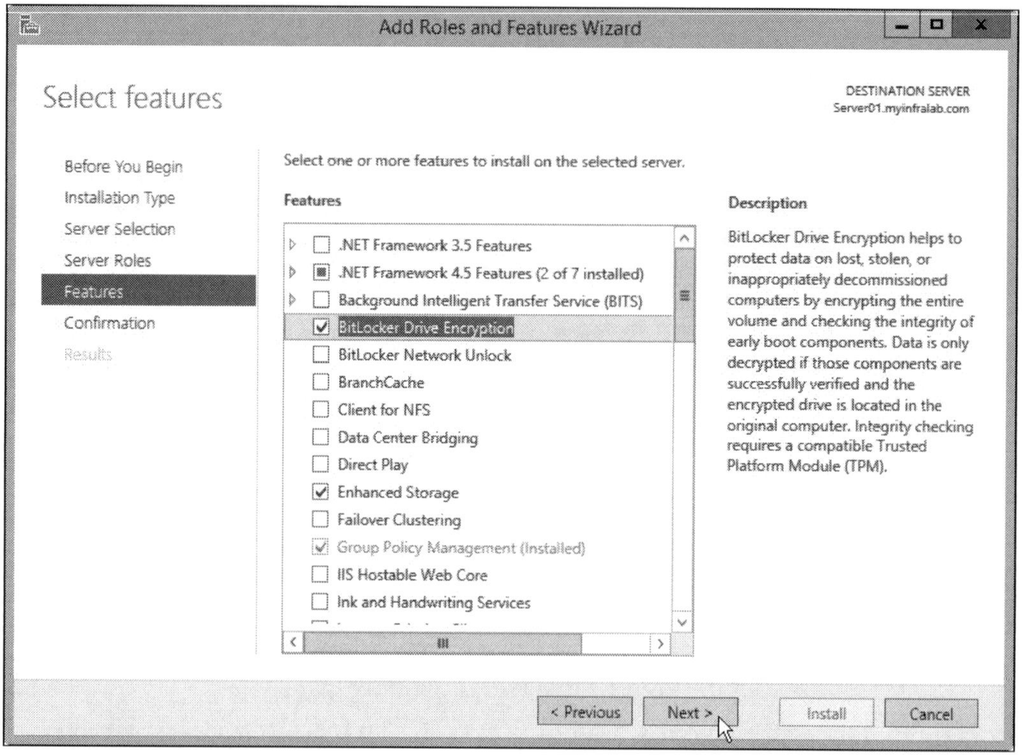

9. You should restart the server after the BitLocker feature installation so you can select the **Restart the destination server automatically if required** option from the **Confirm installation sections** window. Click on **Install** to continue with the installation process.

10. Select **Yes** to confirm the automatic restart option.

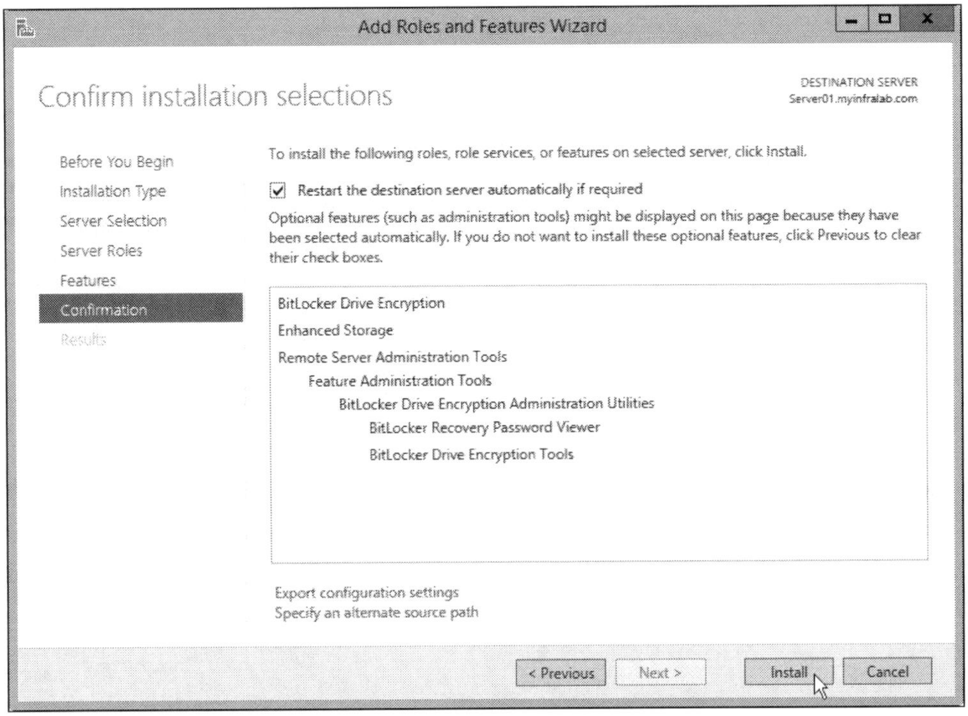

11. You will see the status and progress in the **Installation Progress** window. Since you have selected the automatic restart option, the server will be restarted after the feature installation. For whatever reason, if automatic restart is not an option, you can uncheck the **Restart the destination server automatically if required** option in step 9 and restart the server manually after the installation.

12. After the reboot, the server will open the **Add Roles and Features Wizard** window. Check the status of the installation process. Click on **Close** to close the wizard window.

Verifying the encryption status

Before you enable or disable the encryption, the best practice is to verify the current status of the encryption. PoweShell is going to be your best option here as well. The Microsoft BitLocker PowerShell module provides cmldlets that can be used to manage and control BitLocker encryption on a server.

> You can use the `Get-Command -Module BitLocker` cmdlet to get the list of available and supported commands from the BitLocker PowerShell module.

The following instructions provide an option to verify the current encryption status on a server:

1. Log on to the server with administrative credentials. Open the PowerShell command window.
2. Enter the `Get-BitLockerVolume` cmdlet. You can verify the **VolumeStatus** value as shown in the following screenshot:

PS C:\> Get-BitLockerVolume
ComputerName: SERVER01
VolumeType Mount Point CapacityGB VolumeStatus Encryption Percentage KeyProtector
OperatingSystem C: 248.92 FullyDecrypted 0 {}
Data E: 48.83 FullyDecrypted 0 {}

3. Alternately, you can use `Manage-bde.exe -Status` to verify the current encryption status. You can verify the **Conversion Status** value as shown in the following screenshot:

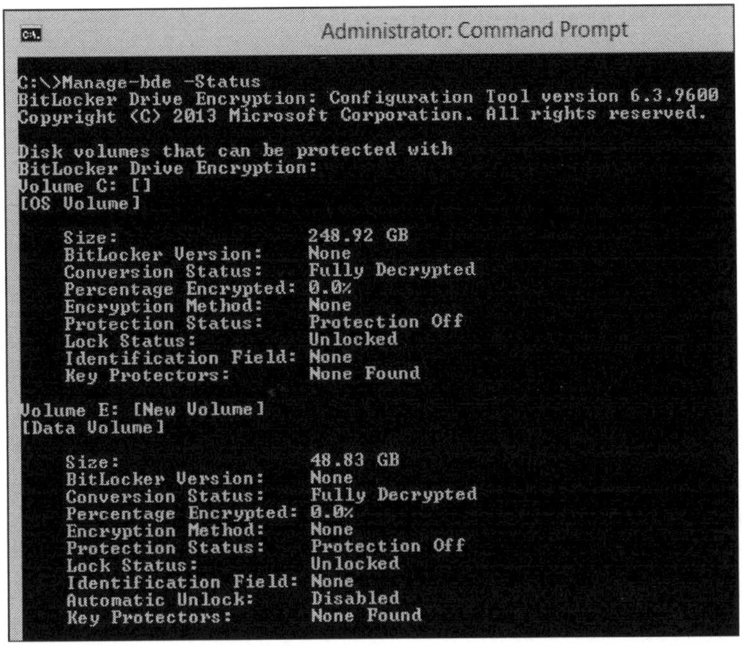

Administrator: Command Prompt
C:\>Manage-bde -Status
BitLocker Drive Encryption: Configuration Tool version 6.3.9600
Copyright (C) 2013 Microsoft Corporation. All rights reserved.
Disk volumes that can be protected with
BitLocker Drive Encryption:
Volume C: []
[OS Volume]
Size: 248.92 GB
BitLocker Version: None
Conversion Status: Fully Decrypted
Percentage Encrypted: 0.0%
Encryption Method: None
Protection Status: Protection Off
Lock Status: Unlocked
Identification Field: None
Key Protectors: None Found
Volume E: [New Volume]
[Data Volume]
Size: 48.83 GB
BitLocker Version: None
Conversion Status: Fully Decrypted
Percentage Encrypted: 0.0%
Encryption Method: None
Protection Status: Protection Off
Lock Status: Unlocked
Identification Field: None
Automatic Unlock: Disabled
Key Protectors: None Found

4. Once you have verified the encryption status, the next step in the process is to enable or disable the data encryption.

Encrypting data volume

There are a few options available for encryption when using Microsoft BitLocker. You can use a hardware or software method. If your server has a **Trusted Platform Module (TPM)** chip, the operating system volume can be encrypted using TPM. TPM controls the encryption keys. The TPM chip has to verify the state of the computer before the key can be accessible. Since our goal is to protect the data on a file server, I will be explaining an option using Microsoft BitLocker to encrypt the data without using TPM, and in our case, the access mechanism will be protected and controlled using an Active Directory security group.

The `Enable-BitLocker` PowerShell cmdlet can be used to encrypt the data. Since it is a file server and the goal is to protect sensitive data, you will be using `AdAccountOrGroup` as the Key Protector.

The following step-by-step instructions will provide a method to encrypt data on a file server:

1. Log in to the server with administrative credentials. Open the PowerShell command window.
2. From the PowerShell window, enter the following command:

```
Enable-BitLocker -MountPoint"E:" -EncryptionMethod Aes256
-AdAccountOrGroup"MyInfraLab\HR Admin" -AdAccountOrGroupProtector
```

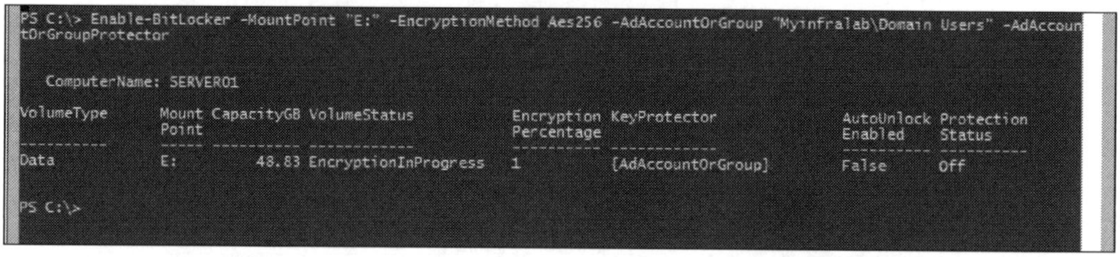
PS C:\> Enable-BitLocker -MountPoint "E:" -EncryptionMethod Aes256 -AdAccountOrGroup "Myinfralab\Domain Users" -AdAccountOrGroupProtector
ComputerName: SERVER01
VolumeType Mount Point CapacityGB VolumeStatus Encryption Percentage KeyProtector AutoUnlock Enabled Protection Status
Data E: 48.83 EncryptionInProgress 1 [AdAccountOrGroup] False Off
PS C:\>

In the preceding cmdlet, you are encrypting the `E` drive with the `Aes256` encryption methods. Based on your requirement, you can use either the `Aes128` or `Aes256` encryption method. The **HR Admin** security group from your Active Directory will act as **Key Protector.**

By default, the `Enable-BitLocker` cmdlet will encrypt the entire volume. This encryption process can take a few hours to complete, depending on the data and volume size. The `-UsedSpaceOnly` parameter can be used to save some time by excluding the unused portion of the disk.

Additional protectors such as TPM, PIN, or Recovery Key are required if you are planning to use the `ADAccountOrGroup` protector on an operating system volume. The TPM and PIN encryption methods and instructions are included in the *Hyper-V server* section of this chapter.

You will get the encryption status by double-clicking on the BitLocker icon from the status bar, as shown in the following screenshot:

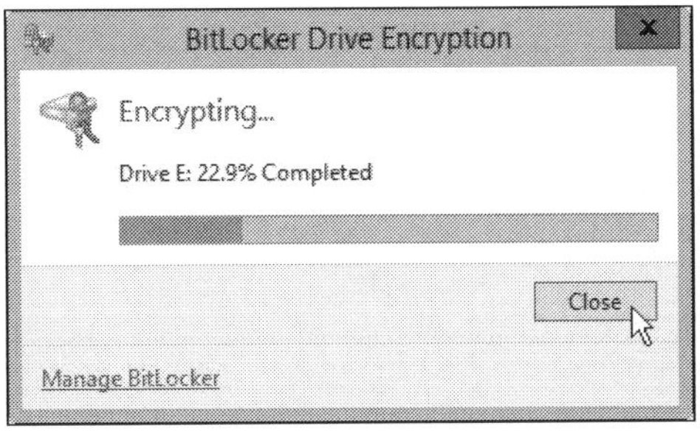

> **Microsoft BitLocker Administration and Monitoring** (**MBAM**) is a centralized administration and management tool for Microsoft BitLocker. It provides many features such as centralized reporting, a self-service portal for recovery, and the ability to validate compliance state. If you have multiple servers and clients using Microsoft BitLocker encryption, you may need to consider this tool for administration.

Managing BitLocker volume

Most administration tasks can be performed using PowerShell cmdlets. Some of the basic functionalities are also available from Windows Explorer, or by going to the properties of the disk or volume.

To administer a BitLocker encrypted volume, you can right-click on the drive and select the **Manage BitLocker** option, as shown in the following screenshot:

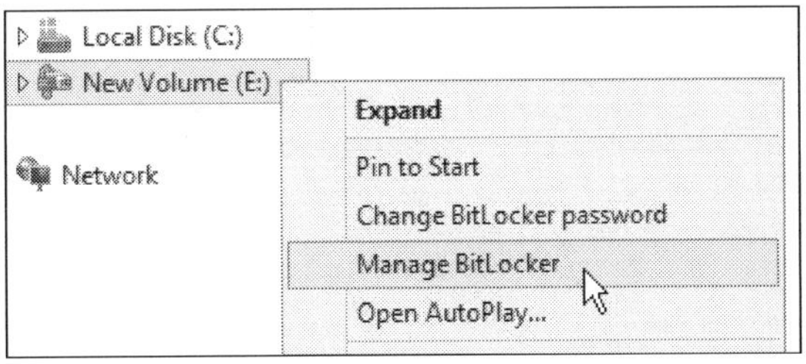

All the available options will be displayed in the **BitLocker Drive Encryption** window, as shown in the following screenshot:

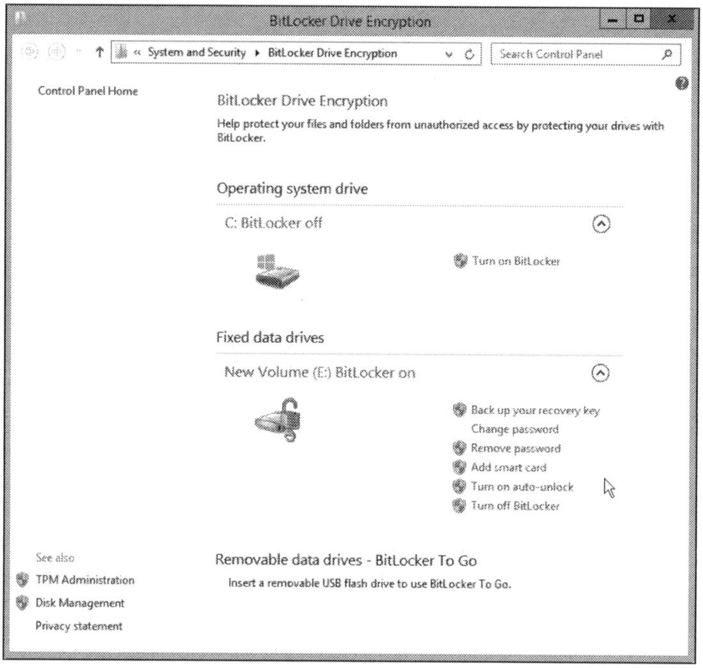

The data protection and security won't complete with an encryption. The encryption has only one security layer to protect the data. You will learn some more advanced techniques such as dynamic access, data classification, file screening, and data expiration in *Chapter 6, Access Control*.

> BitLocker can be used to protect cluster shared volumes and storage area networks. The details and more information can be found at `http://technet.microsoft.com/en-us/library/dn383585.aspx`.

Print server

Securing printers and print servers is vital in ensuring the security of an organization and their resources. These security configurations should start from the foundation level—the operating system. Then, you can apply appropriate **Group Policy Objects** (**GPO**), ACL, and so on to make the printing infrastructure more secure. The process and configuration details are included in the following sections.

An administrator can use the following task list as a starting point for their print server security configuration:

- **Operating system type**: Use the Windows Server Core operation system
- **Baseline security**: Create and implement server baseline security
- **Print server role feature integrity**: Continuously monitor and validate roles and features
- **Printer drive security and protection**: Ensure printer driver security and appropriate GPOs
- **Printer share security and protection**: Ensure printer and share security using GPOs and other policy mechanisms

You will see the details of these tasks in the following sections.

Applying baseline security

For hardening print servers, you can start with Microsoft SCW and Microsoft SCM for creating and applying baseline polices. At the time of writing this book, Microsoft SCM offers 203 security setting recommendations for Windows Server 2012 print servers, as shown in the following screenshot:

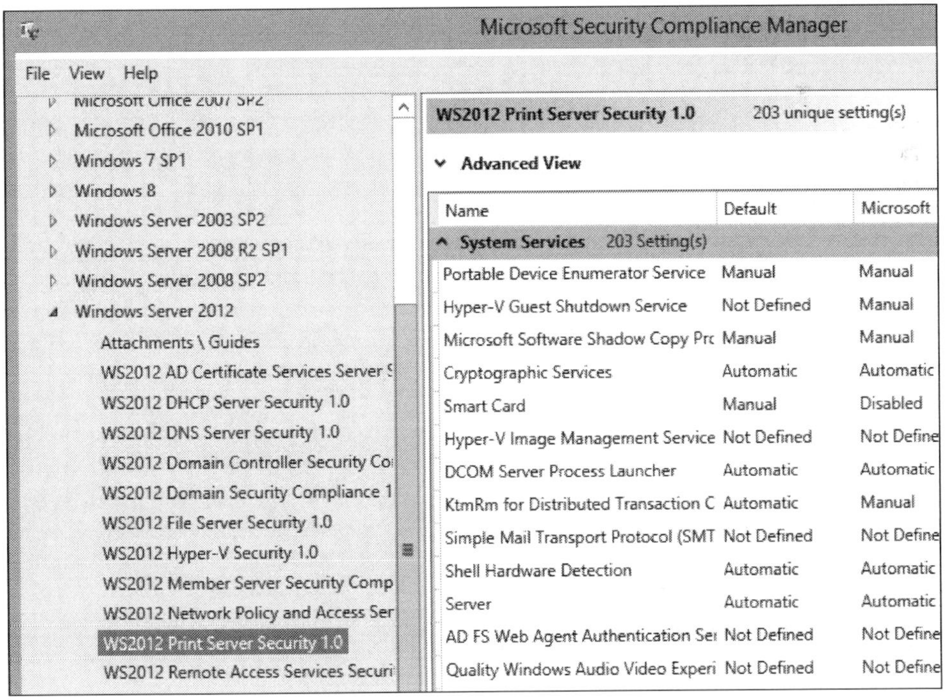

The next step in the process is to apply these polices onto your print servers. This can be achieved by manually applying these templates onto the server or applying them using a GPO or some other automated mechanism. The configuration and step-by-step implementation details are explained in *Chapter 1, Operating System and Baseline Security*, and *Chapter 2, Native MS Security Tools and Configuration*.

The print server role security

The **Printing and Documenting** service in Windows Server 2012 offers a few services such as **Print Server**, **Distributed Scan Server**, **Internet Printing**, and **LDP** service, as shown in the following screenshot:

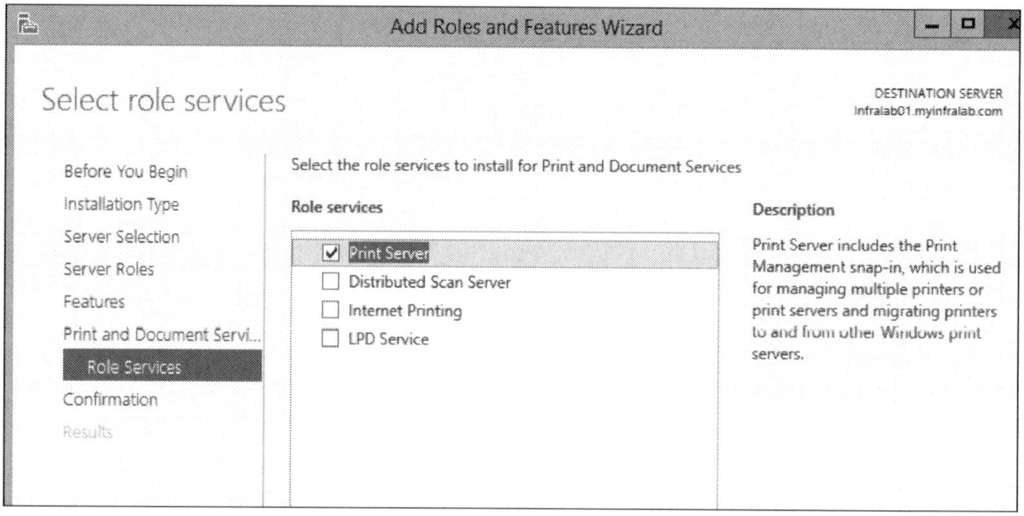

Installing **Print Server** may not impact the overall security of the server. However, some of the features such as **Internet Printing** can adversely impact the overall security if you don't properly monitor and apply the appropriate security baseline and take appropriate security measures. **Internet Printing** is an IIS-based service. Microsoft IIS based security components must be configured to ensure maximum security.

The `Get-WindowsFeature | Where-Object Installed` cmdlet will provide a list of installed roles and features on the server. If you want to filter only the **Printing** and **Documenting Service** details, you can use the `Get-WindowsFeature Print*` cmdlet, as shown in the following screenshot:

```
PS C:\> Get-WindowsFeature Print*

Display Name                                            Name
------------                                            ----
[X] Print and Document Services                         Print-Services
    [X] Print Server                                    Print-Server
    [X] Distributed Scan Server                         Print-Scan-Server
    [ ] Internet Printing                               Print-Internet
    [X] LPD Service                                     Print-LPD-Service
```

Based on your requirement, you can create a printer baseline policy and compare it against all print servers to ensure the integrity of these servers and roles. I have provided a PowerShell-based script in *Chapter 3, Server Roles and Protocols*, which can be used to achieve this goal.

Print server access mechanisms

Security threats and attacks such as **Man-In-the-Middle** attacks can alter the SMB package during transit. In order to ensure authenticity, these packages must be evaluated before communication can be permitted. The digital signing of an SMB package in Windows Server can be used to verify these packages. So it is recommended to enable **Digitally Sign Communication** for print servers. If you are using Microsoft SCW or SCM, these sets of configurations are included as part of baseline security. If there is no other business or technical requirements, it is recommended to implement these configurations for your servers.

These policies and configuration details are located in the **Computer Configuration | Policies | Windows Settings | Security Settings | Local Policies | Security Options** section of the GPO. There are two settings in the **Microsoft Network Client** section to support **Digitally Sign Communication**—**Digitally Sign Communications** (always) and **Digitally Sign Communications** (if server agrees). The **Digitally Sign Communications** (if server agrees) configuration will negotiate with the client on SMB packet signing. The **Digitally Sign Communications** (always) configuration will not communicate with the client without using SMB packet signing. More theoretical details and explanation can be found at `http://technet.microsoft.com/en-us/library/cc728025(v=WS.10).aspx`.

The printer driver security and installation

As a next step, you need to ensure the printer driver security on a print server. On Windows Server 2012, it is recommended to use the V4 driver whenever possible. The printer driver can be installed or updated using the Print Management console, or using the `Add-PrinterDriver` PowerShell cmdlet.

The Point and Print Restrictions configuration provides an additional set of security features to enhance the security of the print server. These settings can be configured using Group Policy Objects. These GPO settings are located at **User Configuration** | **Policies** | **Administrative Templates** | **Control Panel** | **Printers**.

> Windows Server 2012 servers support secure **Web Services on Devices** (**WSD**) printing without any additional encryption technologies such as IPSEC or IPsec.

By default, only the local administrator on a machine can install and update the printer drivers. Giving administrator permission to end users can open a huge security threat to any organization.

The following steps provide instructions on configuring the Point and Print Restrictions GPO to allow an end user to download and install printer drivers from a print server without administrator permissions on the local machine:

1. Open **Group Policy Management Console** (**GPMC**).
2. Right-click on the appropriate GPO and click on **Edit**.
3. Navigate to **User Configuration** | **Policies** | **Administrative Templates** | **Control Panel** | **Printers**.

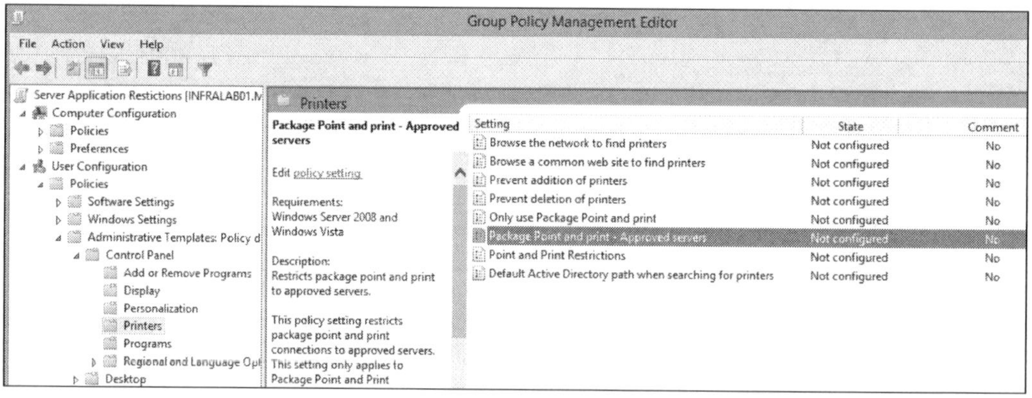

From the **Printers** settings page, you can configure different settings based on your security requirements.

Print server and share permissions

By default, the **Everyone** special group has the **Print** permission on all the installed printers, as shown in the following screenshot:

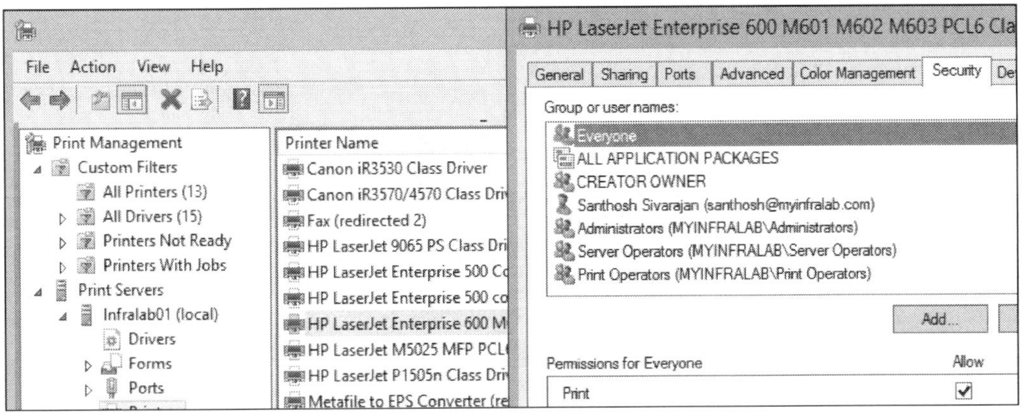

The Everyone special group

By default, it's an inheritance permission from the printer server itself. From a security perspective, the best practice is to remove the **Everyone** group, unless you have some valid technical or business reason to keep them. Some automated printer deployment mechanisms using **GPO** or **Group Policy Preference** (**GPP**) may require the **Print** permission for all domain users. In that scenario, you can replace the **Everyone** group with the **Authenticated Users** group.

The following steps explain the process to modify the default print server permission using the **Print Management** console:

1. Open the **Print Management** console by navigating to **Server Manager** | **Tools** | **Print Management**.
2. Expand the **Print Server** node. Right-click on your print server and select **Properties**.

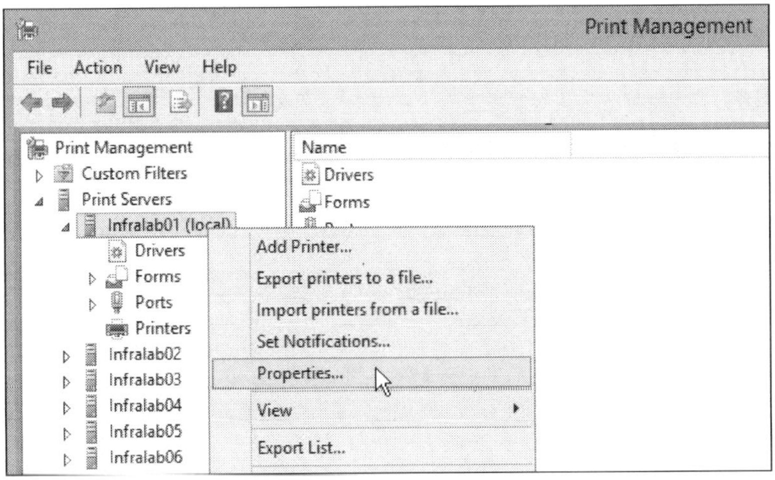

3. From the **Security** tab, unselect the **Print** permission.

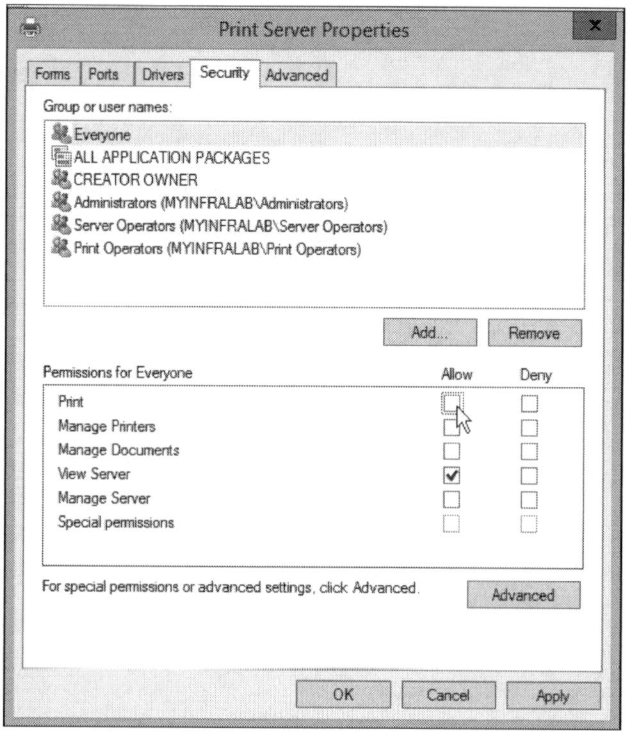

4. Click on **Apply** and **OK** to complete this operation.

This configuration will be the new default configuration for all the new printers installed on this print server. Depending on your requirements, you can delegate or customize the administrative permission requirements from this console as well by following the preceding instructions.

> The print server can also be managed by using a PowerShell cmdlet. The set of print server cmdlets are available in the `PrintManagement` PowerShell module.

Hyper-V servers

In this section, your goal is to protect your Microsoft Hyper-V servers using native and built-in tools. As mentioned in the earlier sections of this book, we can divide an application server into four different components: server type, operating system, access mechanism, and data.

If there are no other business or technical requirements, it is recommended to use the Windows Server Core operating system for Hyper-V servers.

Applying baseline security

For this application, we will again start with baseline security. Based on your business and technical requirements, baseline policies can be created and implemented using Microsoft SCW and Microsoft SCM. The Hyper-V security template is available by default in Microsoft SCM. It can be customized based on your requirements. The details of these tasks are included in *Chapter 1, Operating System and Baseline Security*, and *Chapter 2, Native MS Security Tools and Configuration*.

From Microsoft SCM, you can select the correct baseline policy based on the role of the server. Since you are working with Hyper-V servers, you can select the **Hyper-V Security V1.0** policy from the list, as shown in the following screenshot:

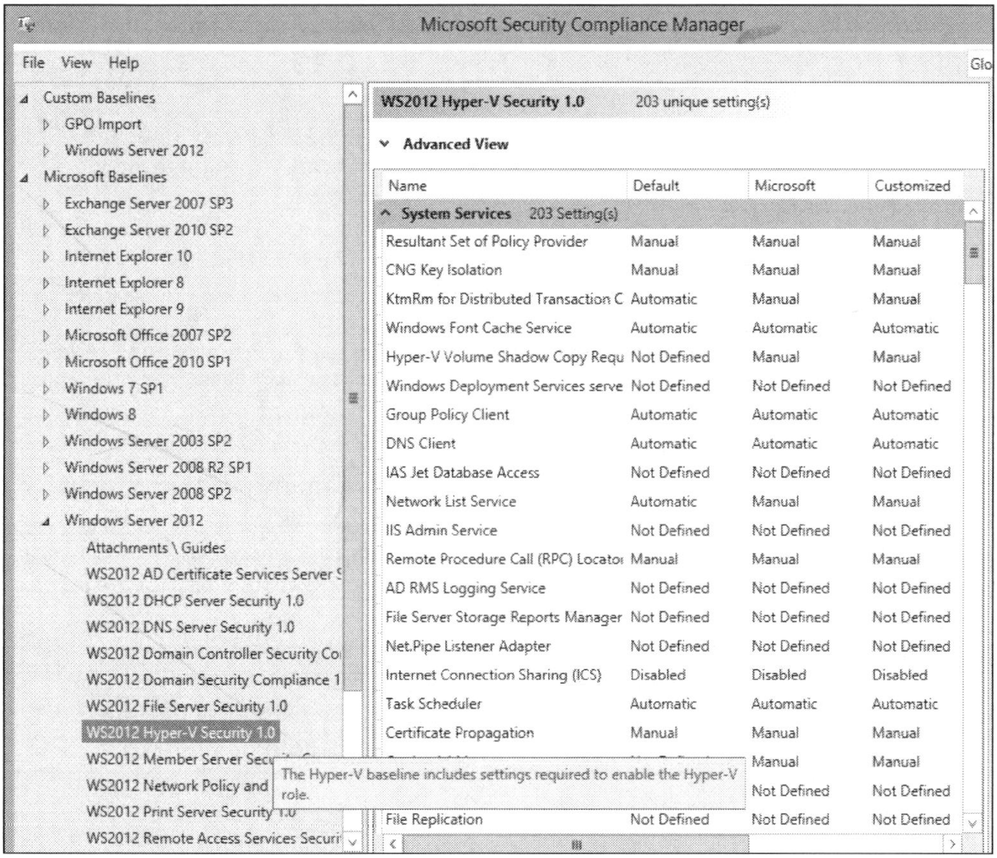

The configuration and implementation details of these polices are explained in *Chapter 1, Operating System and Baseline Security*, and *Chapter 2, Native MS Security Tools and Configuration*. You can apply these policies onto Hyper-V hosts and guest servers. The guest baseline policy will be based on the application running on that server.

Securing the access mechanism

Prior to Windows Server 2012, providing a Hyper-V administration role without granting a local administration permissions was a challenge. The role-based administrator using Microsoft Authorization Manager was popular in those days. In Windows Server 2012, Microsoft has introduced a new local security group called **Hyper-V Administrators** to overcome these limitations. The members of **Hyper-V Administrators** will have full permission on a Hyper-V server without having local administrator permissions. This is officially called **Simplified Authorization**.

You can see more details of Simplified Authorization at `http://technet.microsoft.com/en-us/library/hh831410.aspx`.

> Even though the **Authorization Manager** (**Azan**) tool is included in Windows Server 2012 R2 servers, role-based administration using Azan is not supported on Windows Server 2012 R2 Hyper-V.

Guard protection

In Windows Server 2012, Microsoft has introduced two types of additional *guard* protection in Hyper-V servers—DHCP Guard and Router Guard. In an enterprise, unauthorized systems and devices can be an enormous security threat. These rouge devices can act on behalf of the network security and other services to access sensitive information. The DHCP Guard option will determine whether a DHCP server message should be accepted or denied. The best practice recommendation is to enable the DHCP Guard option on all non-DHCP servers and disable on all DHCP servers. By enabling the Router Guard option, the Hyper-V server will discard the Redirect and Router advertisement messages. Keep in mind that enabling this option will have minimal impact on the Hyper-V server. This is the reason it is not enabled by default.

Enabling the guard protection

The following provides the details of enabling DHCP Guard and Router Guard on a Hyper-V server:

1. Open **Hyper-V Manager**. From the middle pane, right-click on the guest server and select **Settings**.

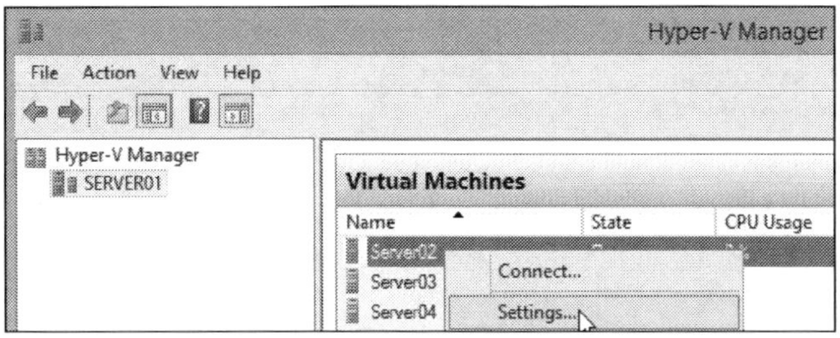

2. Expand the **Network Adaptor** section and select **Advanced Features**.
3. From the **Advanced Features** window, you can enable **DHCP guard** and **Router guard**:

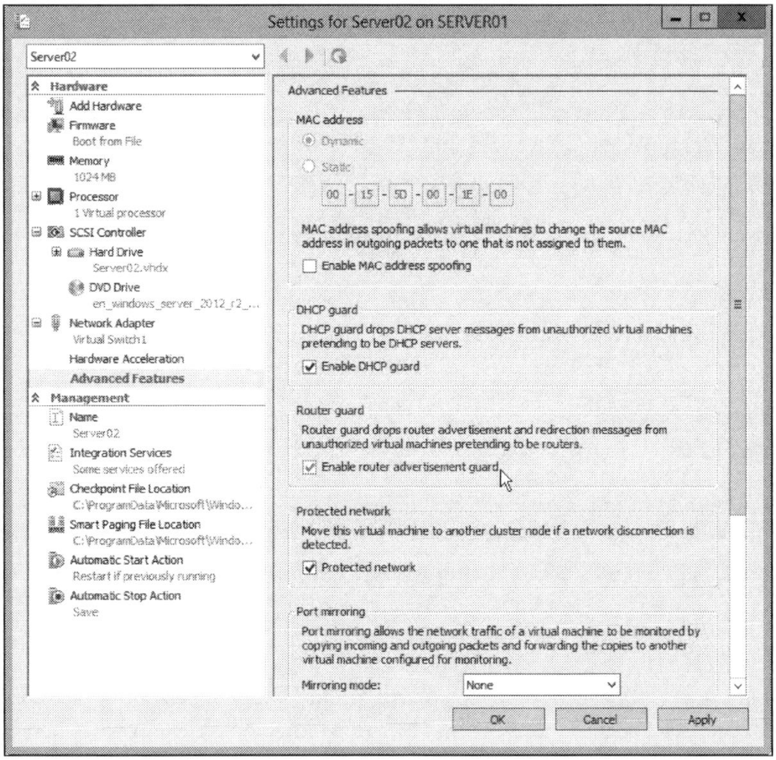

The guard protection can be enabled or disabled using the `Set-VMNetworkAdapter PowerShell` cmdlet. It can be applied based on the network adaptor name or server name.

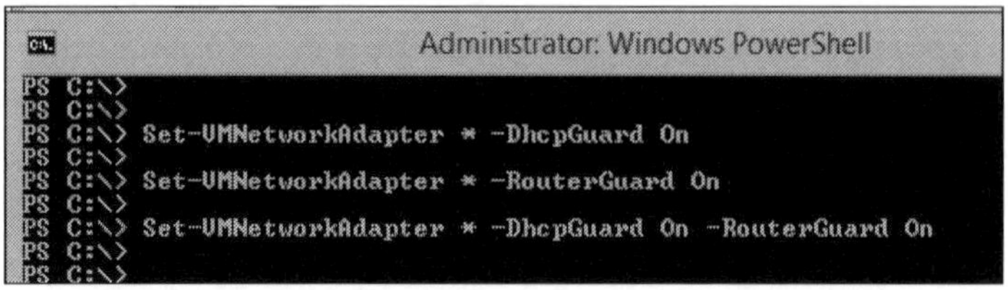
Administrator: Windows PowerShell
PS C:\>
PS C:\>
PS C:\> Set-VMNetworkAdapter * -DhcpGuard On
PS C:\>
PS C:\> Set-VMNetworkAdapter * -RouterGuard On
PS C:\>
PS C:\> Set-VMNetworkAdapter * -DhcpGuard On -RouterGuard On
PS C:\>
PS C:\>

Encrypting Hyper-V host servers

I introduced BitLocker encryption in the previous section of this book. BitLocker encryption can be applied to Hyper-V hosts to ensure data protection. The Hyper-V guest encryption is not supported. Since Hyper-V guest files (VHDX) are physically located on a Hyper-V host volume, the best practice is to encrypt the drive using Microsoft BitLocker. If you are planning to use TPM and PIN encryption, you need to make sure the TPM chip is enabled in the BIOS. Also, if you are planning to partition the disk, you need two NTFS partitions– one for the operating system and one for the system volume.

The `Enable-BitLocker` PowerShell cmdlet can be used to encrypt the data or drive. Since it is a Hyper-V server and the goal is to protect virtual server files, you will be encrypting the drive using TPM and PIN Key. The PIN needs to be converted to a secure string using the `ConvertTo-SecureString` cmdlet, but it can be used.

The following step-by-step instructions will provide a method to encrypt data on a Hyper-V server:

1. Log in to the server with administrative credentials. Open the PowerShell command window.
2. From the PowerShell window, enter the following command:

   ```
   $SecurePIN = ConvertTo-SecureString "1212" -AsPlainText -Force
   ```

3. This cmdlet will convert `1103 pain test` to a secure string and store the value in the `SecurePIN` variable.
4. The next step in the process is to enable the encryption of the drive using TPM and the previously created secure PIN. To enable the encryption, enter the following PowerShell cmdlet.

   ```
   Enable-BitLocker -MountPoint "E:" -EncryptionMethod Aes256 -
   UsedSpaceOnly -Pin $SecurePIN -TPMandPinProtector
   ```

In the preceding cmdlet, you are encrypting the `E` drive with the `Aes256` encryption methods. Based on your requirement, you can use either the `Aes128` or `Aes256` encryption method. In this scenario, you are using TMP and PIN for encryption. An Active Directory security group can also be used as Key Protector. These details are included in the *Encrypting data volume* section of this chapter.

I don't think I can conclude the Microsoft virtualization section without mentioning the Microsoft **System Center Virtual Machine Manager (SCVMM)**. In an enterprise, the SCVMM can provide an enterprise solution for managing and deploying virtual servers.

> Encryption using **Encrypting File System (EFS)** is not supported on a Hyper-V volume.

Internet Information Services

Version 8.0 of web server (IIS) is the default version included with Windows Server 2012. In Microsoft terms, it is considered as secured by default. However, based on your requirements, you may need to tweak the configuration to achieve maximum security. Also, the modular approach of web server in Windows Server 2012 will help you to select or deselect web server components during the installation. Only required and selected components will be on the server. The other web server components and modules can be installed on an as-needed basis. The default installation will only support the static components to support maximum threat.

An administrator can use the following task list as a starting point for their web server security configuration:

- **Operating system type**: Use the Windows Server Core operating system
- **Baseline security**: Create and implement server baseline security
- **Web server component selection**: Install only the required components
- **Web server role feature integrity**: Continuously monitor and validate roles and features
- **Web server security and protection**: Configure the access mechanism using dynamic IP restrictions, SSL, certificates, and so on

> Some of the generic web server best practice recommendations can be found at `http://technet.microsoft.com/en-us/library/jj635855.aspx`.

Applying baseline security

Based on your business and technical requirements, baseline polices can be created and implemented using Microsoft SCW and Microsoft SCM. I discussed the importance of baseline security in *Chapter 1, Operating System and Baseline Security*, and *Chapter 2, Native MS Security Tools and Configuration*. Since your application is running on a Microsoft Windows server, as a security administrator, your job must start from a platform level. So let's start our journey with the implementation of baseline security for your application server.

From Microsoft SCM, you can select the correct baseline policy based on the role of the server. Since you are working with web server, you can select the **Web Server Security V1.0** policy from the list, as shown in the following screenshot:

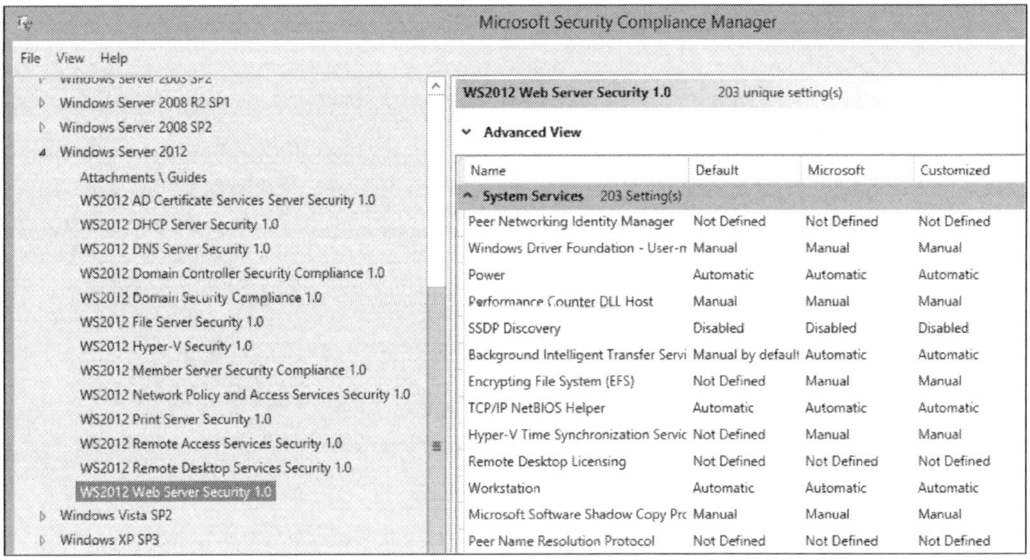

The next step in the process is to apply these polices on your application servers. This can be achieved by manually applying this template onto a server or by applying using GPO, or some other automated mechanism. This configuration and step-by-step implementation details are explained in *Chapter 1, Operating System and Baseline Security*, and *Chapter 2, Native MS Security Tools and Configuration*.

Securing web server components

It is important that you continuously monitor the web server components and features to ensure the maximum security of the server. If some of the web server features are not in use, it must be disabled or uninstalled. You can use the `Get-WindowsFeature Web* | Where-Object Installed` cmdlet to generate a list of installed web server components from a server, as shown in the following screenshot:

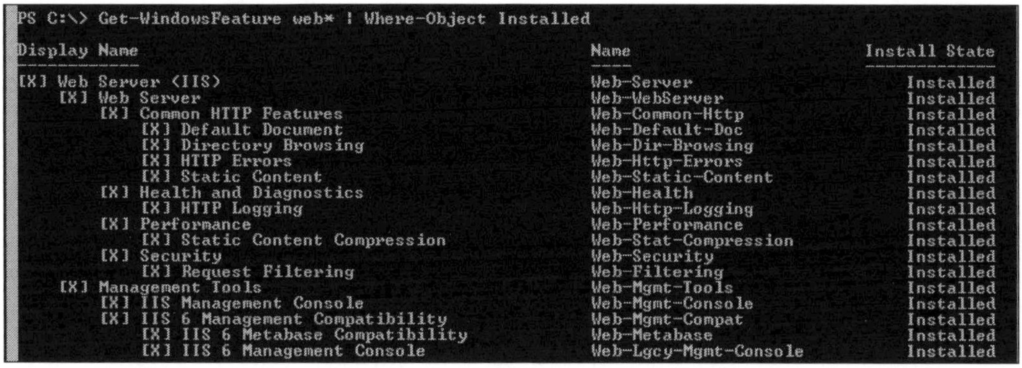

```
PS C:\> Get-WindowsFeature web* | Where-Object Installed

Display Name                                            Name                       Install State
------------                                            ----                       -------------
[X] Web Server (IIS)                                    Web-Server                     Installed
    [X] Web Server                                      Web-WebServer                  Installed
        [X] Common HTTP Features                        Web-Common-Http                Installed
            [X] Default Document                        Web-Default-Doc                Installed
            [X] Directory Browsing                      Web-Dir-Browsing               Installed
            [X] HTTP Errors                             Web-Http-Errors                Installed
            [X] Static Content                          Web-Static-Content             Installed
        [X] Health and Diagnostics                      Web-Health                     Installed
            [X] HTTP Logging                            Web-Http-Logging               Installed
        [X] Performance                                 Web-Performance                Installed
            [X] Static Content Compression              Web-Stat-Compression           Installed
        [X] Security                                    Web-Security                   Installed
            [X] Request Filtering                       Web-Filtering                  Installed
    [X] Management Tools                                Web-Mgmt-Tools                 Installed
        [X] IIS Management Console                      Web-Mgmt-Console               Installed
        [X] IIS 6 Management Compatibility              Web-Mgmt-Compat                Installed
            [X] IIS 6 Metabase Compatibility            Web-Metabase                   Installed
            [X] IIS 6 Management Console                Web-Lgcy-Mgmt-Console          Installed
```

Also, unused components can be uninstalled using the `Uninstall-WindowsFeature` cmdlet. The following screenshot is an example of removing the `Web-Static-Content` feature from web server:

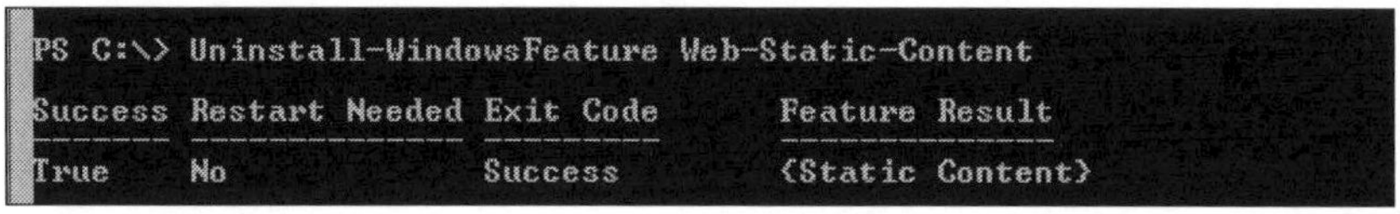

```
PS C:\> Uninstall-WindowsFeature Web-Static-Content

Success Restart Needed Exit Code      Feature Result
------- -------------- ---------      --------------
True    No             Success        {Static Content}
```

Securing the access mechanisms

Based on your requirements, you can enable Windows Integrated Authentication and disable Anonymous Authentication to provide more security for your web server. If it is an internal web server, you may want to allow only Windows Integrated authentication for your web server access. The following section provides the details of enabling or disabling Windows Integrated Authentication and Anonymous Authentication on a web server:

1. Open **Internet Information Manager Console**.

2. Select your **IIS Server**. From the middle pane, double-click on **Authentication**.

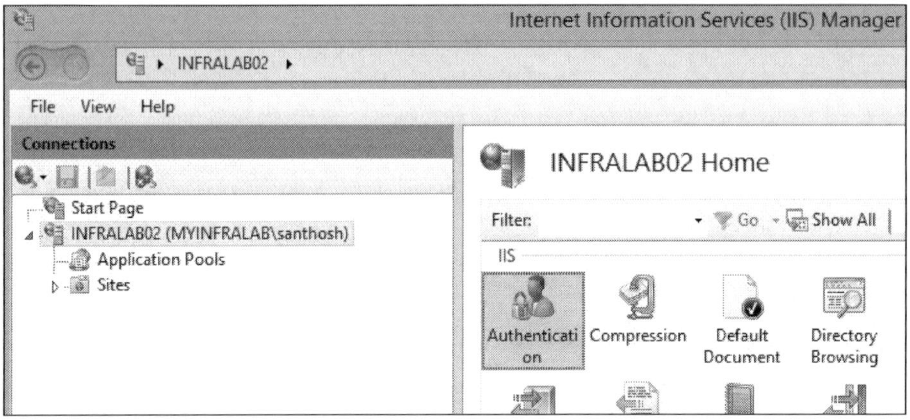

3. From the **Authentication** window, you can right-click on **Windows Authentication** or **Anonymous Authentication** to enable or disable these features, as shown in the following screenshot:

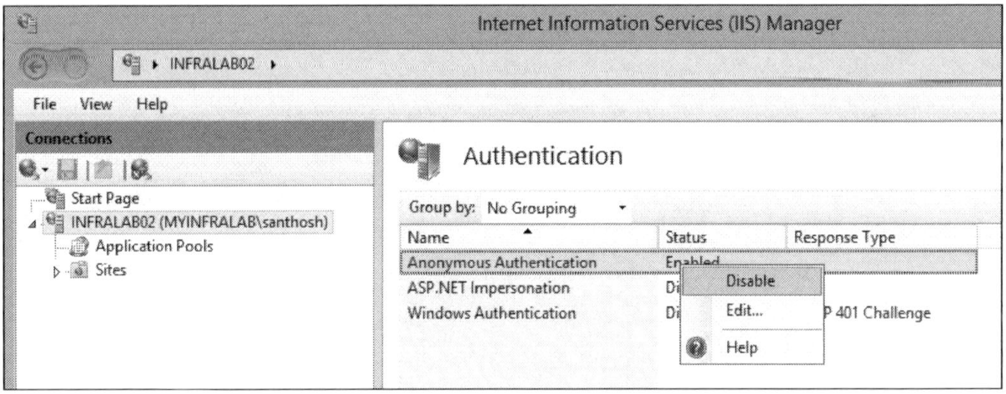

> If you don't see a **Windows Authentication** feature in the **Authentication** window, this feature is not currently installed on the server. You can add this feature using **Add Roles** and the **Features** wizard. The **Windows Authentication** feature is located in **Web Server (IIS)** | **Web Server** | **Security**.

Adding dynamic IP restrictions

The built-in dynamic IP address and domain restriction features of web server provide protection against **Denial of Service** (**DoS**) and **Brute Force** attacks. If you want to take advantage of these features, they have to be installed using the **Add Roles and Features** wizard. These features are located in **Web Server (IIS)** | **Web Server** | **Security** | **IP and Domain Restriction**. The following steps will provide you the details of configuring these components on web server:

> The details of DoS can be found at `http://en.wikipedia.org/wiki/Denial-of-service_attack`. The details of Brute Force attacks can be found at `http://en.wikipedia.org/wiki/Brute-force_attack`.

1. Open the **Internet Information Manager** console.
2. Select **IIS Server**. From the middle pane, under IIS, double-click on the **IP Address and Domain Restriction** icon.

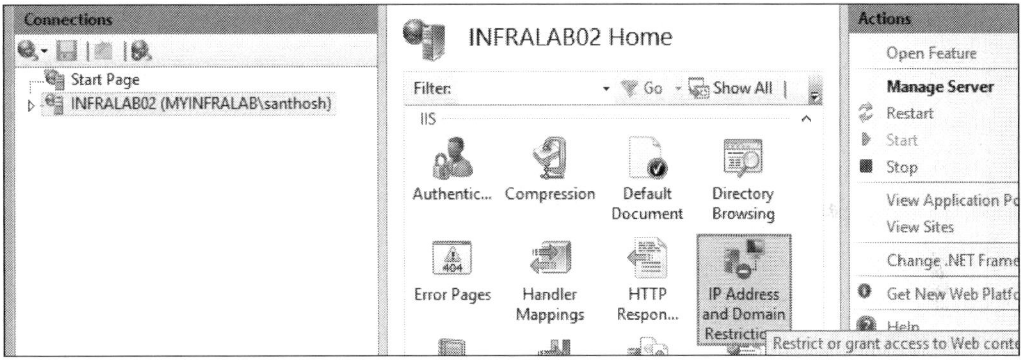

Selecting the IP Address and Domain Restriction option

3. From the **Action** pane you can do the following:
    - You can restrict web server access by allowing or denying a single or range of IP addresses using the **Add Allow Entry** or **Add Deny Entry** option.

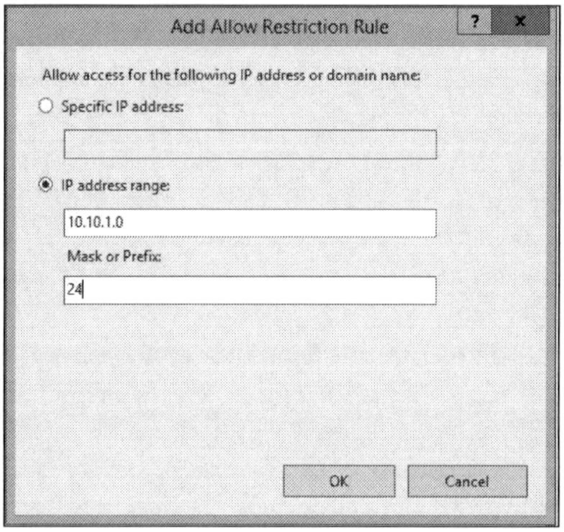

    - You can enable the **Dynamic IP Address** restriction using the **Edit Dynamic Restriction** option.

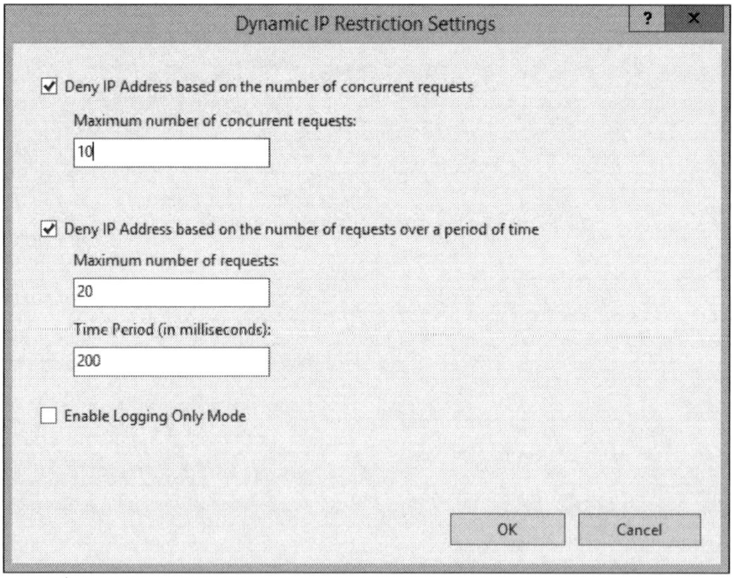

4. Click on **OK** to complete the configuration.

Summary

Since installed applications can change the state of the server, maintaining the integrity and security can be a challenge for any organization. In this chapter, you have gone through a few options to secure popular application services such as file, print, and virtual servers. The method of classifying your application server components into server type, operating system, access mechanism, and data can apply to any server, regardless of which application you are using on the server. The methods mentioned in the chapter can be used as a general guideline for your application security requirement. It is always recommended to validate your security policies in an isolated development environment prior to implementing in production.

The next chapters in this book will provide methods for securing Microsoft network services-related components such as Active Directory, Domain Name Service, **Dynamic Host Configuration Protocol** (DHCP), and so on.

5
Network Service Security

At this stage, we have gone through baseline security, operating system, and application-related security details. Now it is time for us to focus on network services and infrastructure-related aspects of security.

In this chapter, you will learn about the following topics:

- Active Directory and Domain Controller security
- Securing network services such as DNS and DHCP
- Group Managed Service Accounts (gMSA)
- The Enhanced Mitigation Experience Toolkit (EMET)

My goal is to provide you with an option to secure your Microsoft infrastructure platform using native Microsoft tools and technologies. Since Microsoft Active Directory is the core platform for all Microsoft-related technologies, we will start with the Domain Controller and Active Directory. Active Directory Domain Services is a server role that runs on a Windows server, so all the security concepts that you have learned in the previous chapters will be applicable here as well. It is critical to implement all baseline policies to stabilize the environment before you can adopt any custom configurations. So we will start with implementing the baseline polices for Active Directory and Domain Controllers.

Baseline policies

When talking about baseline policies, we need to consider two sets of polices. One is for Active Directory itself, and the second one is for Domain Controllers. **Domain Controllers** (**DCs**) are the backbone of Active Directory. When you install and configure Active Directory Domain Services on a Windows server, it will become a Domain Controller in an Active Directory Forest or Domain. Since they are the foundation of Active Directory, security hardening should start from this level.

We are again going to use and rely on **Microsoft Security Compliance Manager (SCM)** to generate the recommended policy for Domain Controllers. As stated in the previous chapters, these policies can be reviewed and modified based on your business and technical requirements before applying them in your organization. For Active Directory, there are two baseline polices available in Microsoft SCM: Domain Controller Security and Domain Security.

> Windows Server 2012 Active Directory installation, configuration, and upgrade details can be found in the book *Instant Migration from Windows Server 2008 and 2008 R2 to 2012 How-to, Packt Publishing*.

From Microsoft SCM, you can select the correct baseline policy based on the role of the server. Since you are working with Domains and Domain Controllers, you can select **Domain Controller Security Compliance 1.0** and **Domain Security Compliance 1.0** policies from the list, as shown in the following screenshot:

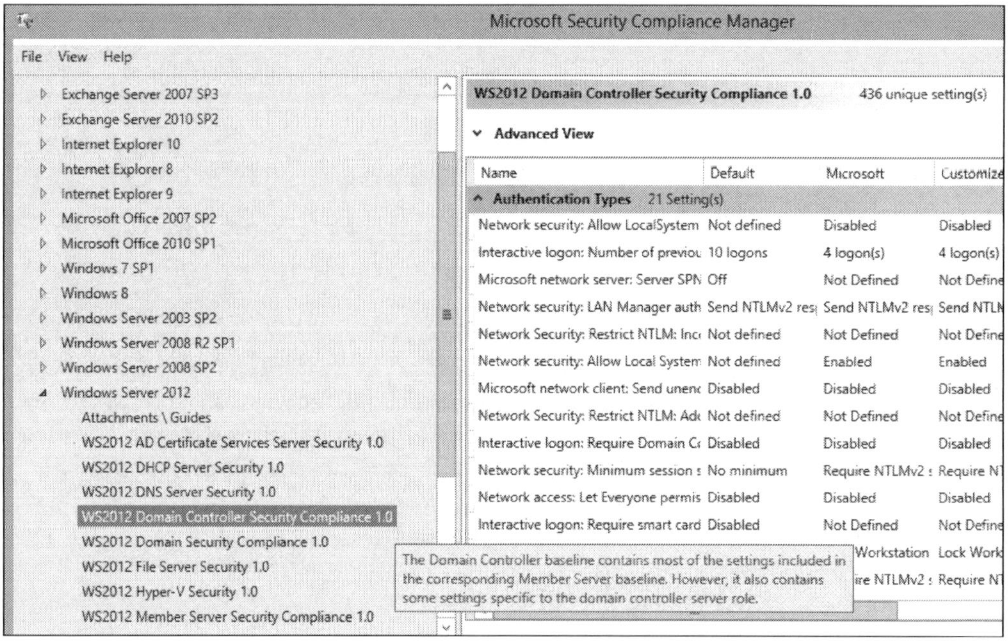

Domain Controllers

The next step in the process is to apply these polices onto your Domain Controller servers. Since this is a Domain policy, it is recommended to use a GPO-based mechanism. You can refer to *Chapter 1, Operating System and Baseline Security*, and *Chapter 2, Native MS Security Tools and Configuration*, for implementing these polices in an enterprise environment.

Read-only Domain Controllers

Microsoft has introduced the concept of **Read-only Domain Controllers (RODCs)** concept with Windows Server 2008. As its name implies, an RODC provides a read-only copy of the Active Directory database. This means any database change can only occur in a rewritable Domain Controller. These changes will be replicated to an RODC during normal Active Directory replication. An RODC can provide a secure mechanism for any organization where the physical security cannot be assured. Since an RODC doesn't store or cache any passwords, even if there is a security compromise, malicious users will not be able to access any password information from an RODC.

> Since an RODC has a read-only database, some applications may not function with RODCs. You need to verify with your application vendor before using RODCs.

The first Domain Controller cannot be an RODC.

> More information about RODCs can be found at `https://technet.microsoft.com/en-us/library/cc771030(v=ws.10).aspx`.

Installing RODCs

The following section provides a step-by-step instruction on how to create and configure an RODC in an existing Active Directory environment:

1. Open **Server Manager**. From the dashboard, navigate to the **All Servers** grouping on the left-hand side pane.
2. From the **Server Name** box, right-click on the appropriate server and select the **Add Roles and Features** option. You can also select **Add Roles and Features** from the **Manage** menu in the command bar. If the correct server is not listed here, you can manually add them from the **Manage** tab on the top right-hand side and select **Add Server**. If you are running **Server Manager** from the local server, you can select **Add Roles and Feature** from the dashboard itself.
3. Click on **Next** in the **Welcome** window.
4. In the **Select Installation Type** window, select **Role based or Feature based installation**. Click on **Next**.

5. In the **Select destination server** window, select the **Select a server from the server pool** option and the pick the correct server from the **Server Pool** box. Click on **Next**.
6. In the **Select server roles** window, select **Active Directory Domain Services**. You will see a pop-up window, as shown in the following screenshot, to confirm additional features that are required for Active Directory Domain Servers. Click on **Add Features** and then click on **Next** to continue.

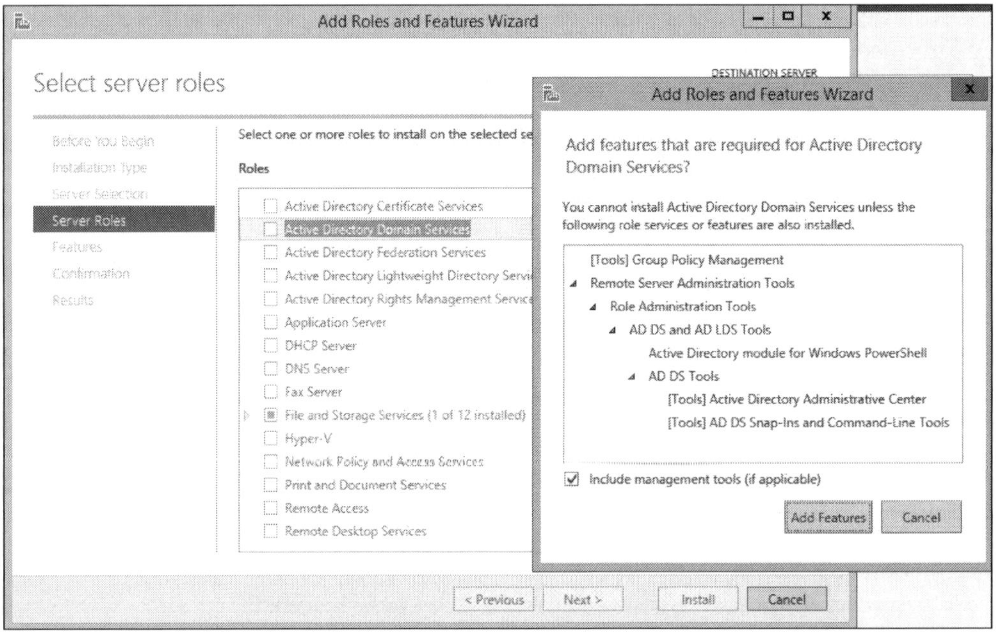

7. Accept the default values and click on **Next** in the **Select features** window.
8. Click on **Next** in the **Active Directory Domain Services** window.
9. In the **Confirm Installation Selections** window, select the **Restart the destination server automatically if required** option, as shown in the following screenshot. In the pop-up window, click on **Yes** to confirm the restart option and click on **Install**. This will begin the installation process.

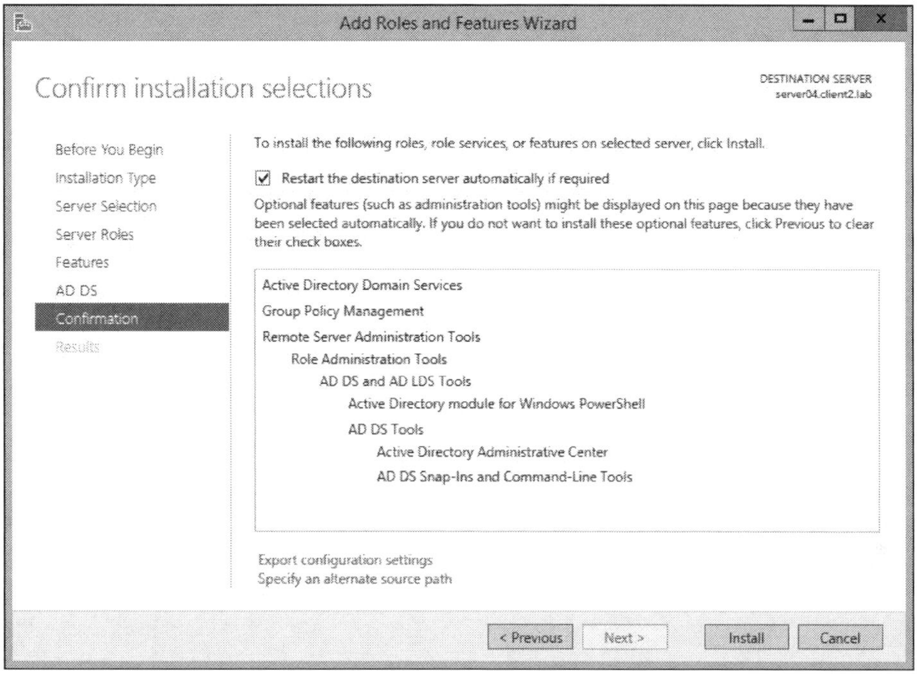

10. You will see the progress in the installation window itself. This window can be closed without interrupting the installation process. You can get the status update from the notification section in the command bar as well.
11. The **Post-deployment Configuration** option needs to be completed after the Active Directory Domain Services role installation. This process will promote the server as a Domain Controller. From the notification window, select the **Promote this server to a domain controller** hyperlink.

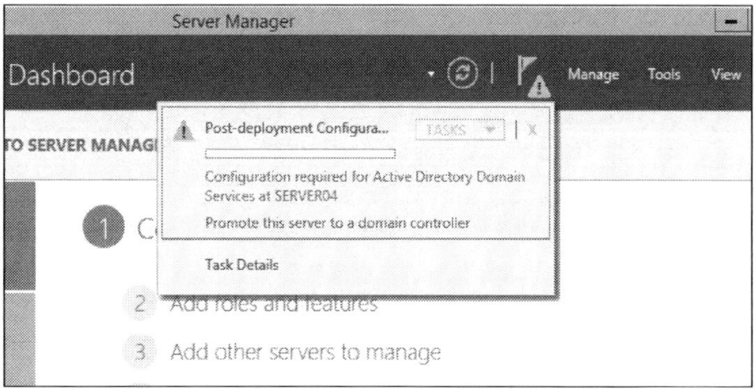

12. From the **Deployment Configuration** window, select **Add an additional domain controller for an existing domain**. Click on **Next**. You can specify alternative credentials for the Domain Controller promotion, if required, from this screen.

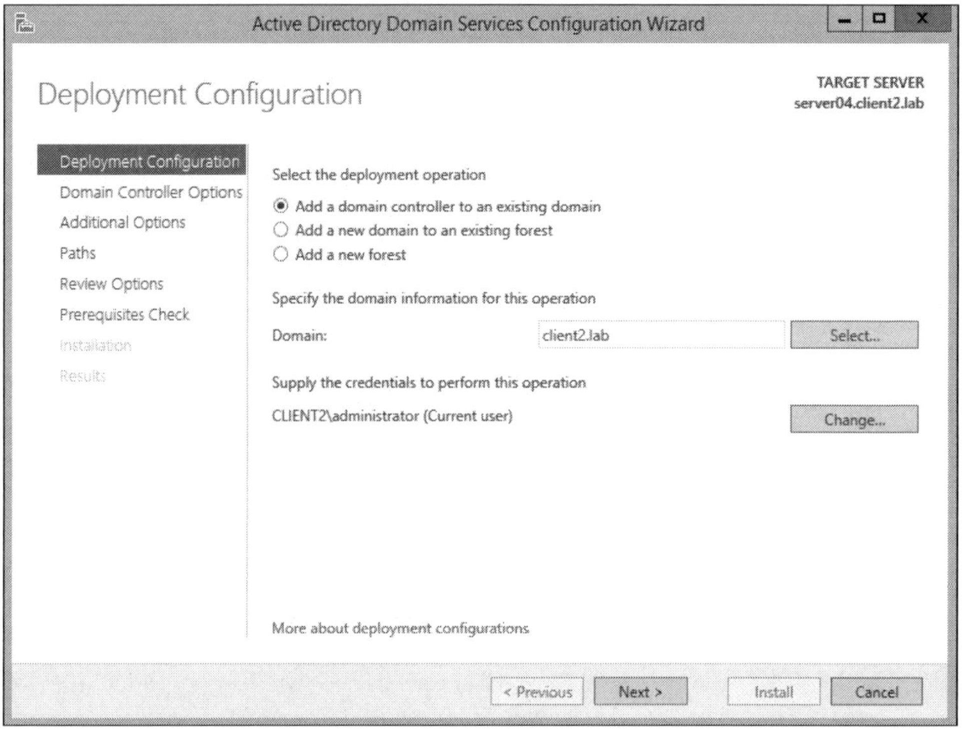

13. In the **Domain Controller Options** window, select the following checkboxes:
    - **Domain Name System (DNS) server**
    - **Global Catalog (GC)**
    - **Read-only Domain controller (RODC)**
    - **Site name for this domain controller**

Enter the **Site Name** and **Directory Service Restore Mode (DSRM)** values in the appropriate section. Click on **Next** to continue with the installation process.

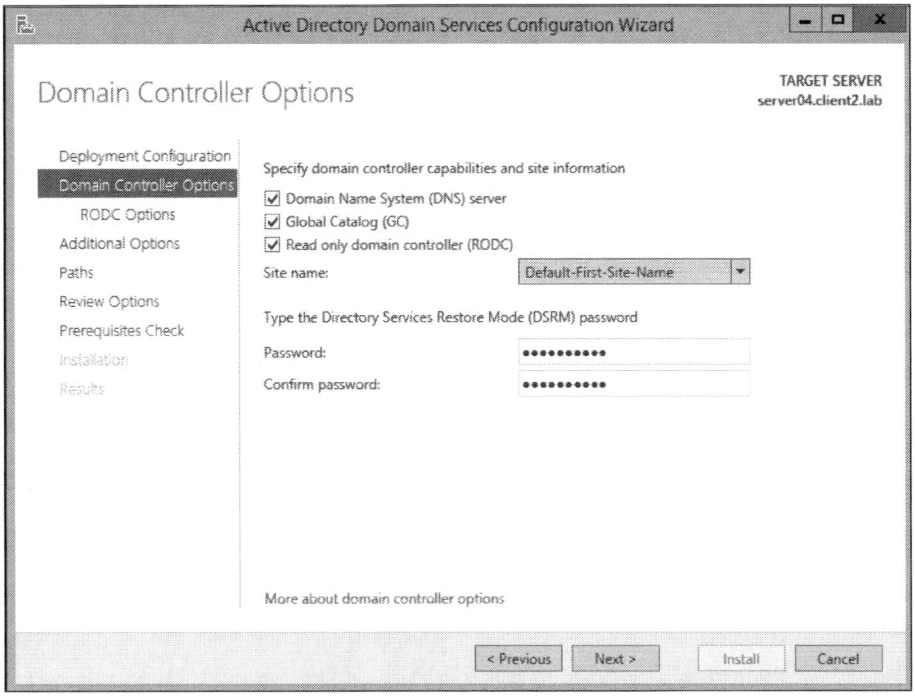

14. In the **RODC Options** window, you can modify the following configurations based on your requirements:
    - **Delegated Administrator Account**
    - **Accounts that are allowed to replicate passwords to the RODC**
    - **Accounts that are denied from replicating passwords to the RODC**

Select the appropriate options. Click on **Next** to continue.

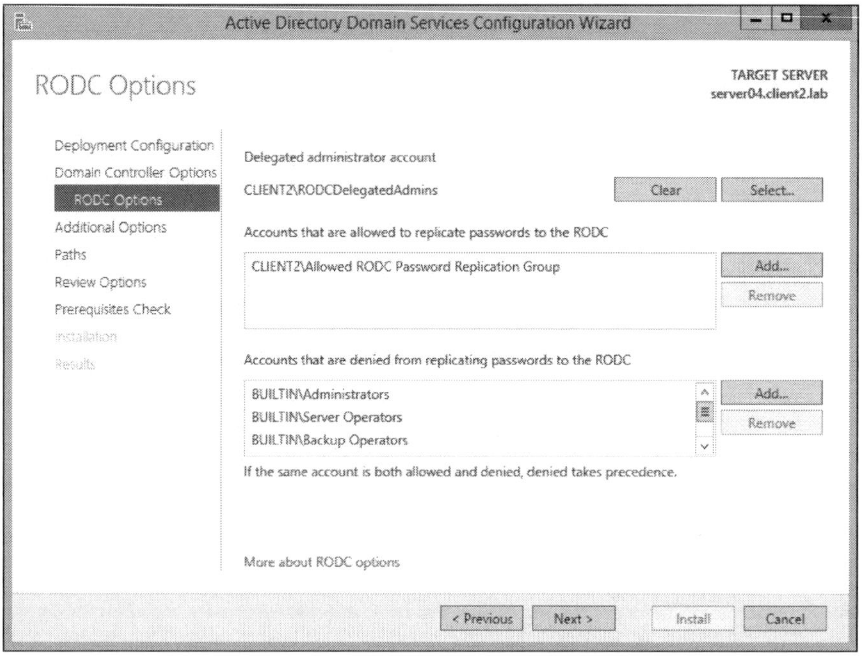

15. Accept the default options in the **Additional Options** window, unless you have technical reasons to modify these. Click on **Next**.
16. In the **Paths** window, you can specify the **AD Database**, **Log**, and **SYSVOL** locations. Select the appropriate locations and then click on **Next**. Review the Microsoft **Infrastructure Planning and Design** (**IPD**) guides (`http://msdn.microsoft.com/en-us/library/cc196387.aspx`) for best practice recommendations. For performance improvements, it is recommended to place database, log, and so on in separate drives.
17. You can review the selected options and settings from the **Review Options** window. These settings can be exported to a PowerShell script by clicking on the **View Script** option in the bottom-right corner of the screen. This script can be used for future Domain Controller deployments. Click on **Next** to continue with the installation.
18. The prerequisite checking process will happen in the background. You will see the result in the **Prerequisites Check** window. This is a new enhancement in Windows Server 2012. Review the result and click on **Install**.
19. The progress and status of the Domain Controller promotion will display in the **Installation** window.

20. This server will be restarted after the installation. Click on **Close** to complete the installation process.

Configuring RODCs

You can complete the configuration of an RODC using the following instructions:

1. Open **Active Directory Users and Computer** and navigate to the **Domain Controllers** OU.
2. Select the newly promoted Domain Controller and go to **Properties**.
3. From the **Password Replication Policy** tab, you can modify the cached password replication behavior. Users or groups can be directly added to the default group, which is the **Allowed RODC Password Replication** group.

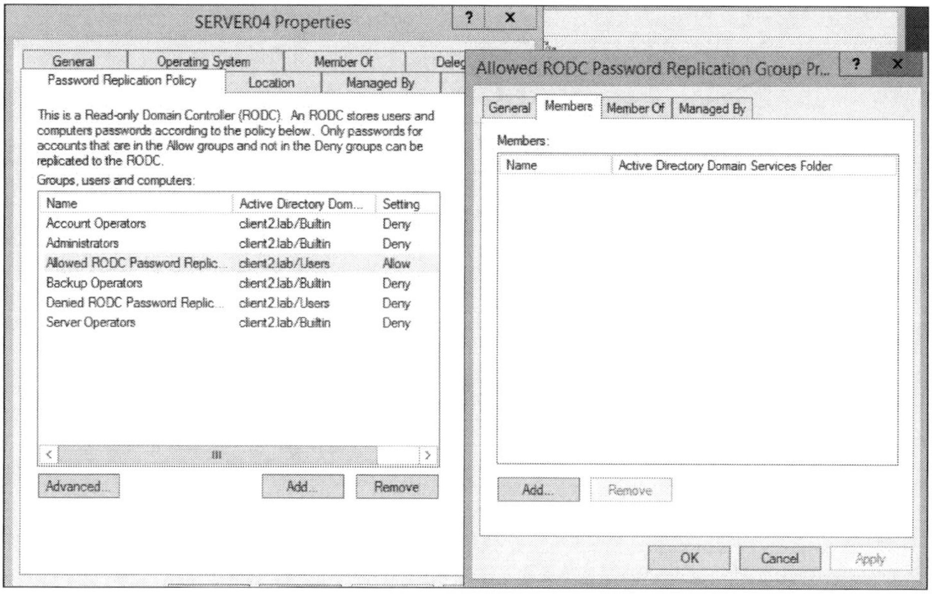

4. To add a custom group, click on the **Add** button in the **Password Replication Policy** tab.

5. Select **Allow passwords for the account to replicate to this RODC**. Click on **OK**.

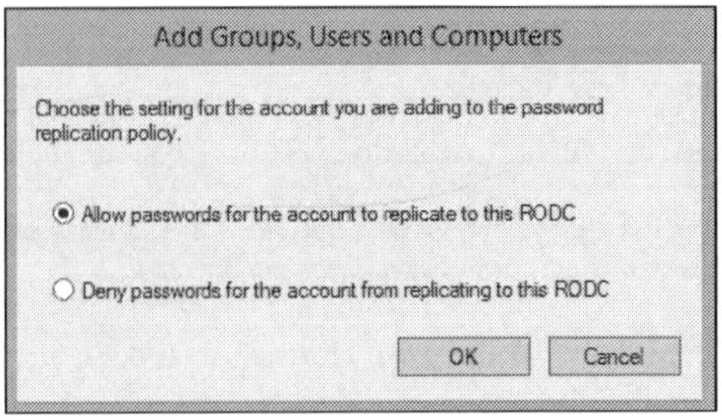

6. From the **Select Users, Computers, Service Accounts, or Group** window, select the appropriate users or group. Click on **OK** twice to complete this process.

By default, the Domain Controller will use all the RPC high ports for replication. If there is a security requirement, this default behavior can be changed by enabling some of the ports on the firewall and modifying the registry on the Domain Controller.

> The Microsoft TechNet articles `http://support.microsoft.com/kb/224196` and `http://technet.microsoft.com/en-us/library/dd772723(v=ws.10).aspx` provide more information on this.

An RODC can also be installed using the `Install-addsdomaincontroller` PowerShell cmdlet. The following cmdlet will initiate the RODC installation process:

```
Install-ADDSDomainController -ReadonlyReplica -DomainName MyInfralab.Com
-SiteName Houston -Credentail (Get-Credential)
```

The `-domainname`, `-readonlyreplica`, `-sitename`, and `-credential` parameters are all required. The preceding command uses the `Get-Credential` PowerShell cmdlet to capture the username and password.

Domain Name System

Active Directory and other network services rely highly on name services such as **Domain Name System (DNS)**. When it comes to Active Directory lookup and authentication, it uses DNS to locate appropriate services. Securing these services is also critical to ensuring maximum security in your organization.

An administrator can use the following task list as a starting point when considering a DNS server security method:

- **Operating system type**: Use the Windows Server Core operating system
- **DNS server roles**: Remove unwanted roles and features from the DNS server
- **Zone type**: Enable Active Directory Integrated (ADI) zones
- **Baseline Security**: Create and implement DNS server baseline security
- **Stale Records**: Implement a solution to monitor remote or stale DNS records
- **Secure Update**: Configure a secure update for ADI zones
- **Zone transfer**: Limit the DNS zone transfer to appropriate servers

You will see the details of these tasks in the next sections. Also, if there is no physical security available, you can use DNS on an RODC. RODC installation and configuration details are included in the previous section in this chapter. Keep in mind that on an RODC, the DNS zone will also be read-only.

Applying a DNS baseline policy

For hardening DNS servers, you can start with Microsoft SCW and Microsoft SCM for creating and applying baseline policies. At the time of writing this book, Microsoft SCM offers 203 security setting recommendations for Windows Server 2012 DNS servers, as shown in the following screenshot:

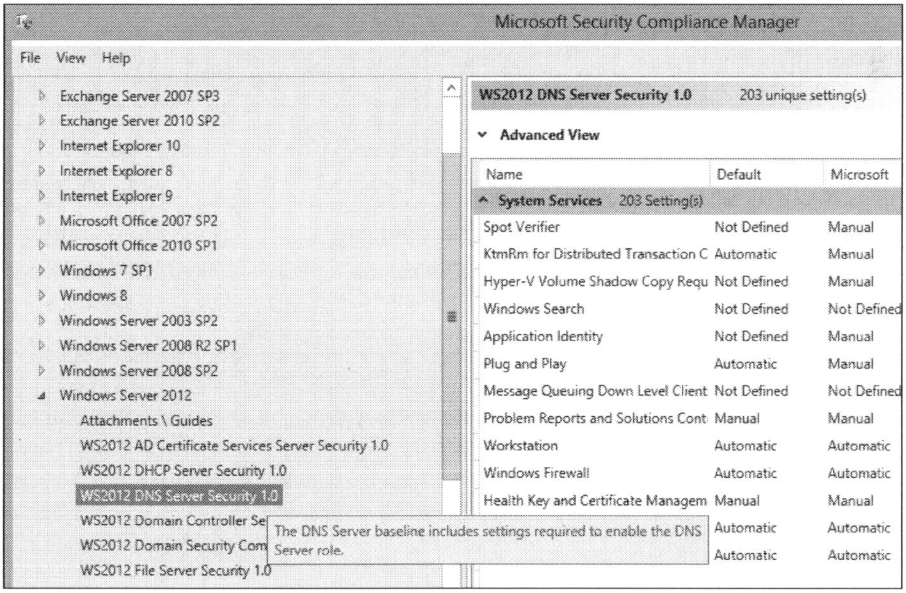

The next step in the process is to apply these policies onto your DNS servers. This can be achieved by manually applying these templates onto the server or applying them using a GPO or some other automated mechanism. The configuration and step-by-step implementation details are explained in *Chapter 1, Operating System and Baseline Security*, and *Chapter 2, Native MS Security Tools and Configuration*.

Enabling Scavenging on a DNS server

Unused or stale DNS records can be a security threat. The proper management of DNS records is essential to ensure maximum security for your DNS server as well as the entire network infrastructure. The details of these records and other security details can be found at `https://technet.microsoft.com/en-us/library/cc759204(v=ws.10).aspx` and `https://technet.microsoft.com/library/security/ms08-037`. DNS Aging and Scavenging is not a new concept in DNS. This option can provide an automated mechanism to control and manage DNS records based on the update interval or time. The following section provides the details of enabling Aging and Scavenging in an Active Directory environment:

1. Open **DNS Manager**
2. Select your DNS server and select the **Set Aging/Scavenging for All Zone** option.

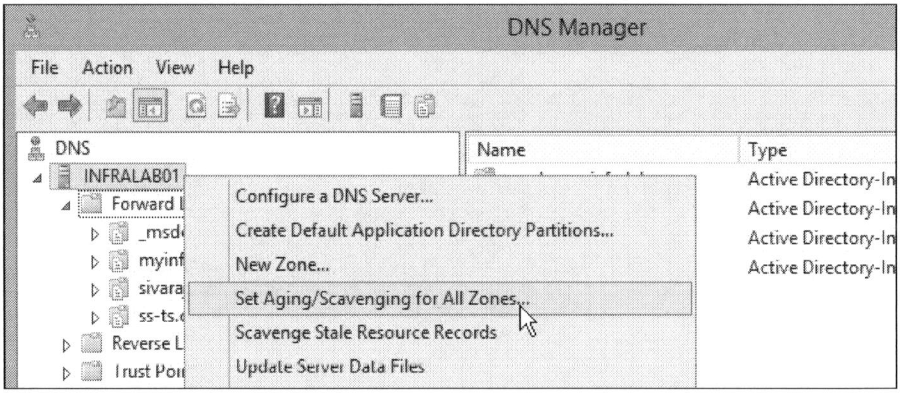

3. From the **Set Aging/Scavenging** window:
   - Select the **Enable automatic scavenging of stale records** option.
   - In the **No-refresh interval and Refresh interval** section, select an appropriate interval of time based on your requirements:

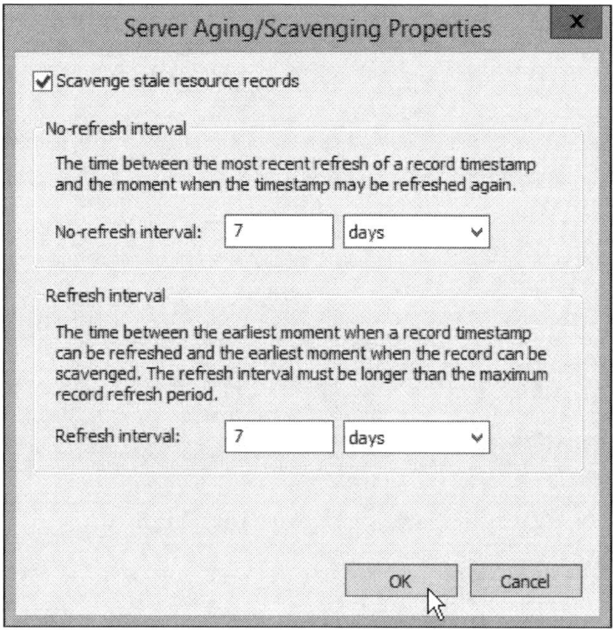
Server Aging/Scavenging Properties
Scavenge stale resource records
No-refresh interval
The time between the most recent refresh of a record timestamp and the moment when the timestamp may be refreshed again.
No-refresh interval:
7
days
Refresh interval
The time between the earliest moment when a record timestamp can be refreshed and the earliest moment when the record can be scavenged. The refresh interval must be longer than the maximum record refresh period.
Refresh interval:
7
days
OK
Cancel

4. Click on **Apply** and **OK** to complete this operation.

Enabling Scavenging on a DNS zone

You can also enable Aging and Scavenging on a DNS zone. The following instructions can be used to complete the configuration:

1. Open **DNS Manager**.

2. Navigate to **DNS zone**. Right-click on the zone and go to **Properties**.

3. From the **Set Aging/Scavenging Properties** window:

    ◦ Select the **Enable automatic scavenging of stale records** option.

    ◦ In the **No-refresh interval and Refresh interval** section, select an appropriate interval of time based on your requirements:

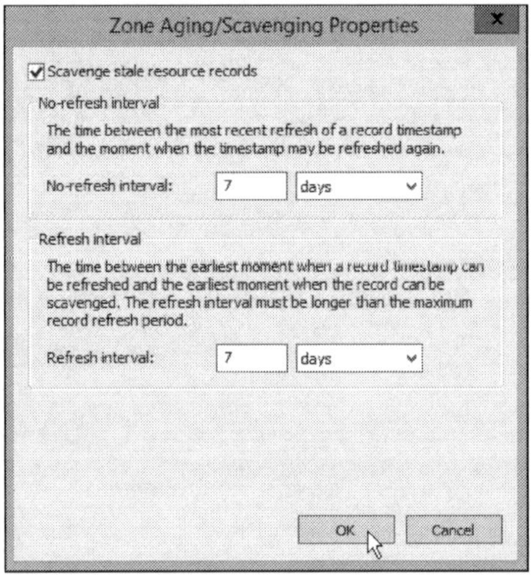

The stale records can also be removed manually from the zone by going to the **Properties** of the zone and selecting the **Scavenge Stale Resource Records** option, as shown in the following screenshot:

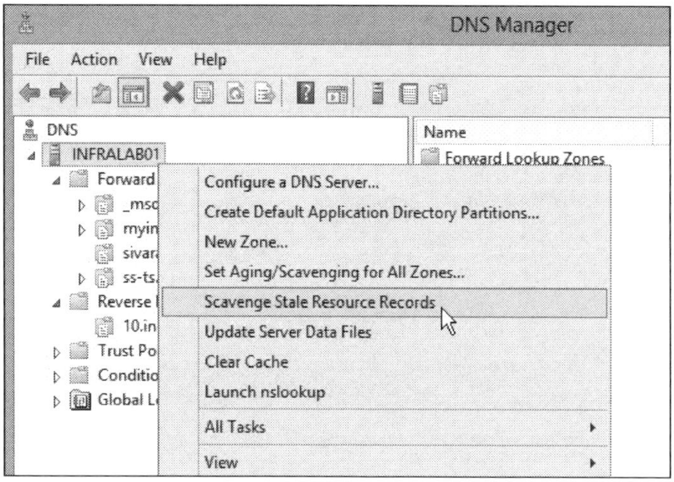

Securing DNS dynamic updates

The Microsoft DNS supports non-secure and secure updates as the dynamic updates for its DNS zones. For Active Directory integrated zones, you can use secure updates to enhance the security of the dynamic registration process. The following instructions can be used to enable secure updates on a DNS zone:

1. Open **DNS Manager**.
2. Navigate to **DNS zone**. Right-click on the zone and go to **Properties**.

3. From the **Properties** tab, select **Dynamic updates** as **Secure only**. Click on **OK**.

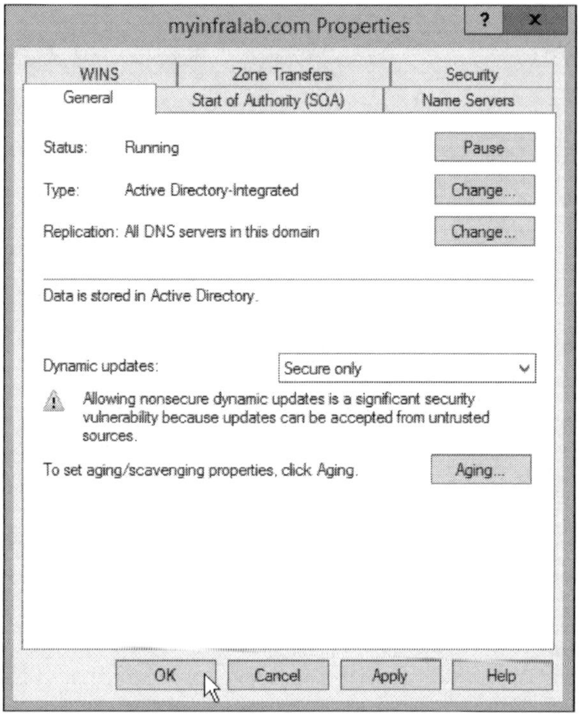

Cache poisoning attacks

I don't think I can conclude the DNS security section without mentioning the **Domain Name System Security Extensions (DNSSEC)** and DNS cache locking features. DNS cache poisoning attacks can be prevented by using DNSSEC. By default, Windows Server 2012 and Windows 8 operating systems support DNSSEC. DNSSEC protects DNS zones by using a digital signature. The DNS cache locking feature will protect the cached records by not allowing anyone to overwrite them within the **Time To Live (TTL)** period. More information on DNSSEC can be found at `https://technet.microsoft.com/en-us/library/jj200221.aspx`.

Dynamic Host Configuration Protocol

Dynamic Host Configuration Protocol (DHCP) provides an automated mechanism to assign IP addresses to the network clients. In Windows Server, it is a server role that can be added using Server Manager.

An administrator can use the following tasks in their checklist when considering a DHCP server security method:

- **Operating system type**: Use the Windows Server Core operating system
- **DHCP server roles**: Remove unwanted roles and features from the DHCP server
- **Baseline security**: Create and implement DHCP server baseline security
- **Exclusion and reservation**: Create a proper exclusion and reservation range
- **Administration**: Restrict DHCP administration access
- **Access policy**: Configure policy-based access

The details of these tasks are included in the following sections.

Applying a DHCP baseline policy

Like with the other services, I will again start with baseline policies. These baseline policies are included in Microsoft SCM, as shown in the following screenshot. The details of configuration and implementation are included in *Chapter 1, Operating System and Baseline Security*, and *Chapter 2, Native MS Tools and Security Configuration*.

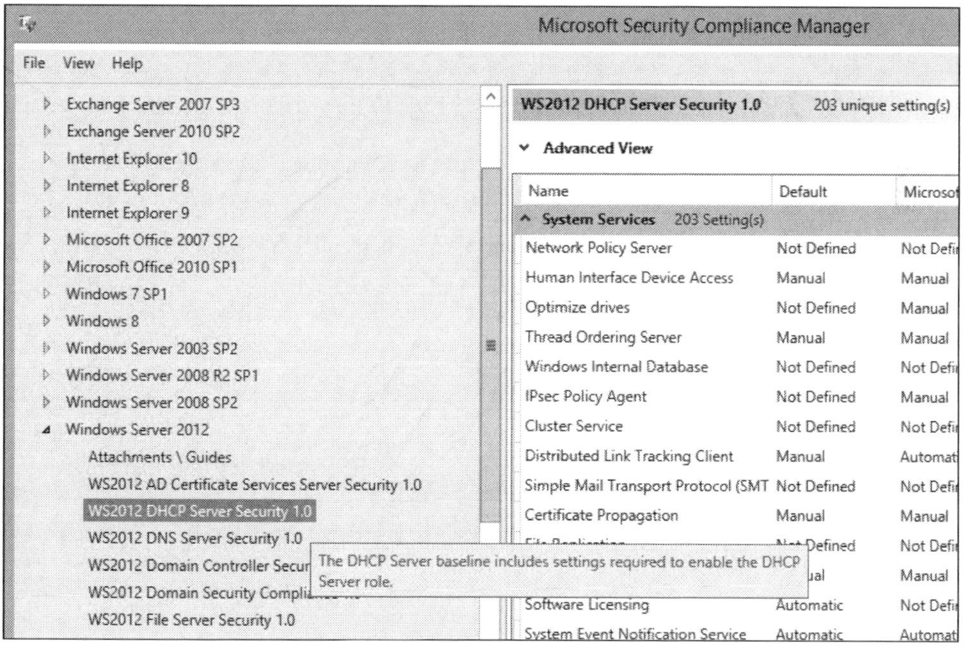

Baseline policies

Controlling and segregating IP address allocation

Virtualization and **bring your own devices** (**BYOD**) are very common in enterprises these days. The reservation, exclusion range, and **Policy Based Assignment** (**PBA**) mechanisms can provide better classification, segmentation, and control over your IP address allocation mechanism.

Configuring PBA

Windows Server 2012 provides an option to assign IP addresses based on the following:

- Vendor class
- User class
- MAC address
- Client identification
- Fully qualified domain name
- Relay agent information

Your implementation scenario can be different based on your requirements. In the following section, we will be configuring a policy based on **Fully Qualified Domain Name** (**FQDN**). This is useful if you are operating in a multi-domain environment or going through a merger or acquisition:

1. Open the **DHCP** console and expand the scope.
2. Right-click on the **Policy** node and select **New Policy**.

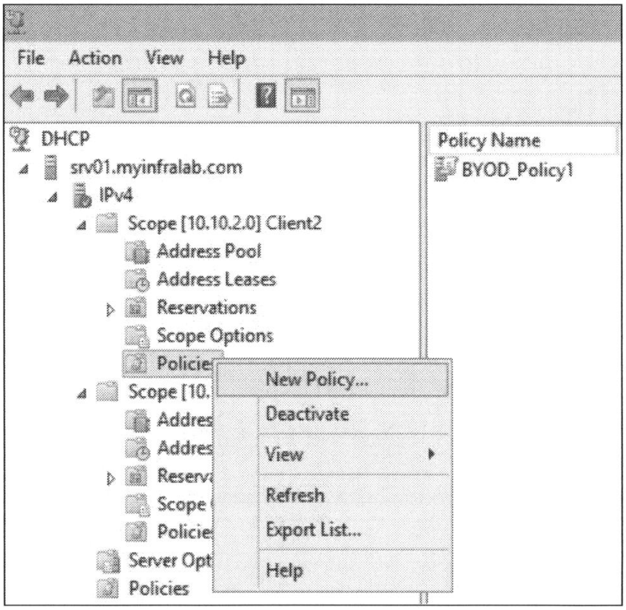

3. Enter the name and description for the policy in the **Policy based IP Address and Option Assignment** window. Click on **Next**.
4. In the **Configure Conditions for the policy** window, select the **Add** option.
5. In the **Add/Edit Condition** window, select the appropriate criteria and value based on your requirement. In this exercise, we will be selecting **Fully Qualified Domain Name (FQDN)**:
    - From the **Criteria** drop-down box, select **Fully Qualified Domain Name (FQDN)**.
    - From the **Operator** drop-down box, select **Equals**.
    - In the **Value** column, enter the FQDN of your domain.
    - If you want to use a wildcard, use the **Prefix wildcard (*)** or **Append wildcard (*)** checkboxes.

- Click on **Add** to create the condition.
- Click on **OK** to continue with the operation.

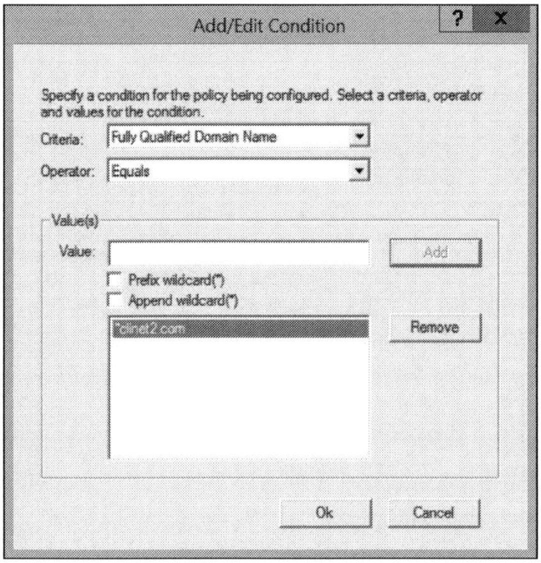
Add/Edit Condition
Specify a condition for the policy being configured. Select a criteria, operator and values for the condition.
Criteria:
Fully Qualified Domain Name
Operator:
Equals
Value(s)
Value:
Add
Prefix wildcard(*)
Append wildcard(*)
*clinet2.com
Remove
Ok
Cancel

6. Click on **Next** in the **Configure Conditions for the Policy** window.

DHCP Policy Configuration Wizard
Configure Conditions for the policy
A policy consists of one or more conditions and a set of configuration settings (options, IP Address) that are distributed to the client. The DHCP server delivers these specific settings to clients that match these conditions.
A policy with conditions based on fully qualified domain name can have configuration settings for DNS but not for options or IP address ranges.
Conditions
Operator
Value
Fully Qualified Domain Name
Equals
*client2.com
AND
OR
Add...
Edit...
Remove
< Back
Next >
Cancel

The Confgure Conditions for the Policy window

7. In the **Summary** window, click on **Finish** to complete the operation.

These are scope-based policies. A scope can have multiple polices. If a client request matches the policies configured on the scope, the DHCP server will assign the first available IP address based on your policy configuration.

Securing DHCP administration

In Windows Server 2012, the built-in DHCP administration groups such as DHCP administrators and DHCP users are not created during the DHCP role installation. The members of the DHCP administrators group will have full administrative access to the DHCP service. The members of DHCP users will have view-only access to the DHCP service. Based on your requirements, you can enable these groups using the `Netsh` command. Perform the following steps:

1. Open the command prompt using administrative credentials.
2. Run the `Netsh DHCP Add SerurityGroups` command.

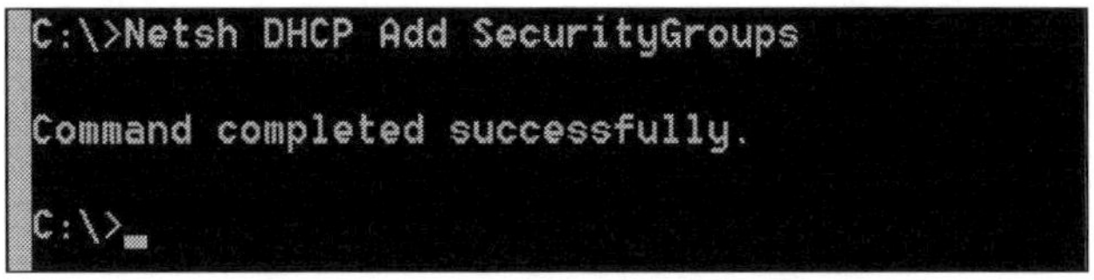

3. This process will enable both DHCP administrators and DHCP users in Active Directory.

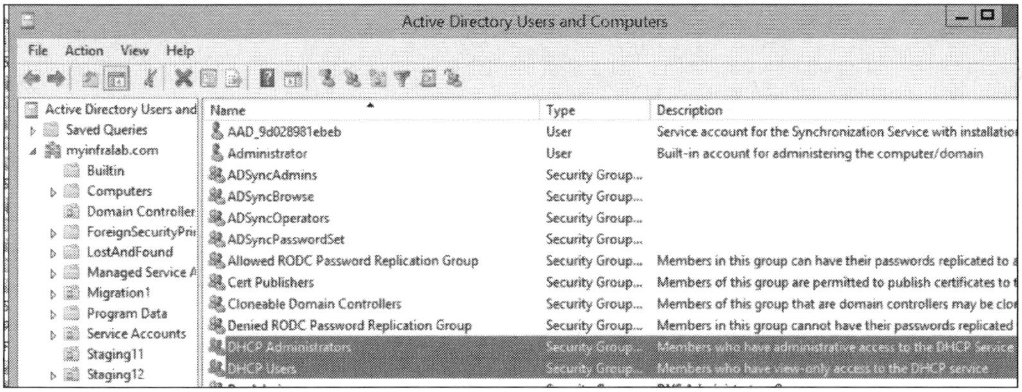

DHCP administrators and DHCP users enabled in Active Directory

4. Restart the DHCP service.

Based on your administration strategy, you can maintain and control the group members using GPOs such as **Restricted Groups**.

IP address and DNS management and monitoring

IP address management and control is a challenge, and this can lead to a security threat for any organization. Microsoft has introduced an **IP Address Management (IPAM)** solution to overcome some of these challenges. It provides a framework to manage and monitor IP addresses and their related infrastructure components such as DHCP and DNS. The installation and configuration of IPAM is beyond the scope of this book. However, it is important for a security administrator to be familiar with and understand the capabilities of this solution.

IPAM has two components: the IPAM server and IPAM client. The IPAM server feature can be added using Server Manager.

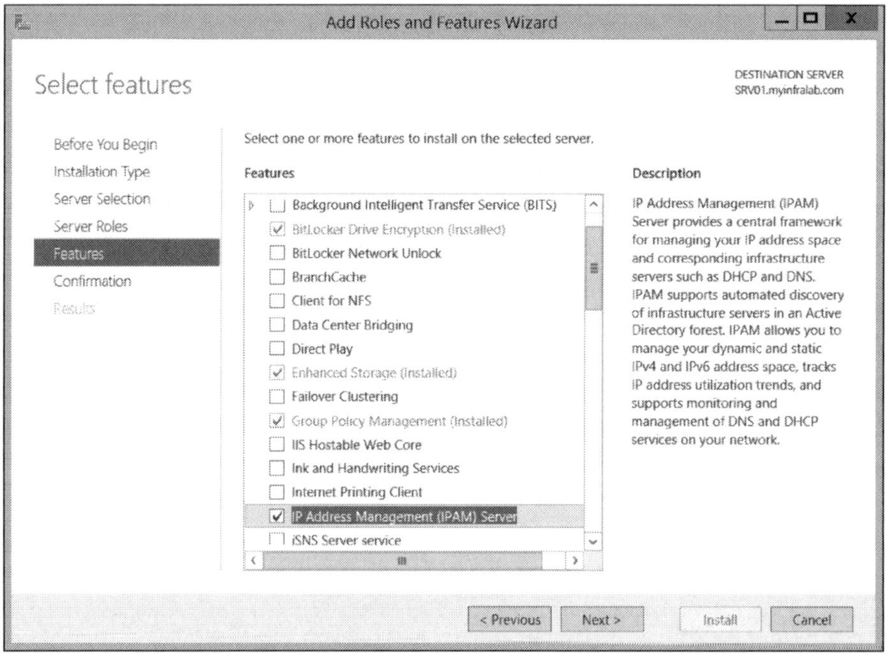

The IPAM client is an administrator tool and is part of the Windows Server **Remote Server Administration Tool (RSAT)**, or you can directly access it from the Server Manager, as shown in the following screenshot:

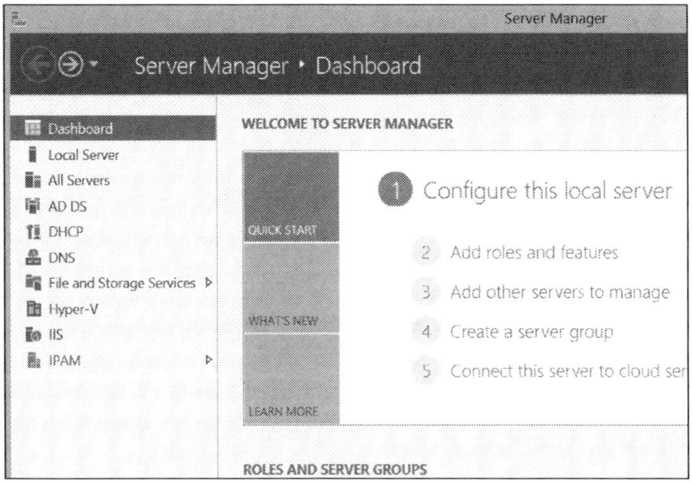

More information about IPAM can be found at `http://technet.microsoft.com/en-us/library/jj878343(v=ws.11)`.

Service accounts

Management of service accounts and passwords can be a challenge. Since these accounts are highly privileged and have unique settings in Active Directory, unmanaged accounts can be a security threat to any organization. Some of these issues are documented at `http://blogs.technet.com/b/askpfeplat/archive/2012/07/16/too-many-admins-in-your-domain-expose-the-problems-and-find-a-solution-don-t-forget-powershell.aspx`. To address some of these issues and to better control these types of highly privileged and special accounts in Active Directory, Microsoft has introduced a concept called **Managed Service Accounts** (**MSA**) in Windows Server 2008. Sometimes it is referred to as standalone MSA. Due to some limitations, this concept wasn't highly adopted in large enterprise environments. With Windows Server 2012, Microsoft introduced an enhancement to MSA called **Group Managed Service Accounts** (**gMSA**). gMSA can provide the same functionality as MSA for multiple or groups of servers. The multiple server support was not supported in the previous version of MSA. MSA can provide easy and automated password and **Service Principle Name** (**SPN**) management options for applications and resources. You will see the details of how to configure and implement gMSA in the following sections.

Group Managed Service Accounts

There are four steps involved in configuring gMSA in an enterprise:

1. Creating a **Key Distribution Service** (**KDS**) root key: The password for gMSA is generated and managed using KDS. You need to create a KDS root key prior to using gMSA in your environment.
2. Creating gMSA: In this step, you will create gMSA for a computer or group of computers.
3. Installing gMSA: After the configuration, you need to install gMSA on the server.
4. Configuring gMSA: Once you have created a KDS root key and gMSA, you can configure the supported application using the newly created gMSA.

> Passwords are maintained by KDS in Active Directory.
>
> Active Directory 2012 is a requirement for gMSA.
>
> Windows Server 2012 Client or Windows 8 is a requirement to use gMSA.

Creating a KDS root key

You will be using the `Add-KDSRootKey` PowerShell cmdlet to create a KDS root key in Active Directory. This cmdlet is part of the Active Directory PowerShell module. You can execute this cmdlet directly from a Domain Controller or a server that has the Active Directory PowerShell module imported. Also, the account must be a member of the domain account or enterprise admin to create a KDS in Active Directory. Perform the following steps:

1. Open the PowerShell command window.
2. From the PowerShell command window, enter the following command:

   ```
   Add-KDSRootKey -EffectiveImmediately
   ```

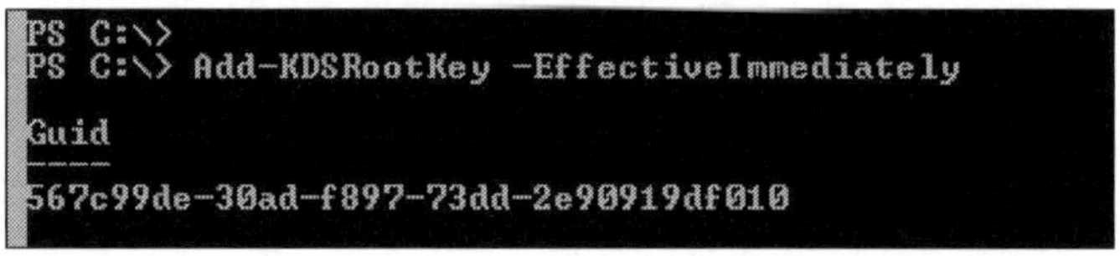
PS C:\>
PS C:\> Add-KDSRootKey -EffectiveImmediately
Guid

567c99de-30ad-f897-73dd-2e90919df010

3. You will need to wait for Active Directory replication to complete before you can proceed to the configuration step.

4. The root key can be verified using Active Directory Site and Service. The **Services Node** has to be enabled (**View** | **Show Services Node**) before you can see the details.

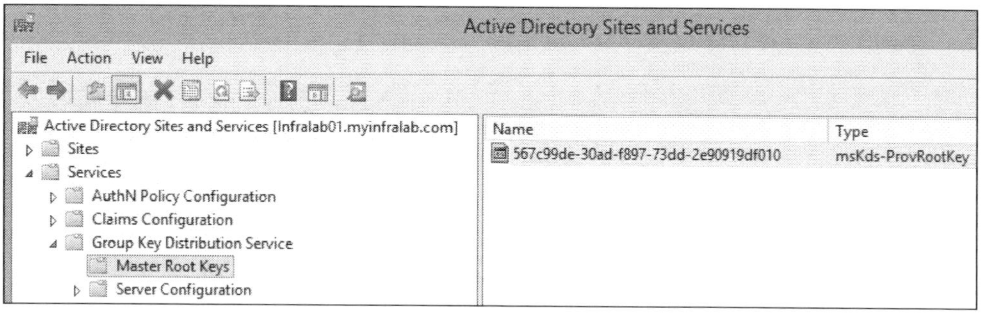

> The Key Distribution Service Key creation can take up to 10 hours to replicate this information across all the Domain Controllers. In a development environment with fewer Domain Controllers, you can reduce this time by using the method mentioned in this TechNet article: `http://technet.microsoft.com/en-us/library/jj128430.aspx`.

Creating Group Managed Service Accounts

The next step is to create a service account using the `New-ADServiceAccount` PowerShell cmdlet. Instead of using a single server name, you can create a security group for your servers and assign gMSA based on that group membership. These servers need to be restarted to get the updated group membership change and token:

> gMSA is only available in Windows Server 2012 Active Directory.
>
> By default, the members of domain admins and account operators have permission to create a `GroupManagedSerivce Account` object in Active Directory.
>
> By default, the password change interval is 30 days. If required, you can change the default value by using the `–ManagedPasswordIntervalInDays` parameter during the service account creation process.

1. Open the PowerShell command window.
2. Enter the following command:

```
New-ADServiceAccount -name gMSAWeb1
-DNSHostName WebFarm1.Myinfralab.com
-PrincipalsAllowedToRetrieveManagedPasswordWebServers
```

3. In the preceding cmdlet, `-name` represents the actual name of the service account, `-DNSHostName` represents the DNS host name of the service, and `PrincipalsAllowedToRetrieveManagedPassword` represents the host members. You can use a single computer name or a group of computers using a security group. In this case, it is a web servers security group.
4. These service accounts will appear in **Managed Services Accounts** contained in **Active Directory Users Computers**.

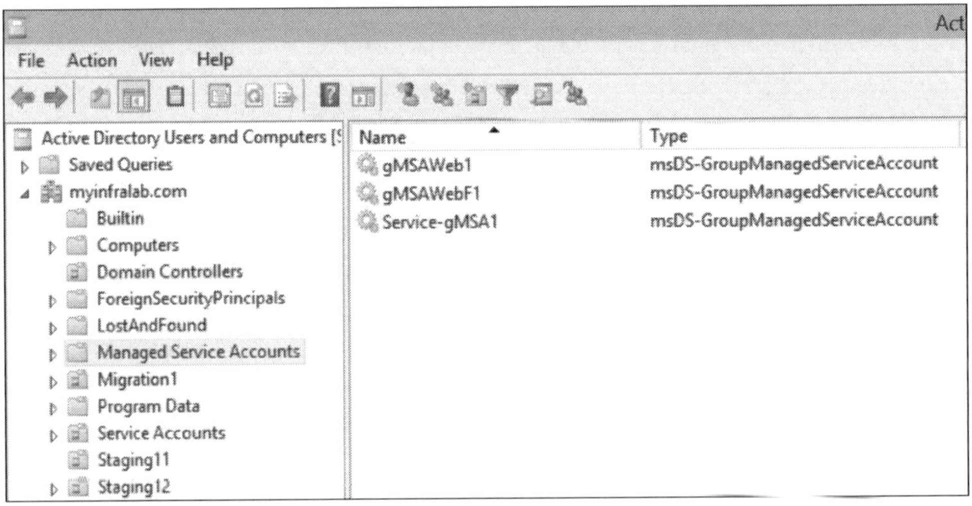

Installing Group Managed Service Accounts

The `Install-AdServiceAccountPowerShell` cmdlet can be used to install a gMSA on a host server:

1. Log on to the host server and open the PowerShell command window.
2. Enter the following command:

```
Install-AdServiceAccountgMSAWeb1
```

3. You can validate the service account using the `Test-AdServiceAccount` PowerShell cmdlet. This command returns a `True` or `False` value based on the configuration:

```
Test-ADServiceAccount -Identity gMSAWeb1
```

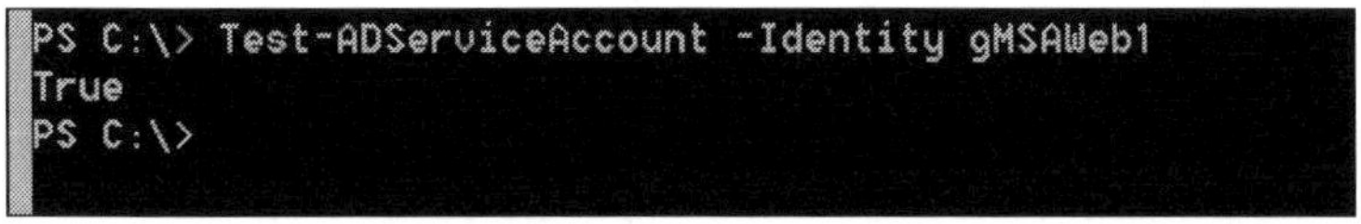

Configuring Group Managed Service Accounts

The final step in this process is to configure the previously created service account inside the application or service. The configuration will depend on your application. If it is just a service, you can modify the **Log On as** account from **Services Managed Console**. A '$' sign must be appended and the password must be blank for these accounts, as show in the following screenshot:

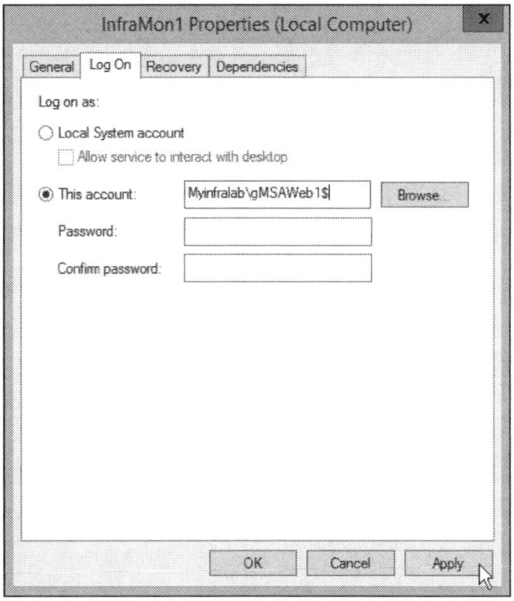

If required, the system will grant **Log On As A Service** permission during this configuration.

Enhanced Mitigation Experience Toolkit

Even though the best practice is to run minimal server roles and third-party applications on a server, sometimes it is required to run some non-Microsoft, non-recommended, and legacy services on an enterprise server. This may be due to some of the business and technical policies in your organization. This brings another type of threat to your organization. Microsoft has a free tool called **Enhanced Mitigation Experience Toolkit** (**EMET**), which can provide another layer of protection for your system and applications. EMET provides multiple mitigation technologies such as:

- **Structured Exception Handler Overwrite Protection** (**SEHOP**)
- **Data Execution Prevention** (**DEP**)
- **Mandatory Address Space Layout Randomization** (**ASLR**)
- **Certificate Trust** (**Pinning**)

The details of these technologies can be found at `http://blogs.technet.com/b/srd/archive/2009/02/02/preventing-the-exploitation-of-seh-overwrites-with-sehop.aspx` and `http://blogs.technet.com/b/srd/archive/2013/05/08/emet-4-0-s-certificate-trust-feature.aspx`.

Depending on the type of your application and server, you can install and configure EMET to enhance the security and minimize the threat.

Installing Enhanced Mitigation Experience Toolkit

The following section provides step-by-step instructions to install EMET on Windows Server 2012:

> The EMET application can be downloaded from the following location: `http://www.microsoft.com/en-us/download/details.aspx?id=43714`.

1. Run the installation by double-clicking on the EMET 5.1 `Setup.msi` file.
2. Click on **Next** in the **Welcome** window.
3. Select the appropriate installation folder or accept the default location in the **Select Installation Folder** window. Click on **Next**.
4. In the **License Agreement** window, accept the license agreement. Click on **Next**.

5. Click on **Next** on the **Confirm Installation** window to start the installation. You will see the installation status in the **Installing EMET 5.1** window.
6. In the EMET configuration window, select the **Use Recommended Settings** option. Click on **Finish**.

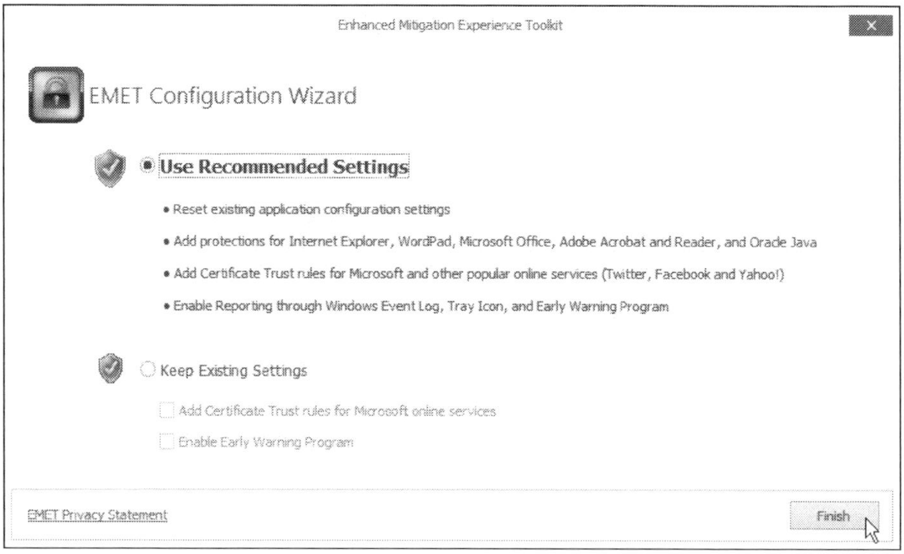
Enhanced Mitigation Experience Toolkit
EMET Configuration Wizard
Use Recommended Settings
• Reset existing application configuration settings
• Add protections for Internet Explorer, WordPad, Microsoft Office, Adobe Acrobat and Reader, and Oracle Java
• Add Certificate Trust rules for Microsoft and other popular online services (Twitter, Facebook and Yahoo!)
• Enable Reporting through Windows Event Log, Tray Icon, and Early Warning Program
Keep Existing Settings
Add Certificate Trust rules for Microsoft online services
Enable Early Warning Program
EMET Privacy Statement
Finish

7. In the **Installation Complete** window, click on **Close** to complete the installation process.

Configuring Enhanced Mitigation Experience Toolkit

If you use the recommended settings during the installation, it will be ready for use with the default configurations. However, based on your requirements and applications running on the server, you may want to customize these settings. The following instructions can be used to administer and customize EMET:

1. Open the EMET console from the **Start** window by entering the `EMET GUI` keyword.

2. From the **Enhanced Mitigation Experience Toolkit** window, select the **App** icon.

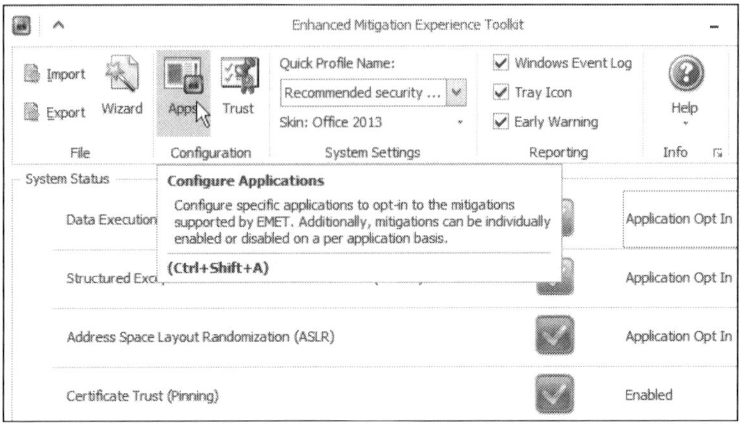

3. From the **Application Configuration** window, select the **Add Application** icon.

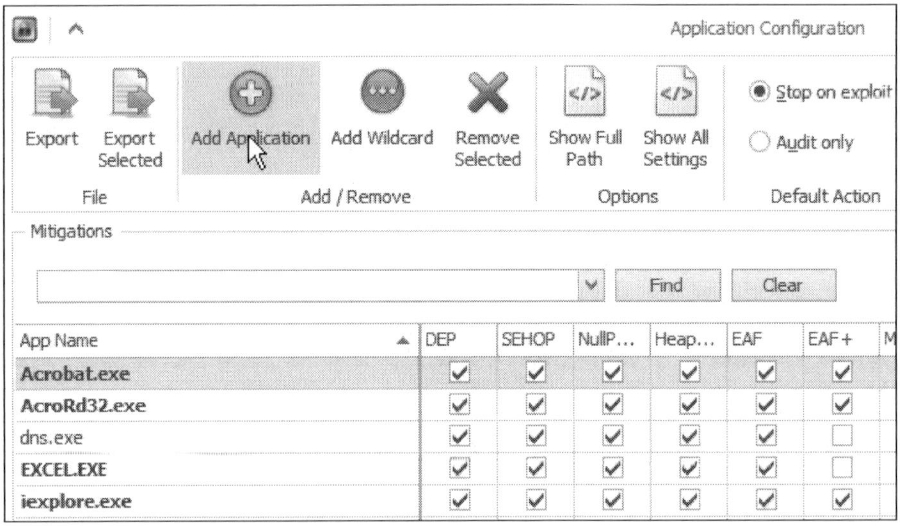

4. In the **Add Application** window, select the executable file for your application. Click on **OK**.

5. This application will be added to the **Application Configuration** window. You can double-click on the application name to customize the mitigation settings, as shown in the following screenshot:

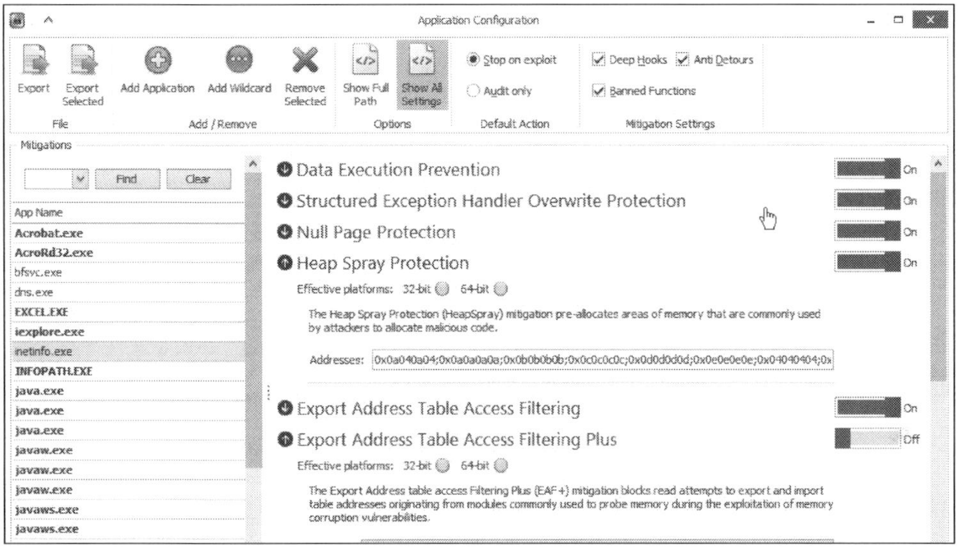

6. The recently added application service needs are started.

The preceding procedure provides an example for adding a custom application into EMET. Based on your application and requirements, you can add more application services to EMET in order to maintain maximum security for your application servers.

Summary

The primary focus of this chapter was to secure the Microsoft network infrastructure and components by using Microsoft tools and methods. We have achieved this by configuring RODCs for an existing Active Directory domain, securing DNS and DHCP using various methods, eliminating the service account password administration and risk by using **Group Managed Service Accounts** (**gMSA**), and by implementing a solution to mitigate application vulnerabilities using **Enhanced Mitigation Experience Toolkit** (**EMET**).

In the next chapter, I will introduce a new and secure access control mechanism for data and file servers. The next chapter will provide some insight into **Dynamic Access Control** (**DAC**) methods, implementation, and configuration details.

6
Access Control

Protecting data and maintaining sensitive data inside the organization is a challenge for any enterprise. Information or data leakage can adversely affect an organization in many ways. Minimizing or controlling access is key in maintaining the integrity and confidentiality of these types of data. In this chapter, you will learn about a new and secure access control mechanism for data and file servers. In a traditional method, there is no easy way to implement an access control mechanism based on the type or class of data. Also, the permissions are based on a static value of the control mechanism.

In Windows Server 2012, Microsoft introduced a new concept called Dynamic Access Control. As it sounds, this method can be used to implement a dynamic access mechanism on an Active Directory resource. This access mechanism can be implemented based on the types and properties of the resources.

The implementation and configuration details of DAC are included in the following sections.

Dynamic Access Control

As mentioned before, **Dynamic Access Control** (**DAC**) was introduced in Windows Server 2012. There are some requirements to support DAC in an enterprise. You need to have at least one Windows Server 2012 Domain Controller and the Active Directory **Forest Functional Level** (**FFL**) must be at least Windows 2003. Also, before you can start using the benefits of DAC, the **Kerberos Key Distribution Center (KDC) support for claims, compound authentication and Kerberos armoring** setting must be enabled on all Domain Controllers.

> The details of DAC can be found at `http://blogs.technet.com/b/windowsserver/archive/2012/05/22/introduction-to-windows-server-2012-dynamic-access-control.aspx`.

On a higher level, the following steps are required to configure and implement a DAC mechanism in an Active Directory environment:

- Enable KDC support
- Create claim type
- Create resource properties
- Create **Central Access Rule** (**CAR**)
- Create **Central Access Policy** (**CAP**)
- Deploy Central Access Policy using GPO
- Configure file shares using Central Access Policy

The following sections provid step-by-step instructions on configuring these components.

Enabling the KDC support

We will start with **Kerberos Key Distribution Center** (**KDC**) support. This is a GPO-based configuration on Domain Controllers. The following instructions can be used to complete this configuration:

1. Open **Group Policy Management Console**.
2. Expand the **Domain Name** node and right-click on **Default Domain Policy GPO**. Select **Edit**.
3. It will open the **Group Policy Management Editor** window. Navigate to **Computer Configuration** | **Policies** | **Administrative Template** | **System** | **KDC**.
4. Select the **KDC** node. From the middle pane, double-click on the **KDC support for claims, compound authentication and Kerberos armoring** setting.
5. Change the configuration type to **Enabled**. Click on **OK**.

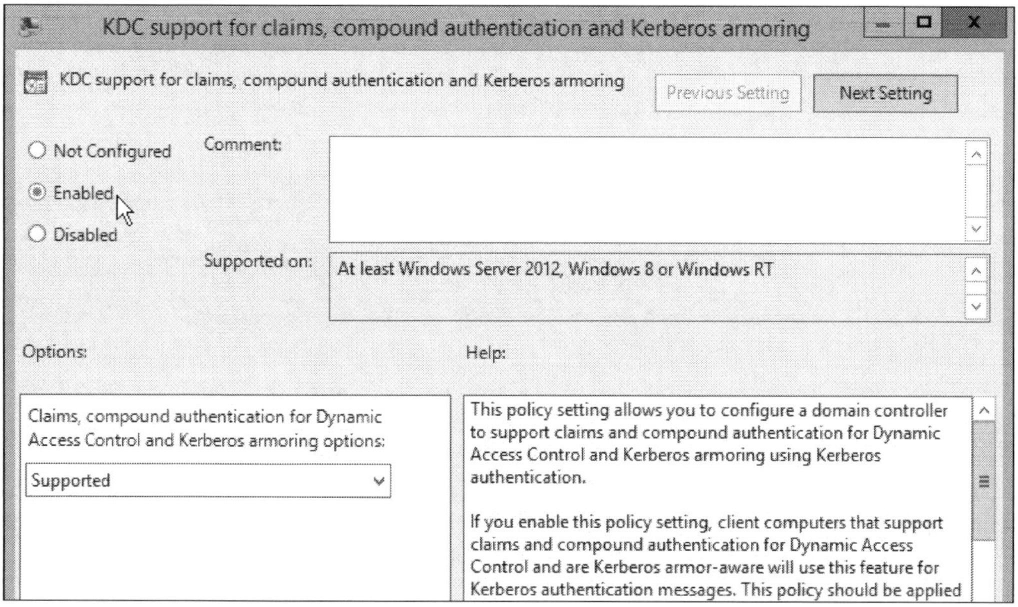
KDC support for claims, compound authentication and Kerberos armoring
KDC support for claims, compound authentication and Kerberos armoring
Previous Setting
Next Setting
Not Configured
Comment:
Enabled
Disabled
Supported on:
At least Windows Server 2012, Windows 8 or Windows RT
Options:
Help:
Claims, compound authentication for Dynamic Access Control and Kerberos armoring options:
Supported
This policy setting allows you to configure a domain controller to support claims and compound authentication for Dynamic Access Control and Kerberos armoring using Kerberos authentication.
If you enable this policy setting, client computers that support claims and compound authentication for Dynamic Access Control and are Kerberos armor-aware will use this feature for Kerberos authentication messages. This policy should be applied

6. Close the **Group Policy Management Editor** window.

If required, update the Group Policy using the `GPUPDATE/Force` command or wait for the AD replication to complete. You need to make sure the new KDC support has been successfully applied on to the Domain Controllers. Once you have the KDC support, you can get started by creating the Dynamic Access Control components. Unlike other options and technologies, there is no dedicated management console for Dynamic Access Control. It is configured by using **Active Directory Administrative Center** (**ADAC**).

In this exercise, your goal is to protect employee information on your file server. You will need to make sure that only employees from the HR group can access the data.

Creating claim types

As the first step in DAC configuration, you will be creating claim types based on your requirements. In this scenario, you need to create a claim type based on department values (HR). So you will be creating a claim type based on the **Department** attribute in Active Directory. The following section provides these instructions.

The details of claim-based identify and access control can be found at `https://msdn.microsoft.com/en-us/library/ff423674.aspx`. Perform the following steps:

1. Open the **Active Directory Administrative Center** console.
2. Select the **Dynamic Access Control** node from the left pane.

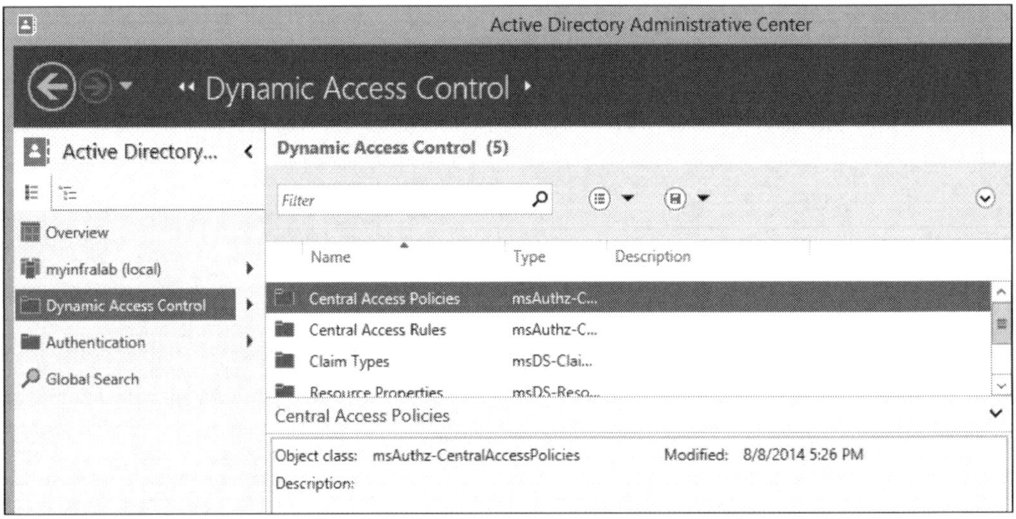

3. Select **Claim Type** from the middle pane. From the right pane, select **New** and then **Claim Type**.
4. From the attribute list, select **Department**.

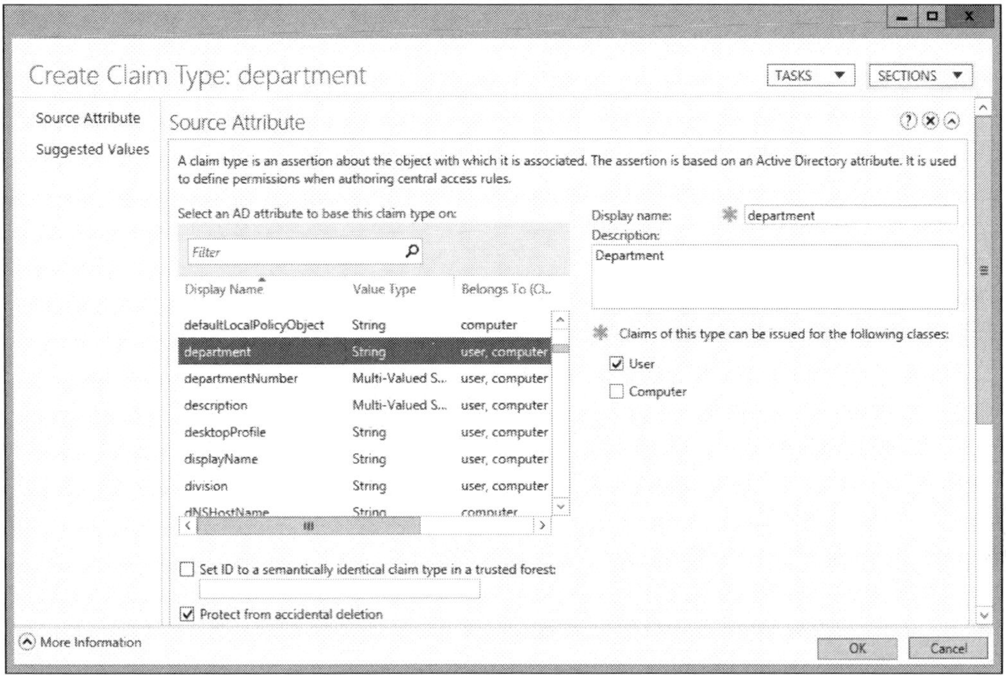

5. In the **Display Name** and **Description** boxes, select an appropriate name and description.
6. From the **Suggested Value** section, click on **Add**. Enter the department name in the **Add a suggested value dialog** box. Click on **OK**.

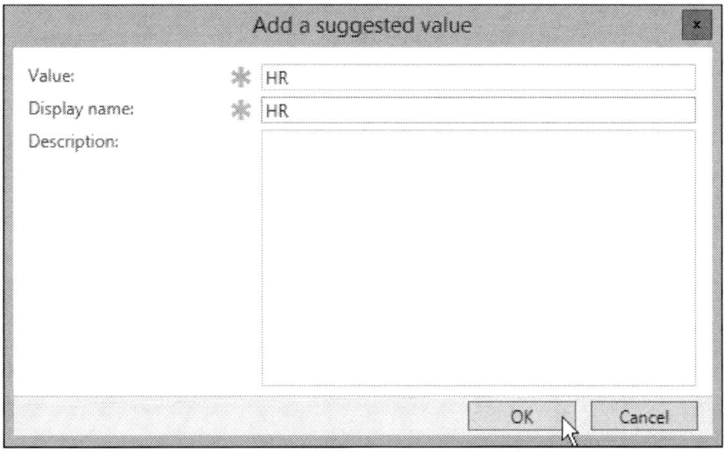

7. Leave **Claim Type** as **User** for this scenario. Click on **OK** to complete the claim type creation process.

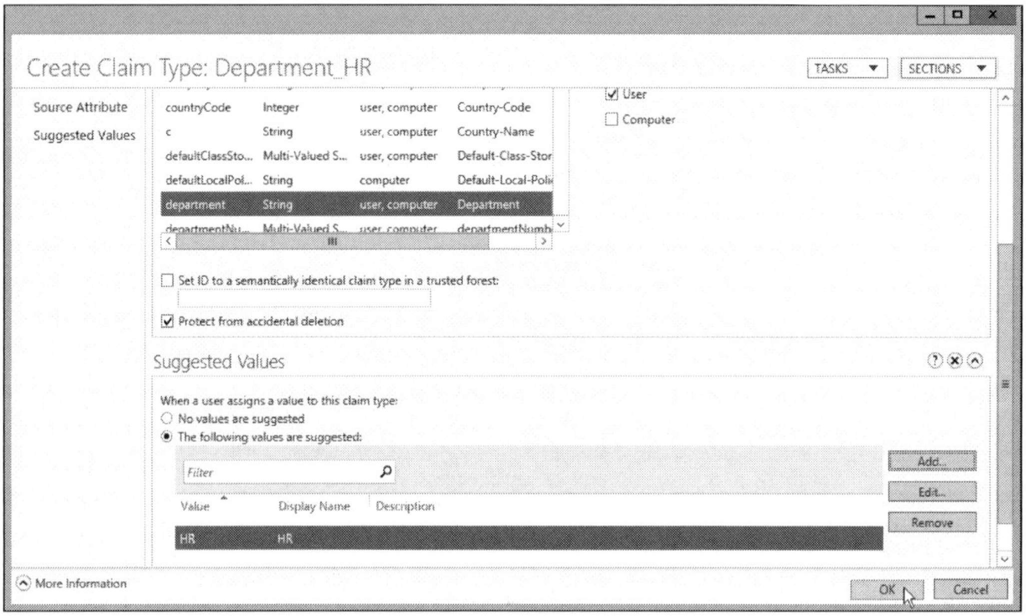

Creating and enabling resource properties

The instructions in the following section provide the details of creating and enabling **resource properties** for the claim type:

1. Select **Resource Property** from the middle pane. From the right pane, select **New** and then select **Reference Resource Properties**.
2. In the **Create Reference Resource Properties** window, select the previously created claim type. Click on **OK**.

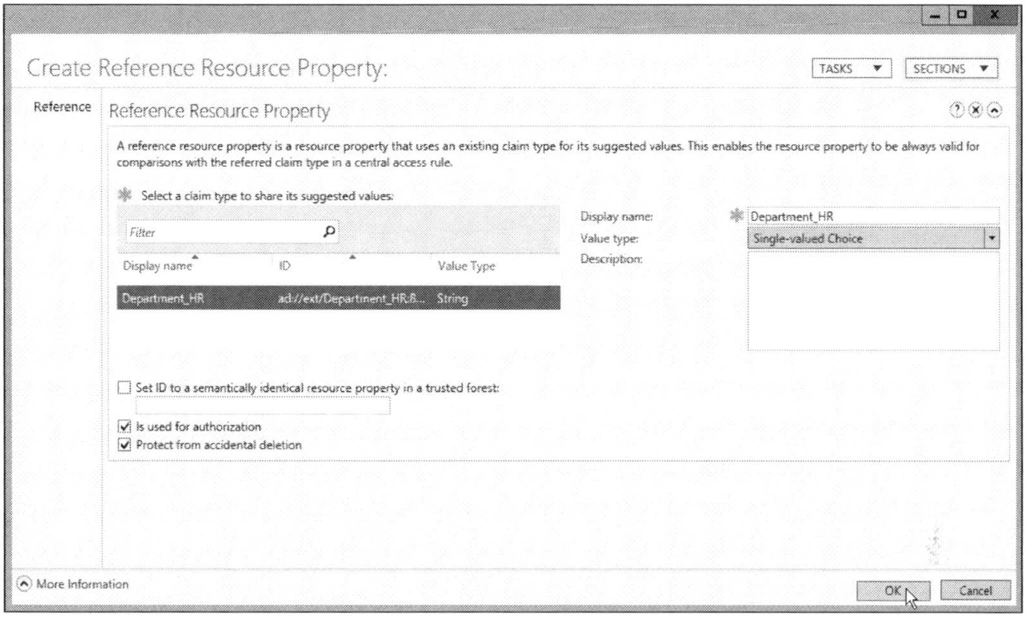

Creating a central access rule

At this stage, you have a claim type and resource properties. Based on this information, you can create access rules. The following instructions can be used to complete this process:

1. Select **Central Access Rule** from the middle pane. From the right pane, select **New** and then **Central Access Rule**.

2. In the **Create Central Access Rule** window:
    - Enter an appropriate name for the access rule in the **Name** box.
    - Leave **Target Resources** as **All Resources**.
    - From the **Permission** section, select the **Edit** button.

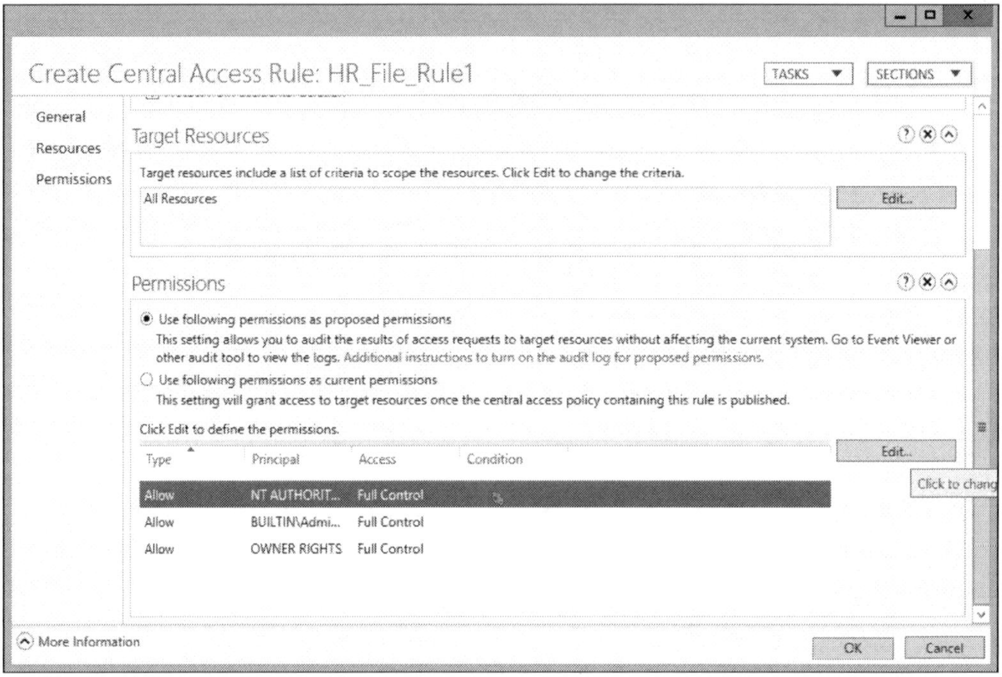
Create Central Access Rule: HR_File_Rule1
TASKS
SECTIONS
General
Resources
Permissions
Target Resources
Target resources include a list of criteria to scope the resources. Click Edit to change the criteria.
All Resources
Edit...
Permissions
Use following permissions as proposed permissions
This setting allows you to audit the results of access requests to target resources without affecting the current system. Go to Event Viewer or other audit tool to view the logs. Additional instructions to turn on the audit log for proposed permissions.
Use following permissions as current permissions
This setting will grant access to target resources once the central access policy containing this rule is published.
Click Edit to define the permissions.
Type
Principal
Access
Condition
Edit...
Allow
NT AUTHORIT...
Full Control
Allow
BUILTIN\Admi...
Full Control
Allow
OWNER RIGHTS
Full Control
More Information
OK
Cancel

    - Select the **Add** option from the **Advanced Security Settings for Permission** window.
    - Click on the **Select a Principal** button to select the appropriate practical account. In this scenario, you will be selecting **Authenticated Users** as the principal.
    - From **Basic Permission section**, select **Full Control.**

- From the bottom pane, select the **Add a Condition** link and enter the appropriate access rules here. In this scenario, you will be using the **Department=HR** condition, as shown in the following screenshot:

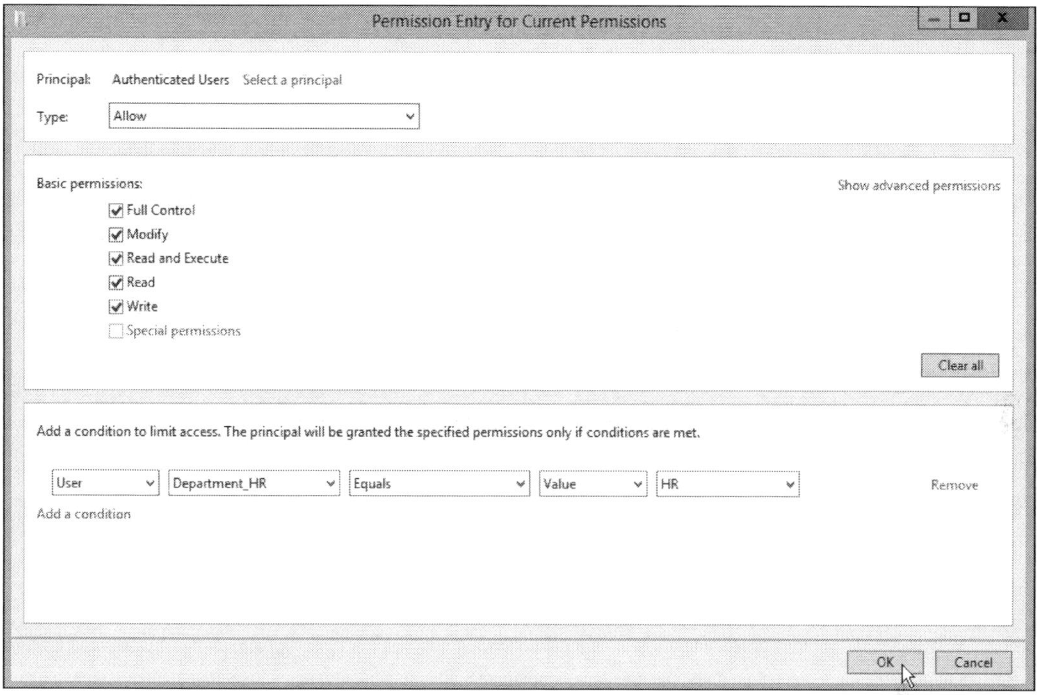

- Click on **OK** twice to complete the operation.

3. Click on **OK** to complete the rule-creation process.

Creating a central access policy

The central access policy comprises of a central access rule. The following instructions provide the details of creating a central access policy based on a previously created central access rule:

> The details of central access policies and rules can be found at `https://technet.microsoft.com/en-us/library/hh831425.aspx`.

1. Select **Central Access Policy** from the middle pane. From the right pane, select **New** and then **Central Access Policy**.
2. On the **Create Central Access Policy** window:
    - Enter an appropriate name for the access policy in the **Name** box.
    - From the **Member Central Access Rules** section, select the **Add** button and select the previously created access rule.

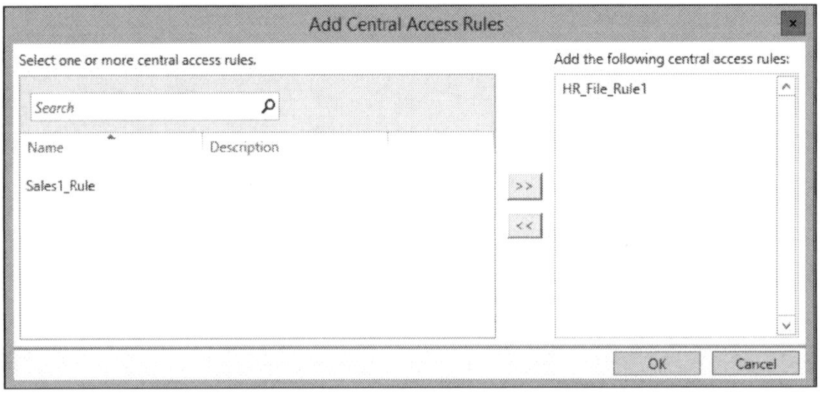

    - The **General Policy** window displays the central access rules, as shown in the following screenshot. Click on **OK** to close the windows.

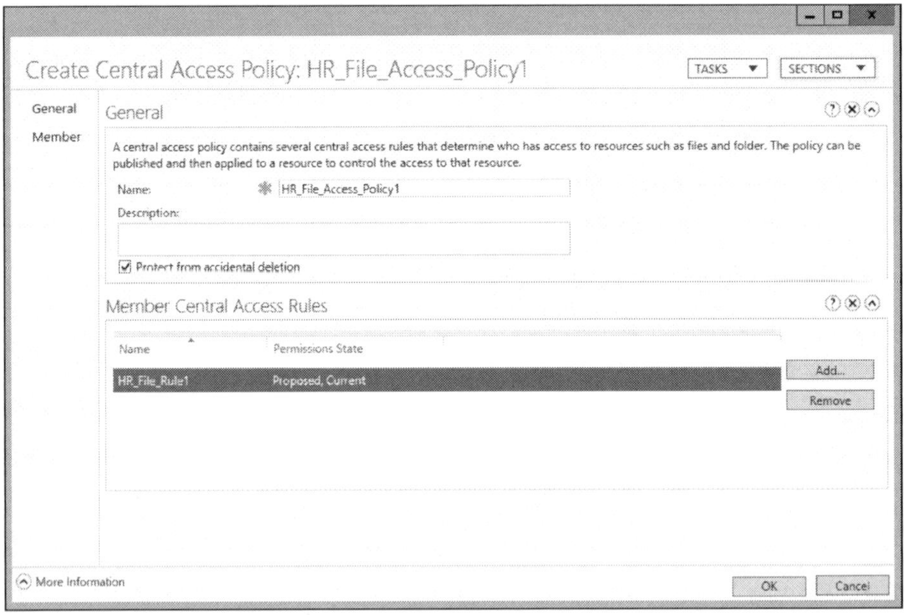

Deploying a central access policy

At this point, you have your access policy ready to be deployed. The deployment of access polices takes place through GPOs. The following section provides an option to deploy these central access polices using the GPMC:

1. Open **Group Policy Management Console**.
2. Expand the **Domain** option and select the appropriate OU. In this scenario, you will be creating a new GPO in **Servers OU**. If you have an existing OU, you can add these settings using the **Edit** option.
3. Right-click on **Servers OU** and select the **Create a GPO in this Domain, and link it here** option.

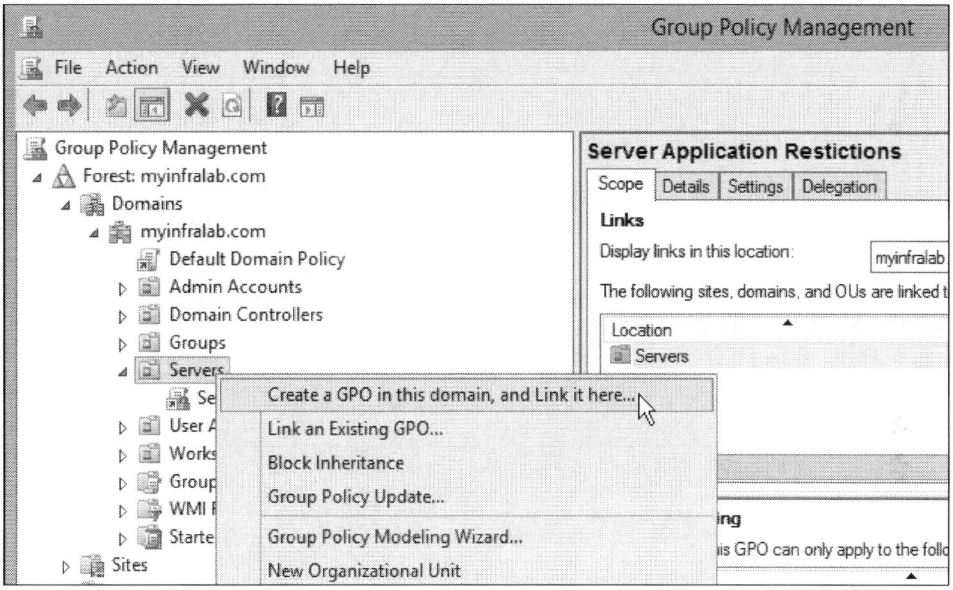

The Create a GPO in this Domain, and link it here option

4. In the **New GPO** window, enter the name for this GPO. Click on **OK**.

5. Right-click on the newly created GPO and select the **Edit** option.

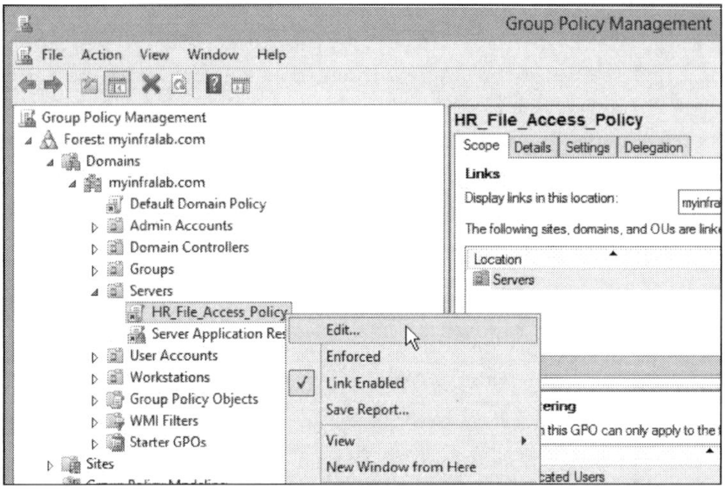

Editing the newly created GPO

6. This will open a **Group Policy Management Editor** window.
7. Expand the **Computer Configuration** node and navigate to **Policies | Windows Settings | Security Settings | File System | Central Access Policy**.
8. Right-click on **Central Access Policy** and select the **Manage Central Access Policies** option.

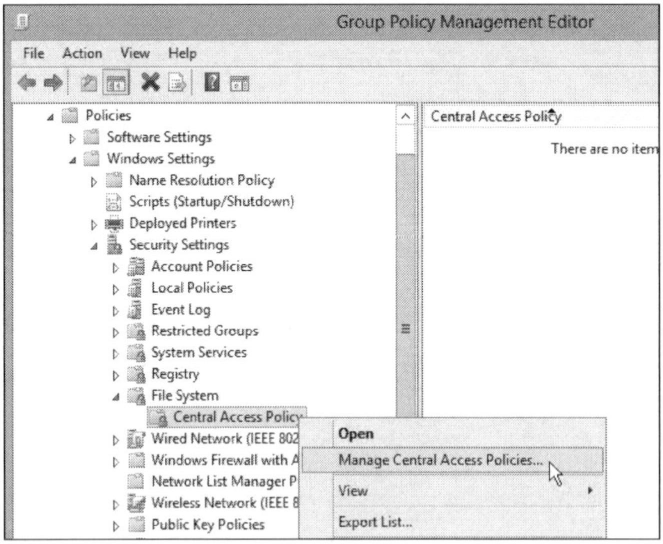

9. From the **Central Access Policy Configuration** window, select the previously created access policy. Click on **Add**, and then on **OK** to complete this operation.

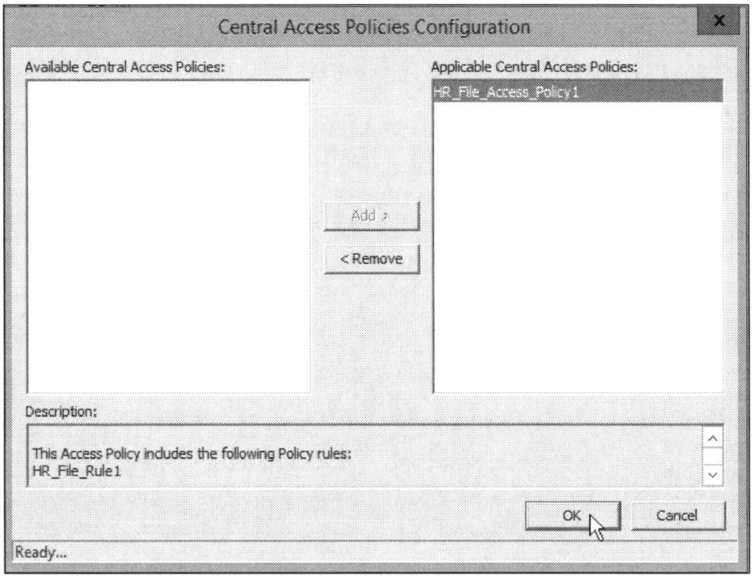

10. Close the **Group Policy Management Editor** window.

The GPO will be applied to all computer objects in **Servers OU**. The GPO can be manually updated by using the `GPUPDATE /Force` command. The `GPRESULT /R` command can be used to verify the applied GPOs on the file server, as shown in the following screenshot:

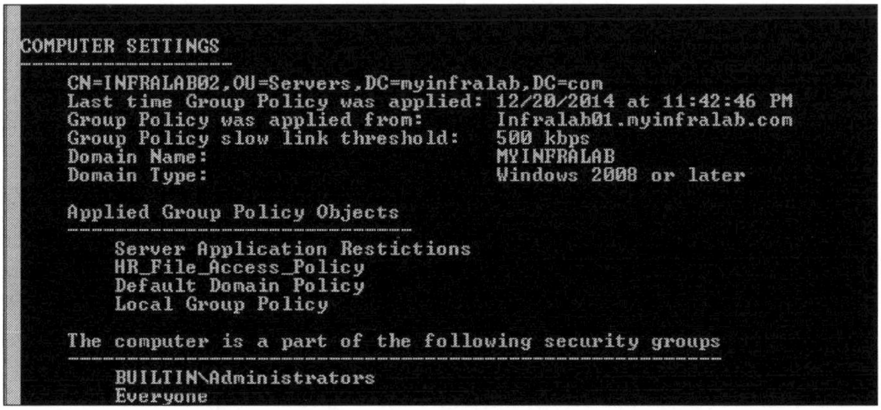

COMPUTER SETTINGS
CN=INFRALAB02,OU=Servers,DC=myinfralab,DC=com
Last time Group Policy was applied: 12/20/2014 at 11:42:46 PM
Group Policy was applied from: Infralab01.myinfralab.com
Group Policy slow link threshold: 500 kbps
Domain Name: MYINFRALAB
Domain Type: Windows 2008 or later
Applied Group Policy Objects
Server Application Restictions
HR_File_Access_Policy
Default Domain Policy
Local Group Policy
The computer is a part of the following security groups
BUILTIN\Administrators
Everyone

Configuring folder permissions on a file server

From an access policy perspective, you have completed all the required tasks. The next step in this process is to apply these access polices to a folder or share them on a file server. The following section explains the steps in detail:

1. Log on to the file server using administrative permission.
2. Right-click on **Folder/Share** and select **Properties**.
3. Select the **Security** tab and click on **Advanced**.
4. In the **Advanced Security Settings** window, you will see a new tab called **Central Policy**. If you don't see the **Central Policy** tab, verify the GPO settings and make sure that they applied on your servers.
5. Select the **Central Policy** tab.
6. From the **Central Policy** window, select the **Change** button.
7. From the drop-down box, select the previously created central access policy. You can click on the policy name to see the permission express configuration details.

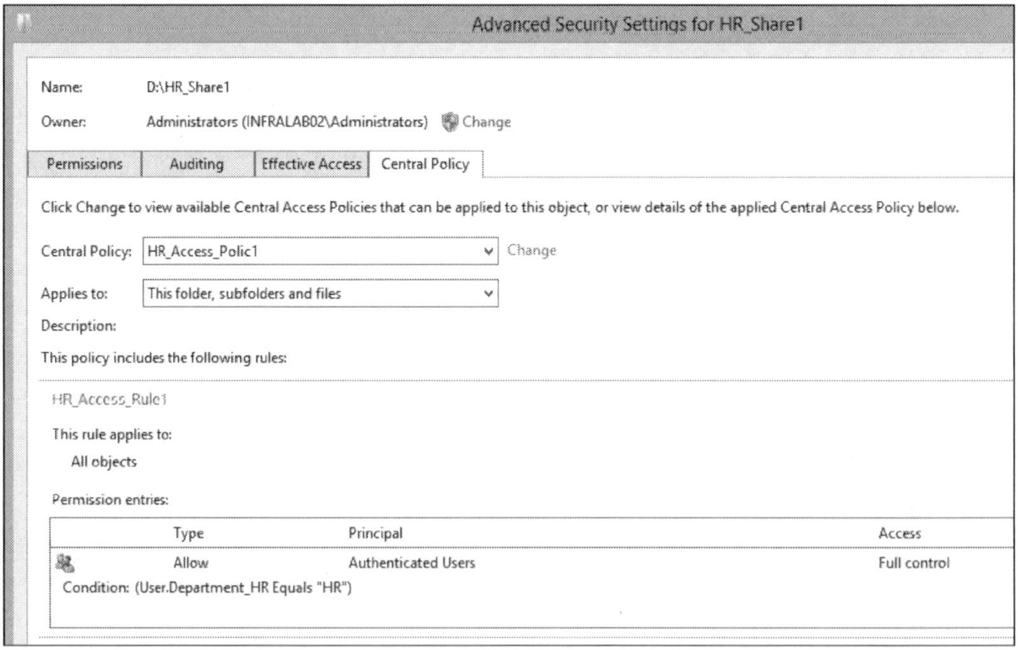

8. Click on **OK** to complete the configuration.

Verifying access the control configuration and permission

The access control policy and effective permission can be verified by using the **Effective Access** option from the **Advanced Security** window:

1. Select **Effective Access** from the **Advanced Security** window.
2. From the **User/Group** section, click on the **Select a user** link.
3. From the **Select Users, Computer, Service Account, or Group** window, select the appropriate user and click on **OK**.
4. Click on **View Effective Access** from the **Advanced Security** window.
5. As shown in the following screenshot, you will see a red **X** indicating the access denied message along with the reason on the right-most column. In this scenario, the access policy was blocking the folder access based on the condition.

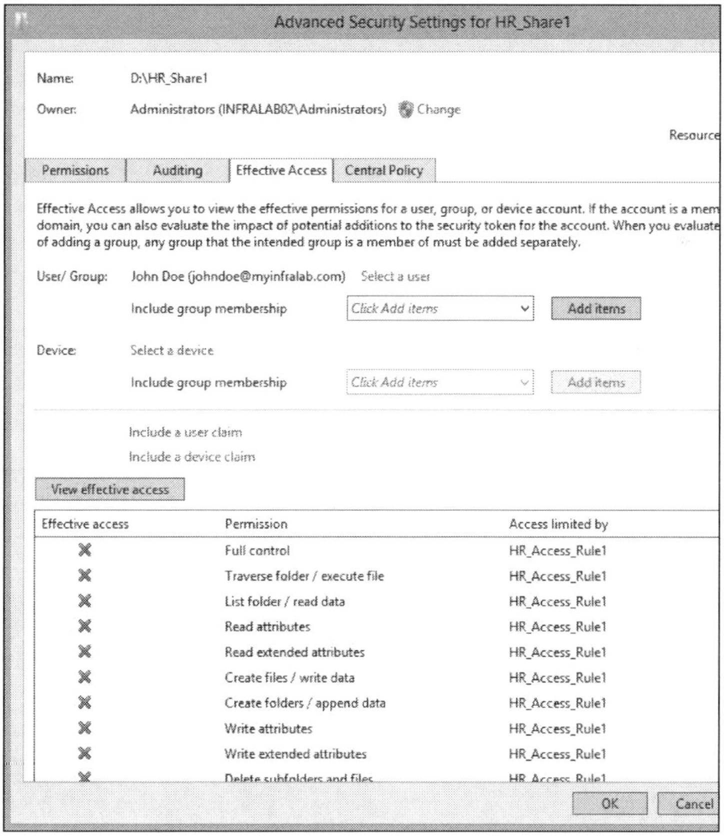

6. Since our access policy was on the **Department** value, for testing purposes, you can change the **Department** value to HR to validate the result.

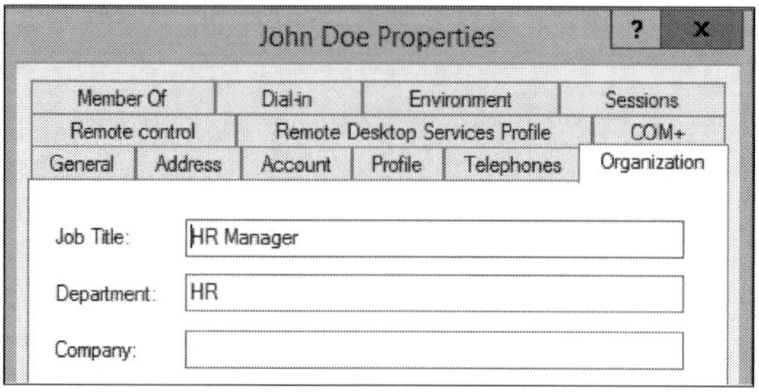

7. As shown in the following screenshot, you will see a green checkmark indicting that full access is granted based on the updated department value in Active Directory.

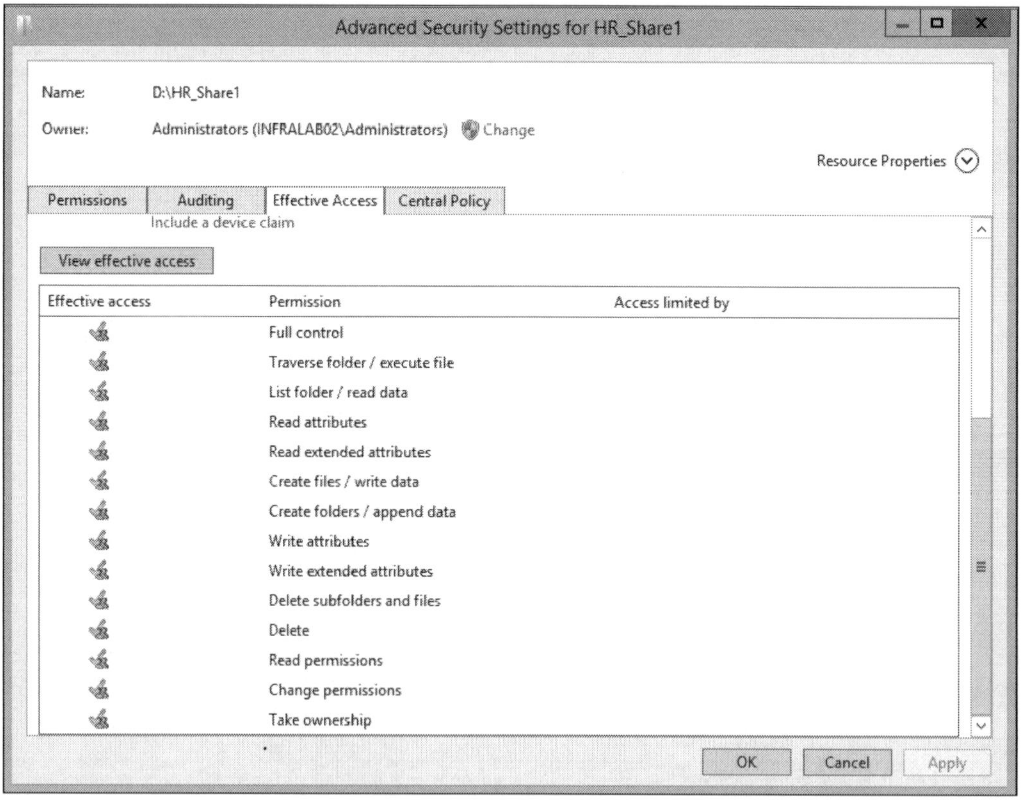

Summary

The goal of this chapter was to establish a secure access mechanism for protecting the data. I believe we can accomplish this task by introducing the concept called Dynamic Access Control. We looked at the DAC configuration and implementation details from an access and security mechanism perspective. File screening and classification can also be integrated with DAC to secure file servers and data. If interested, more information about these technologies can be found at `http://technet.microsoft.com/en-us/library/dn383587.aspx`.

In the next chapter, you will learn how to continually protect your server and server infrastructure using **Windows Server Update Service** (**WSUS**). The automation, implementation, and configuration details of WSUS are included in the following chapter.

7

Patch Management

In the previous chapters, you have seen how we can protect and enhance the security of the Microsoft platform using various tool and technology. It is important that you should continuously maintain the same level of security to ensure the maximum security. The tools mentioned in the previous chapters such as Security Configuration Wizard, Attack Surface Analyzer, and so on can be re-executed to apply the latest security configuration. On the other side, the operating systems and applications are continuously going through a lot of changes and updates from the respective vendors. Keeping up with these updates and installing them are also critical for any organization. An automated way of consolidating these updates and deploying them from a centralized platform would be beneficial. This is where Microsoft **Windows Server Update Services** (**WSUS**) can provide value and play a critical role in the security space. The details, installation, and configuration instructions of Microsoft WSUS are included in this chapter.

Microsoft Windows Server Update Services

The Microsoft **Windows Server Update Services** (**WSUS**) is a patch management solution from Microsoft, which can provide an automated solution to implement the latest updates and service packs for Microsoft server infrastructure. The deployment of these new updates can be controlled through **Group Policy Objects** (**GPOs**).

Based on your organization and network infrastructure, the architecture of the Microsoft Windows Server Update Services can be different. In this chapter, you will see a basic Microsoft WSUS infrastructure, which can be expanded based on your requirements.

In general, the Microsoft WSUS infrastructure requires the following components:

- **WSUS Server Role**: In Windows Server 2012, WSUS is a Server Role, which can be installed using Server Manager. There is no additional software required for WSUS.
- **Database**: The WSUS database contains the configuration details. The **Windows Internal Database (WID)**, Microsoft SQL Server 2012 with SP1, Microsoft SQL Server 2012, Microsoft SQL Server 2008 R2 SP2, and Microsoft SQL Server 2008 R2 SP1 are the supported databases for WSUS.
- **Group Policy Objects**: Group Policy Objects are responsible for deploying WSUS configuration and new security updates and patches.

You will see the installation and configuration details of each of these components in the following sections. Since our primary focus is around Windows Server and server technology, you will see an emphasis around these technologies in this chapter. However, the details included in this chapter can also be applied to client operating systems and applications.

Installing the WSUS web role

The first step in this process is to install Microsoft WSUS Server Role on a designated server. Like any other Server Role, this can also be added through Server Manager. Following are step-by-step instructions on installing and configuring WSUS on a Windows Server 2012 server:

1. Open **Server Manager**.
2. From the **Manage** menu, select the **Add Roles and Features** option.
3. Click on **Next** on the **Before you begin** window.
4. On the **Select installation type** window, select the **Role-based or feature-based installation** option. Click on **Next**.

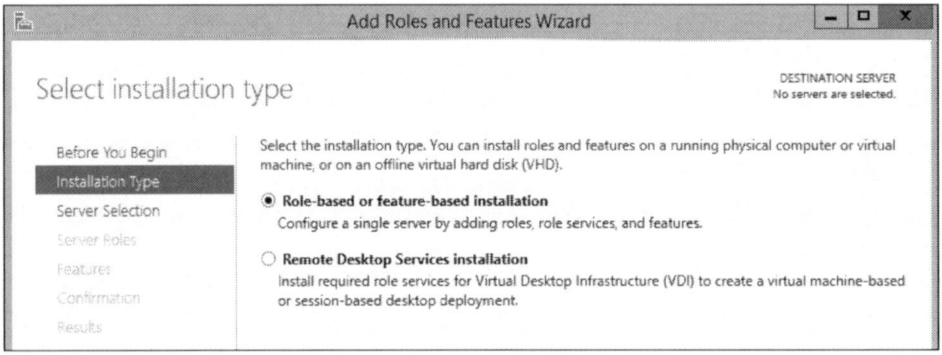
Add Roles and Features Wizard
Select installation type
DESTINATION SERVER
No servers are selected.
Before You Begin
Installation Type
Server Selection
Server Roles
Features
Confirmation
Results
Select the installation type. You can install roles and features on a running physical computer or virtual machine, or on an offline virtual hard disk (VHD).
Role-based or feature-based installation
Configure a single server by adding roles, role services, and features.
Remote Desktop Services installation
Install required role services for Virtual Desktop Infrastructure (VDI) to create a virtual machine-based or session-based desktop deployment.

5. From the **Select destination server** window, select the **Select a server from the server pool** option and select an appropriate server and click on **Next**.

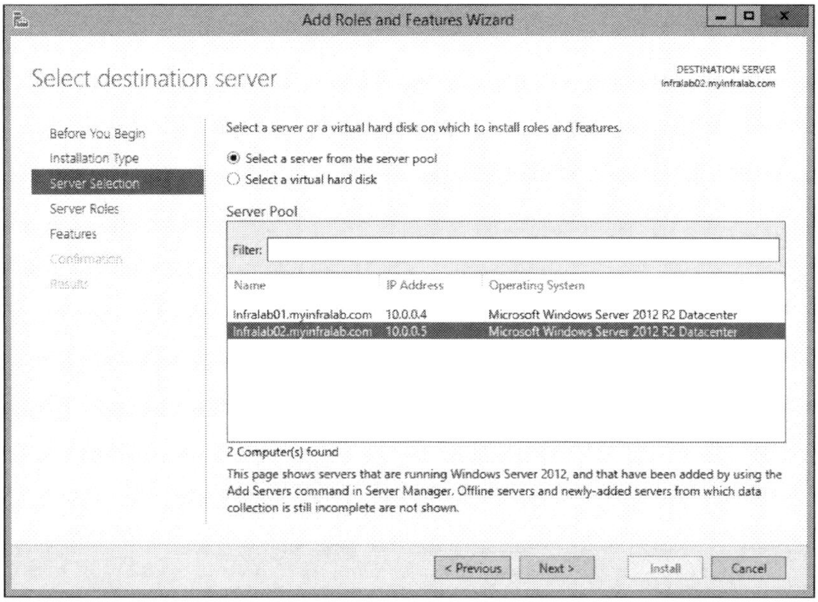

6. From the **Select server roles** window, select the **Windows Server Update Services** role.

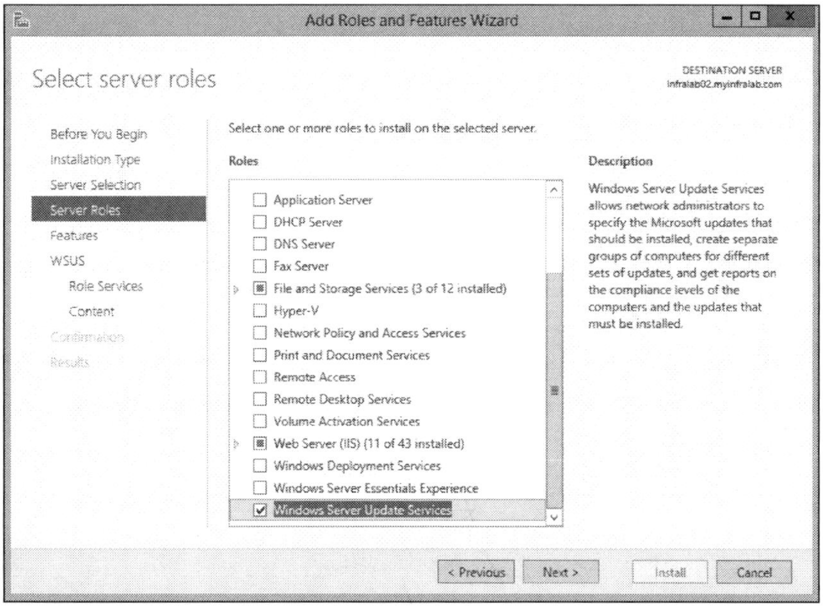

7. Accept the additional feature confirmation by clicking the **Add Features** button. From the **Select server roles** window, select the **Windows Server Update Services** role.

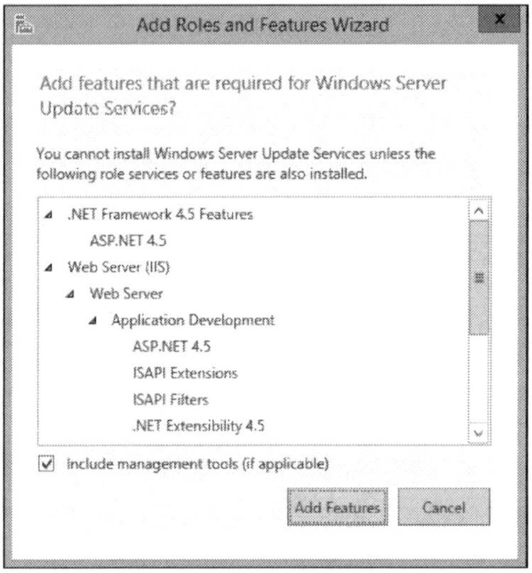

8. Click on **Next** on the **Select server roles** window to continue.
9. On the **Select features** window, click on **Next**.
10. Click on **Next** on the **Windows Server Update Service** window.
11. On the **Select role services** window, accept the default role services. Click on **Next**.

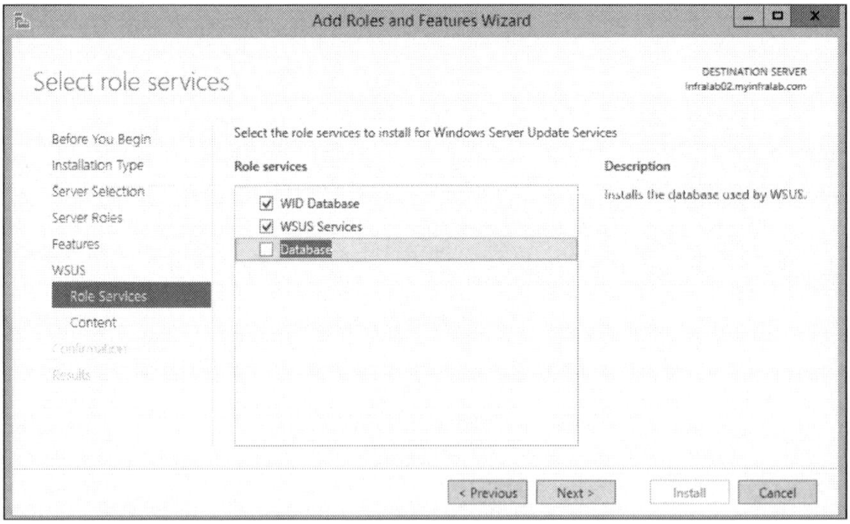

> The database and WSUS service are required components for the WSUS installation. We will be using WID database for this installation.

12. On the **Content location selection** window, enter a location to store updates. Click on **Next**.

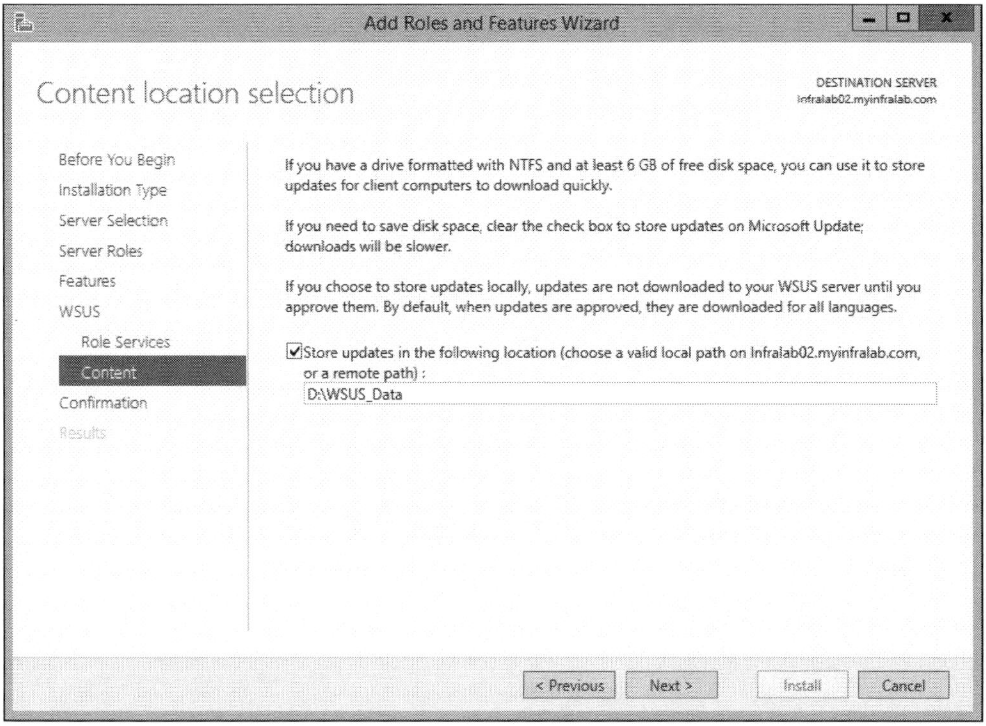
Add Roles and Features Wizard
Content location selection
DESTINATION SERVER
Infralab02.myinfralab.com
Before You Begin
Installation Type
Server Selection
Server Roles
Features
WSUS
Role Services
Content
Confirmation
Results
If you have a drive formatted with NTFS and at least 6 GB of free disk space, you can use it to store updates for client computers to download quickly.
If you need to save disk space, clear the check box to store updates on Microsoft Update; downloads will be slower.
If you choose to store updates locally, updates are not downloaded to your WSUS server until you approve them. By default, when updates are approved, they are downloaded for all languages.
Store updates in the following location (choose a valid local path on Infralab02.myinfralab.com, or a remote path) :
D:\WSUS_Data
< Previous
Next >
Install
Cancel

> This will be the local storage for new updates and patches. If you don't want to store them locally or save the disk space, you can skip this step by unselecting the **Store updates** location checkbox.

13. You can select the **Restart the destination server automatically if required** option from the **Confirm installation sections** window. Click on **Install** to continue with the installation process.
14. You will see the status and progress in the **Installation Progress** window.
15. Click on **Close** to close the wizard window.

Configuring WSUS

The next step is to configure the WSUS. You will see a **Post-deployment Configuration** section in Server Manager, which can be used to complete the configuration. The instructions are included in the following section:

1. Launch the **Post-deployment Configuration** tasks from the Server Manager or from the start screen by typing `Windows Server Update Service`.

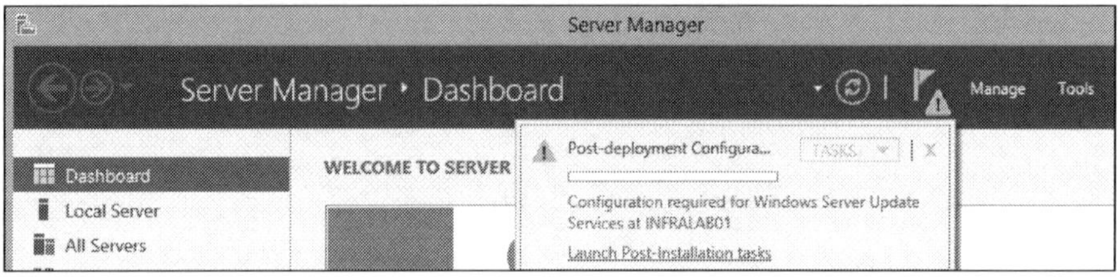

2. Click on **Next** on the **Before You Begin** window.
3. On the **Join the Microsoft Update Improvement Program** window, accept the default configuration and click on **Next**.
4. On the **Choose Upstream Server** window, select the **Synchronize from Microsoft Update** option. Click on **Next**.

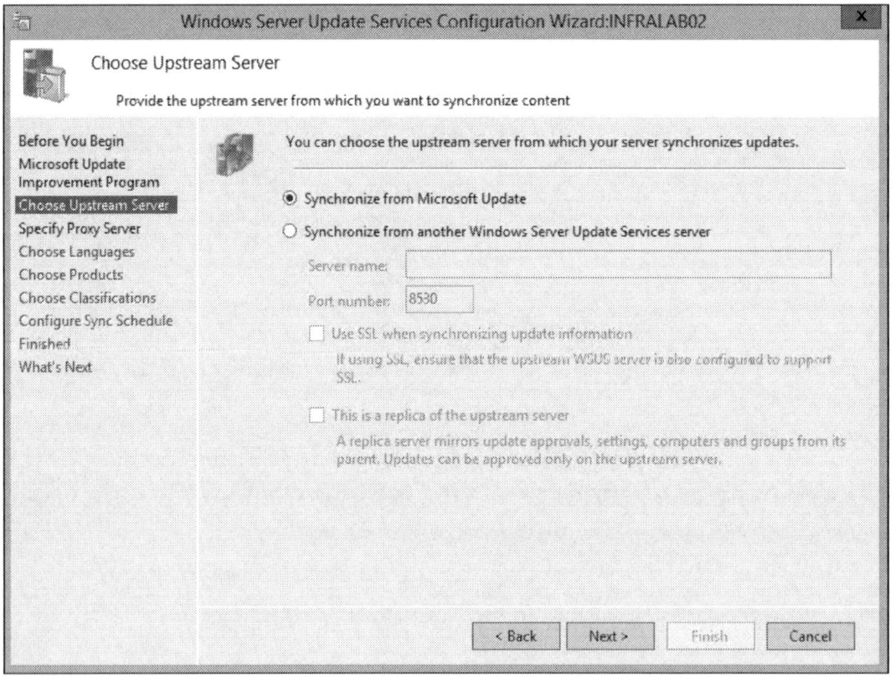

5. If you are using a proxy server for internet or upstream connectivity, enter the information on the **Specify Proxy Server** window. Click on **Next**.

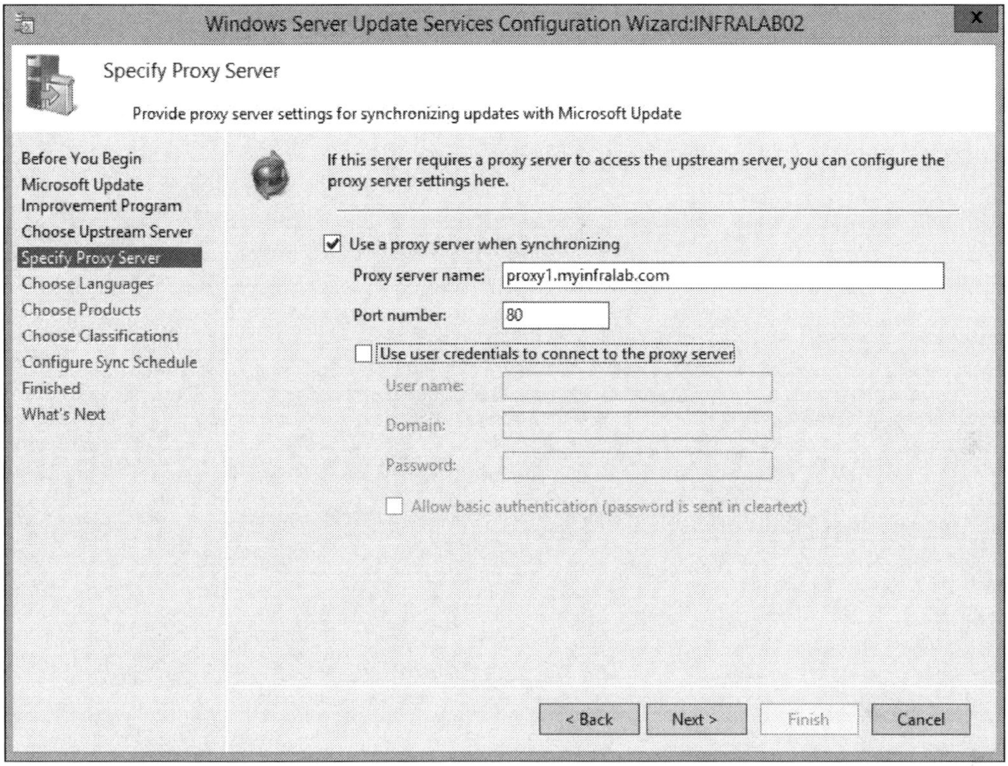

If you are not using a proxy server, you can click on **Next** to continue with the installation.

6. On the **Connect to Upstream Server** window, select the **Start Connecting** button. This will download the product catalogue and update from either an upstream server or from the Microsoft update server. This process can take a few minutes to complete. Once it completes, click on **Next** to continue with the configuration.

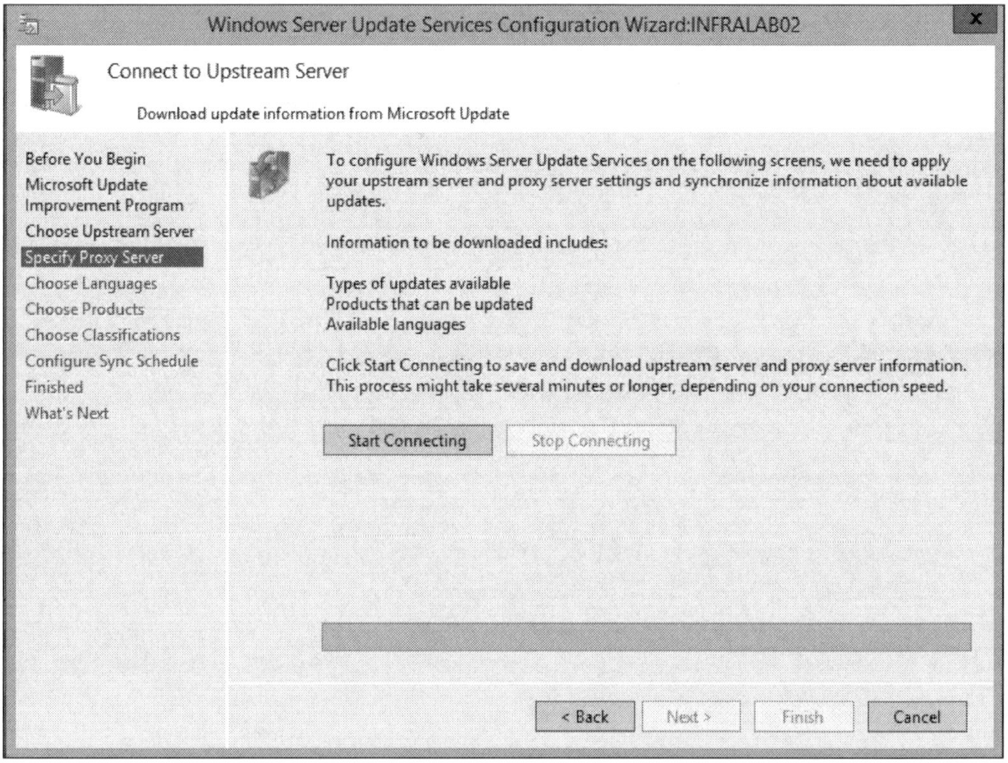
Windows Server Update Services Configuration Wizard:INFRALAB02
Connect to Upstream Server
Download update information from Microsoft Update
Before You Begin
Microsoft Update Improvement Program
Choose Upstream Server
Specify Proxy Server
Choose Languages
Choose Products
Choose Classifications
Configure Sync Schedule
Finished
What's Next
To configure Windows Server Update Services on the following screens, we need to apply your upstream server and proxy server settings and synchronize information about available updates.
Information to be downloaded includes:
Types of updates available
Products that can be updated
Available languages
Click Start Connecting to save and download upstream server and proxy server information. This process might take several minutes or longer, depending on your connection speed.
Start Connecting
Stop Connecting
< Back
Next >
Finish
Cancel

7. On the **Choose Language** window, select the appropriate language based on your requirements. Click on **Next**.
8. On the **Choose Products** window, select the language based on your requirements. For demonstration purpose, you will be selecting **Windows Server 2012 R2** and **Windows Server 2012** here. Click on **Next**.

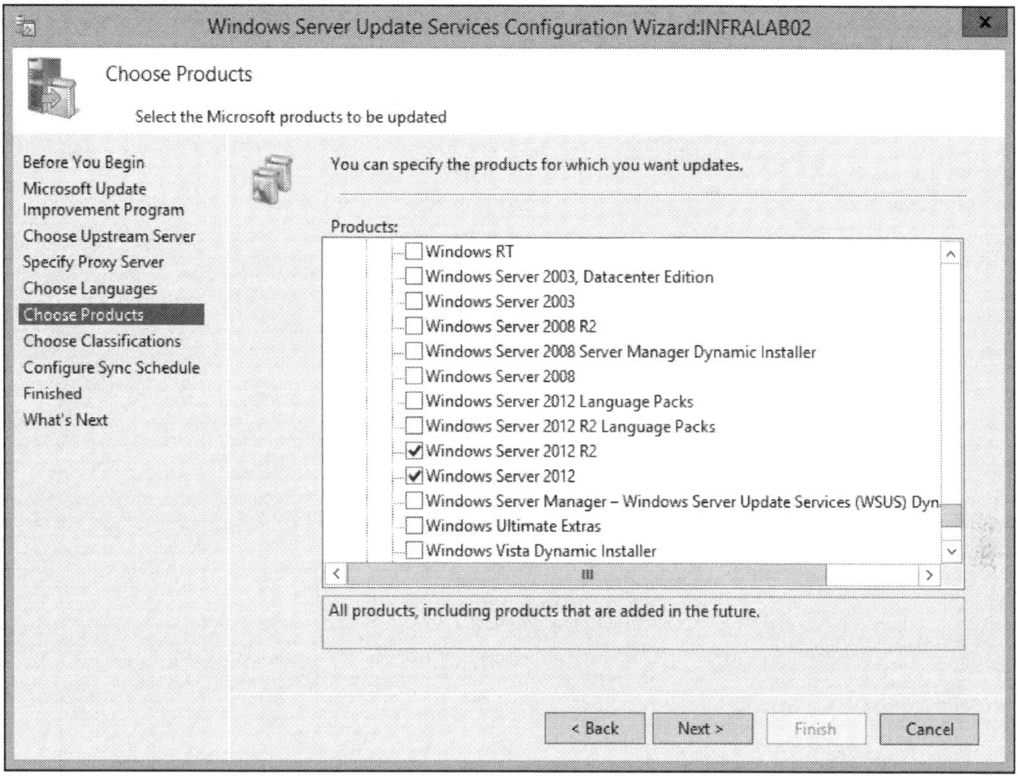

9. On the **Choose Classifications** window select the required options based on your requirements, for example, if your goal is to download only break fixes to a specific problem, you can select the **Critical Update** option. The details of the classifications are provided in the following section:
    - **Critical Updates**: Break fixes for specific issues
    - **Definition Updates**: Update to specific product related definitions, for example, Microsoft Defender
    - **Drivers**: New or updated drivers
    - **Feature Packs**: New and added functionalities of a product
    - **Security Updates**: Security-related updates and fixes
    - **Service Packs**: Service packs, update and hotfixes
    - **Tools**: New and added tools and functionalities
    - **Update Rollups**: Hotfix rollups and updates
    - **Updates**: Non-critical updates to specific issues

10. In this scenario, you will be selecting **Critical Updates**, **Definition Updates**, **Security Updates**, **Service Pack**, **Update Rollups**, and **Updates** as your classification. Click on **Next** to continue.

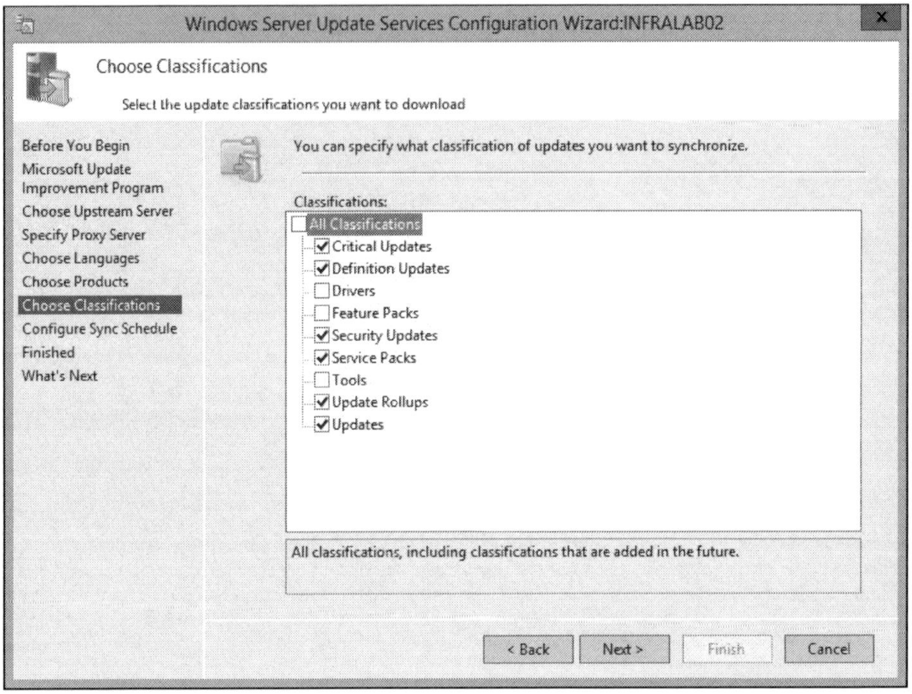

11. On the **Set Sync Schedule** page, you have two options to synchronize the updates from Microsoft. Select the appropriate option based on your requirement. Click on **Next**.

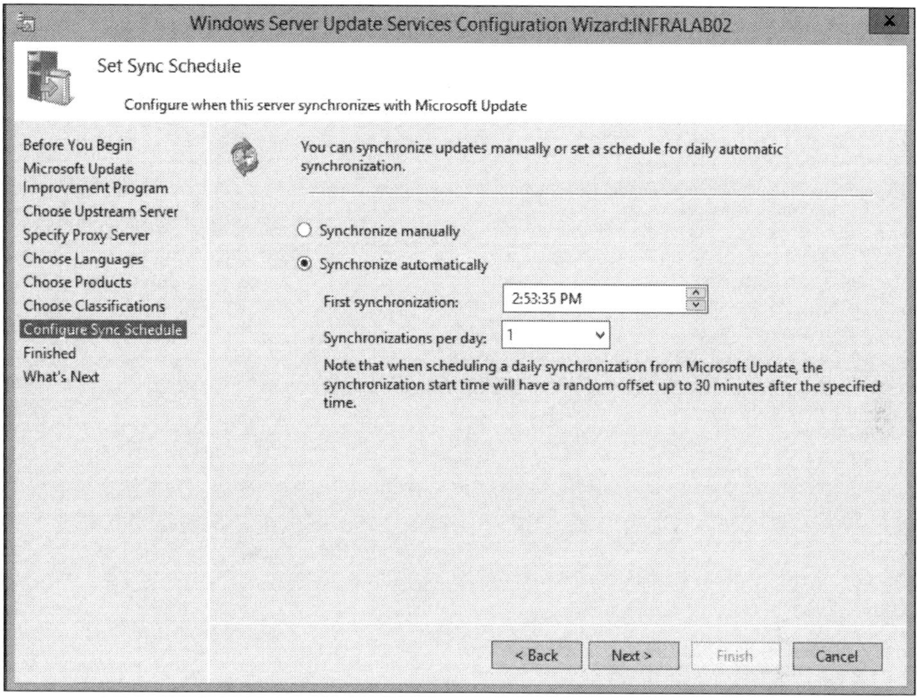

12. Click on **Next** on the **Finished** window.
13. On the **What's Next** window, click on **Finish** to complete the configuration.

At this stage, the configuration of Windows Server Update Services is complete. The next step is to configure the deployment option using Group Policy Objects. There are a few WSUS-related optional configuration components that are available, based on your requirements. These details are included in the following sections.

Configuring and deploying automatic updates

As mentioned earlier, the deployment of these updates is handled by GPOs. By default, the following WSUS GPO settings are included in Active Directory.

Setting	State	Comment
Do not display 'Install Updates and Shut Down' option in Shut Down Windows dialog box	Not configured	No
Do not adjust default option to 'Install Updates and Shut Down' in Shut Down Windows dialog box	Not configured	No
Enabling Windows Update Power Management to automatically wake up the system to install sch...	Not configured	No
Always automatically restart at the scheduled time	Not configured	No
Configure Automatic Updates	Enabled	No
Specify intranet Microsoft update service location	Enabled	No
Automatic Updates detection frequency	Not configured	No
Do not connect to any Windows Update Internet locations	Not configured	No
Allow non-administrators to receive update notifications	Not configured	No
Turn on Software Notifications	Not configured	No
Allow Automatic Updates immediate installation	Not configured	No
Turn on recommended updates via Automatic Updates	Not configured	No
No auto-restart with logged on users for scheduled automatic updates installations	Not configured	No
Re-prompt for restart with scheduled installations	Not configured	No
Delay Restart for scheduled installations	Not configured	No
Reschedule Automatic Updates scheduled installations	Not configured	No
Enable client-side targeting	Enabled	No
Allow signed updates from an intranet Microsoft update service location	Not configured	No

For this scenario, you will be configuring the following two required GPO settings in this section:

- Configure Automatic Updates
- Specify intranet Microsoft update service location

The following step-by-step instructions can be used to complete this configuration:

1. Open **Group Policy Management** console.
2. If you are editing an existing GPO, you can skip to step 3. If you are creating a new GPO, right-click on the **Domain Name** and select the **Create a GPO in this domain, and Link it here** option. Based on your requirement and configuration, you can select the GPO on the OU level.

3. Enter the name for the new GPO in the **New GPO** window. Click on **OK**.

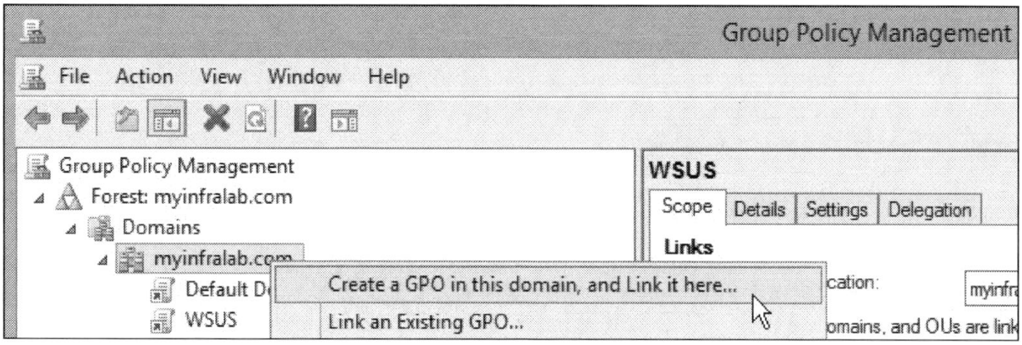

Creating a new GPO

4. Right-click on the **GPO Name** and select **Edit**. This will open the **Group Policy Management Editor** console.

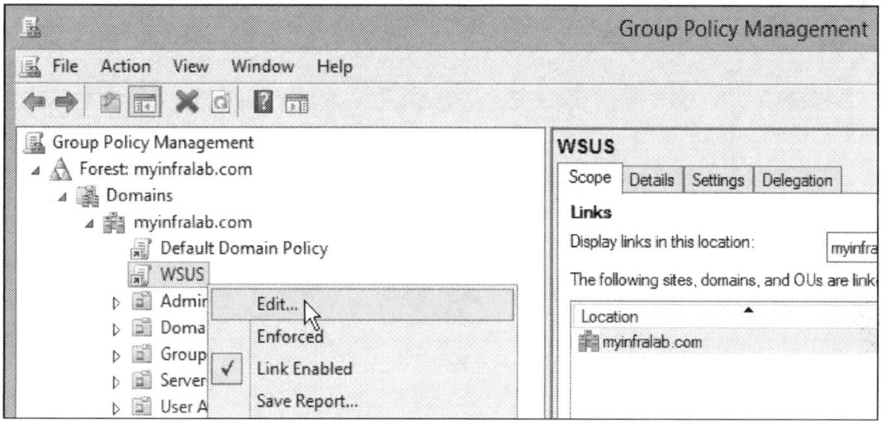

5. Navigate to **Computer Configuration** | **Policies** | **Administrative Templates** | **Windows Components** | **Windows Update**.
6. Select the **Windows Update** node. From the right pane, double-click on the **Configure Automatic Updates** settings.

7. From the **Configure Automatic Updates** window:
   - Select **Automatic Updates** as **Enabled**.
   - Configure **Automatic updating** as **3 - Auto download and notify for install**. You will have four options as shown in the following screenshot. Select the appropriate option based on your requirements.

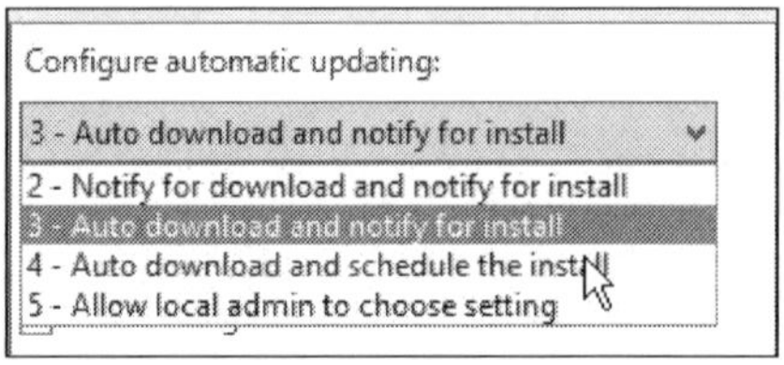

Configure automatic updating:
3 - Auto download and notify for install
2 - Notify for download and notify for install
3 - Auto download and notify for install
4 - Auto download and schedule the install
5 - Allow local admin to choose setting

   - Modify the **Schedule** as appropriate.

8. Click on **Apply** and **OK** to save and complete the automatic update configuration.

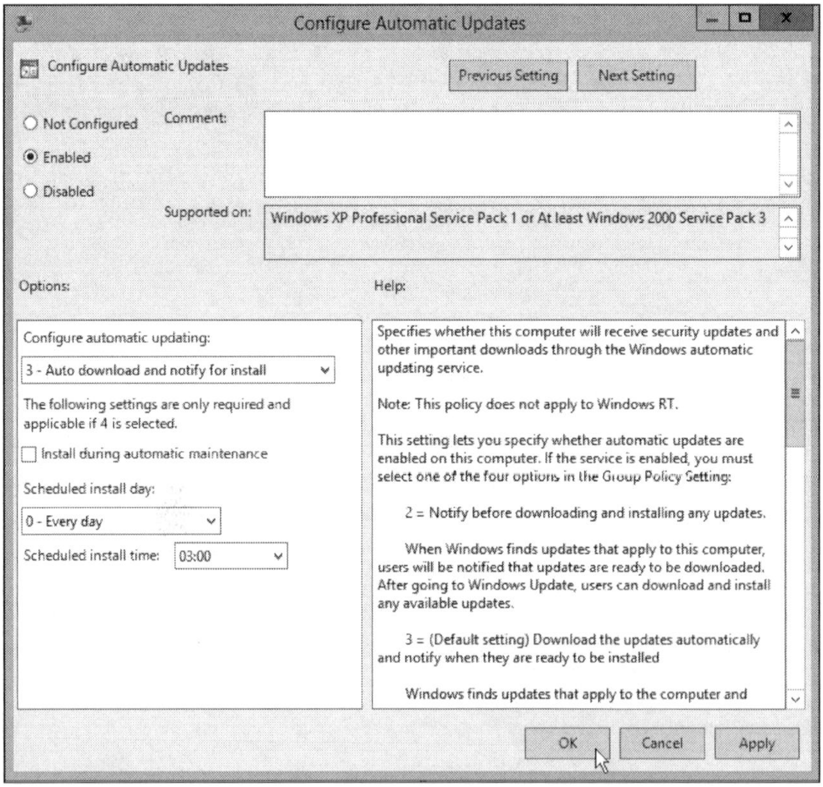

Configure Automatic Updates
Configure Automatic Updates
Previous Setting
Next Setting
Not Configured
Enabled
Disabled
Comment:
Supported on:
Windows XP Professional Service Pack 1 or At least Windows 2000 Service Pack 3
Options:
Help:
Configure automatic updating:
3 - Auto download and notify for install
The following settings are only required and applicable if 4 is selected.
Install during automatic maintenance
Scheduled install day:
0 - Every day
Scheduled install time:
03:00
Specifies whether this computer will receive security updates and other important downloads through the Windows automatic updating service.
Note: This policy does not apply to Windows RT.
This setting lets you specify whether automatic updates are enabled on this computer. If the service is enabled, you must select one of the four options in the Group Policy Setting:
2 = Notify before downloading and installing any updates.
When Windows finds updates that apply to this computer, users will be notified that updates are ready to be downloaded. After going to Windows Update, users can download and install any available updates.
3 = (Default setting) Download the updates automatically and notify when they are ready to be installed
Windows finds updates that apply to the computer and
OK
Cancel
Apply

9. Double-click on the **Specify intranet Microsoft Update Service location** settings. Change the setting to **Enabled**.
    - In the **Set the intranet update service for detecting updates** box, enter the name of the WSUS server.
    - In the **Set the Intranet server** box, enter the name of the WSUS server.

> By default, WSUS server uses port 8530 for HTTP traffic and port 8531 for HTTPS traffic. If you are using HTTPS, you need to enter the correct port information here.

10. Click on **Apply** and **OK** to save and complete the WSUS server configuration.

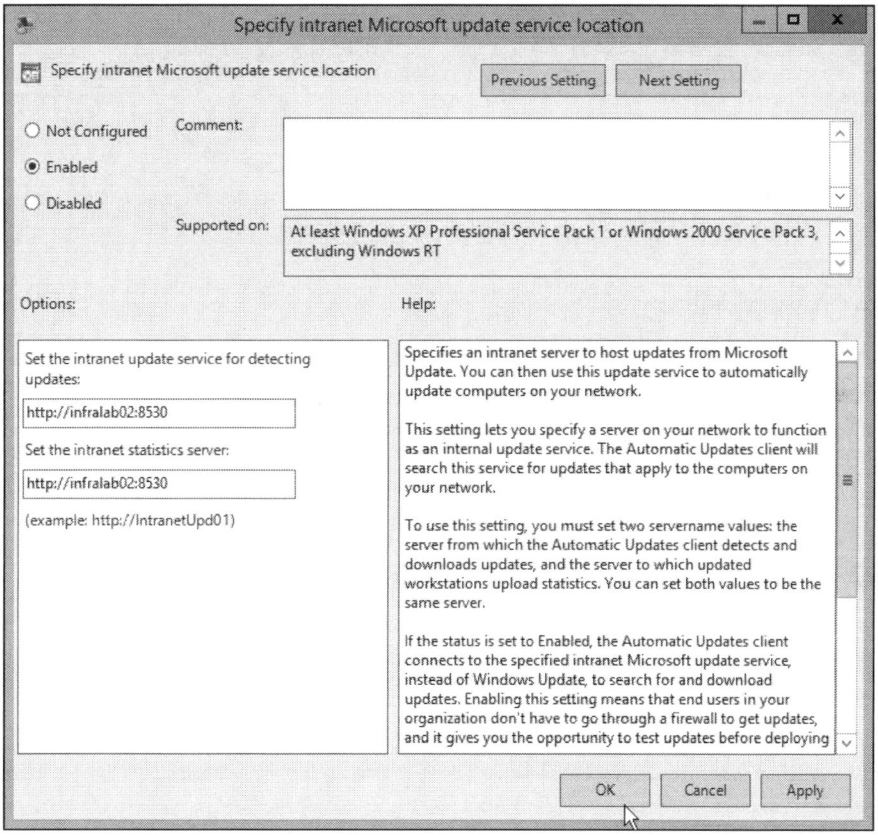
Specify intranet Microsoft update service location
Specify intranet Microsoft update service location
Previous Setting
Next Setting
Not Configured
Enabled
Disabled
Comment:
Supported on:
At least Windows XP Professional Service Pack 1 or Windows 2000 Service Pack 3, excluding Windows RT
Options:
Help:
Set the intranet update service for detecting updates:
http://infralab02:8530
Set the intranet statistics server:
http://infralab02:8530
(example: http://IntranetUpd01)
Specifies an intranet server to host updates from Microsoft Update. You can then use this update service to automatically update computers on your network.
This setting lets you specify a server on your network to function as an internal update service. The Automatic Updates client will search this service for updates that apply to the computers on your network.
To use this setting, you must set two servername values: the server from which the Automatic Updates client detects and downloads updates, and the server to which updated workstations upload statistics. You can set both values to be the same server.
If the status is set to Enabled, the Automatic Updates client connects to the specified intranet Microsoft update service, instead of Windows Update, to search for and download updates. Enabling this setting means that end users in your organization don't have to go through a firewall to get updates, and it gives you the opportunity to test updates before deploying
OK
Cancel
Apply

11. Close the **Group Policy Management Editor** window.

The GPO will be applied to all computer objects based on the location of the GPO. The GPO can be manually updated by using the `GPUPDATE /Force` command. The the `GPRESULT /R` command can be used to verify the applied GPOs on a computer, as shown in the following screenshot:

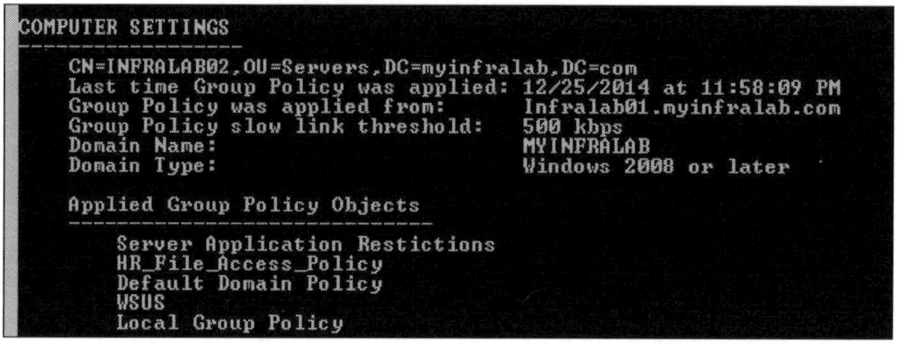
COMPUTER SETTINGS
CN=INFRALAB02,OU=Servers,DC=myinfralab,DC=com
Last time Group Policy was applied: 12/25/2014 at 11:58:09 PM
Group Policy was applied from: Infralab01.myinfralab.com
Group Policy slow link threshold: 500 kbps
Domain Name: MYINFRALAB
Domain Type: Windows 2008 or later
Applied Group Policy Objects
Server Application Restictions
HR_File_Access_Policy
Default Domain Policy
WSUS
Local Group Policy

> The command `wuauclt.exe /detectnow` can be executed from a WSUS client to initiate the WSUS detection.

Administering WSUS

The management and administration of Windows Server Update Service is performed from the **Update Service** management console, which will be installed as part of the WSUS Server Role installation. Explaining each of these components is beyond the scope of the book. However, the details of the administrative tasks required to complete WSUS configuration are included in the following sections.

The WSUS management console can be opened by entering the **Update Service** or **Windows Server Update Service** keyword in the Start screen of your Windows Server 2012. Most of the configuration tasks will be performed from the **Options** node of the WSUS console, as shown in the following screenshot:

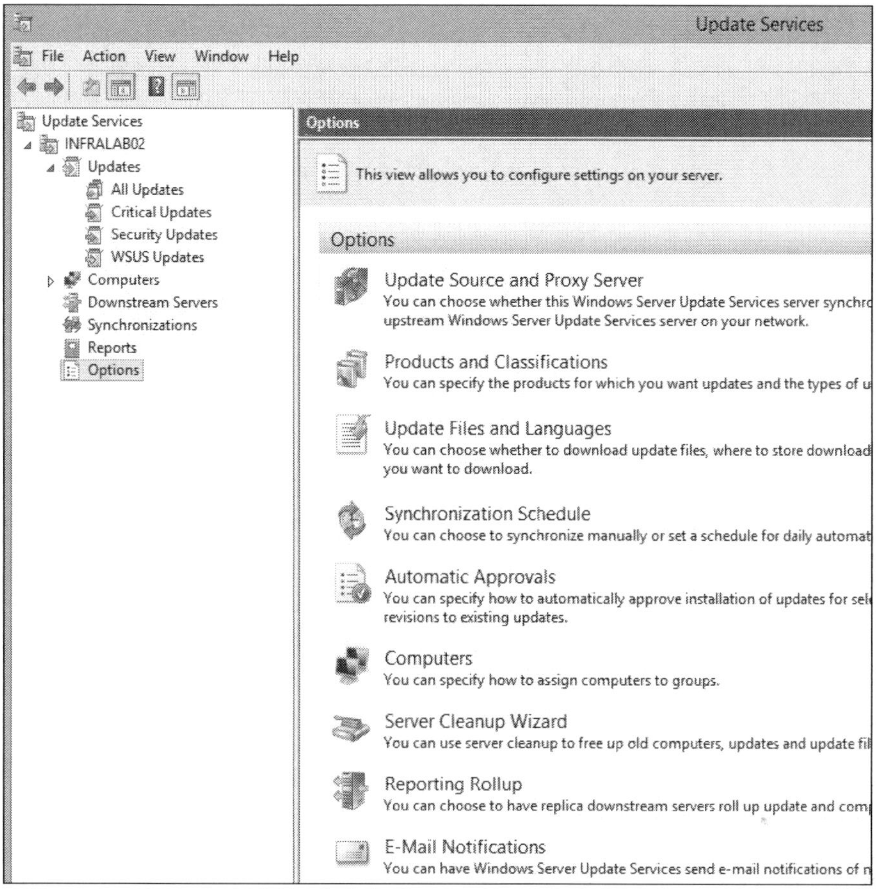
Update Services
File Action View Window Help
Update Services
INFRALAB02
Updates
All Updates
Critical Updates
Security Updates
WSUS Updates
Computers
Downstream Servers
Synchronizations
Reports
Options
Options
This view allows you to configure settings on your server.
Options
Update Source and Proxy Server
You can choose whether this Windows Server Update Services server synchr
upstream Windows Server Update Services server on your network.
Products and Classifications
You can specify the products for which you want updates and the types of u
Update Files and Languages
You can choose whether to download update files, where to store download
you want to download.
Synchronization Schedule
You can choose to synchronize manually or set a schedule for daily automat
Automatic Approvals
You can specify how to automatically approve installation of updates for sel
revisions to existing updates.
Computers
You can specify how to assign computers to groups.
Server Cleanup Wizard
You can use server cleanup to free up old computers, updates and update fi
Reporting Rollup
You can choose to have replica downstream servers roll up update and com
E-Mail Notifications
You can have Windows Server Update Services send e-mail notifications of n

WSUS console - Options

During the installation, you have configured **Product**, **Classification**, **Schedule**, and so on. These settings can be modified from the **Options** node. As shown in the preceding screenshot, you will see a corresponding configuration section on the right pane.

Creating groups

By default, all the WSUS computers will be added to the **All Computers** container inside the WSUS console. A custom computer can be created based on your requirements or needs. As the best practice, I always recommend to create a Test or Pilot container to evaluate the new patches or updates before deploying in production. The following section provides the details on creating a custom group in WSUS:

1. Open the **Windows Server Update Services** console.
2. Expand the **Server** and then **Computers** node. Right-click on the **All Computers** node and select **Add Computer Groups**.

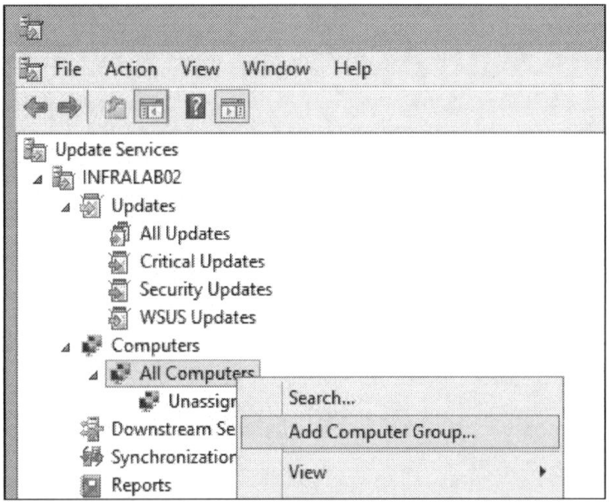

3. Enter the name of the group in the **Add Computer Group** window. Click on **Add**.

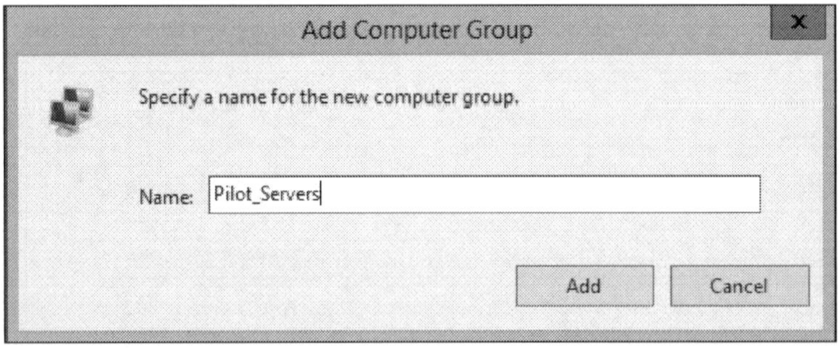

Based on your requirement, computers can be automatically moved to this computer container using Group Policy. The client-side targeting option in GPO will help to achieve this goal. The details are included in the following section. Again, this is an optional configuration based on your requirement:

1. Open the **Group Policy Management** console and edit the previously created WSUS GPO.
2. Navigate to **Computer Configuration | Policies | Administrative Templates | Windows Components | Windows Update**. Select **Windows Update**.
3. Double-click on the **Enable client-side targeting** settings. Change the settings to **Enabled**.
4. Enter the previously created group name in the **Target group name for this computer** window.
5. Click on **Apply** and then **OK** to save and complete the automatic update configuration.

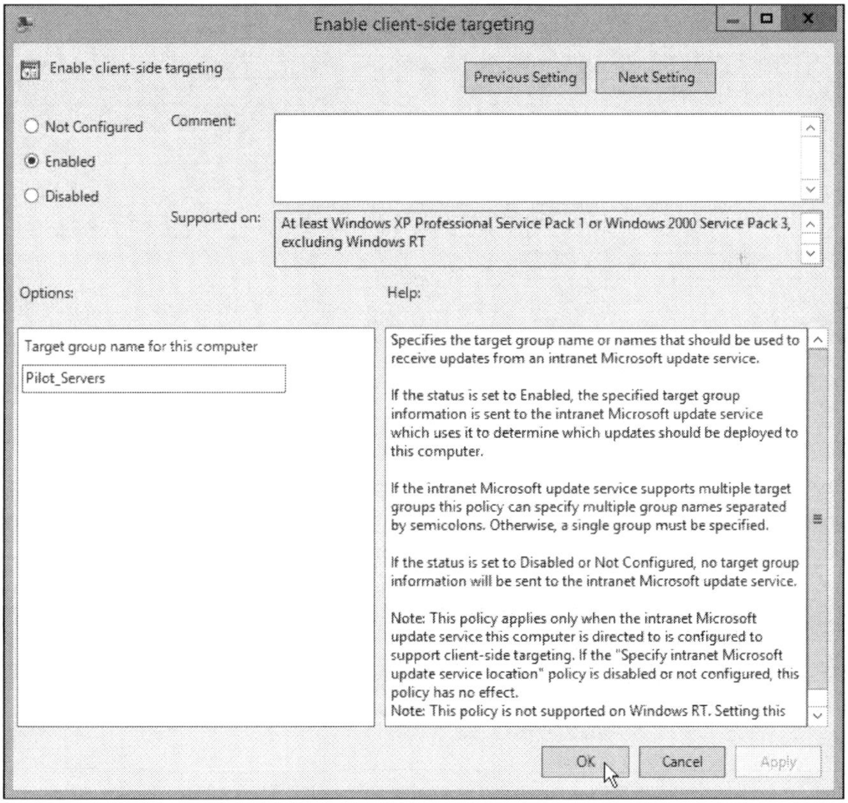
Enable client-side targeting
Enable client-side targeting
Previous Setting
Next Setting
Not Configured
Comment:
Enabled
Disabled
Supported on:
At least Windows XP Professional Service Pack 1 or Windows 2000 Service Pack 3, excluding Windows RT
Options:
Help:
Target group name for this computer
Pilot_Servers
Specifies the target group name or names that should be used to receive updates from an intranet Microsoft update service.
If the status is set to Enabled, the specified target group information is sent to the intranet Microsoft update service which uses it to determine which updates should be deployed to this computer.
If the intranet Microsoft update service supports multiple target groups this policy can specify multiple group names separated by semicolons. Otherwise, a single group must be specified.
If the status is set to Disabled or Not Configured, no target group information will be sent to the intranet Microsoft update service.
Note: This policy applies only when the intranet Microsoft update service this computer is directed to is configured to support client-side targeting. If the "Specify intranet Microsoft update service location" policy is disabled or not configured, this policy has no effect.
Note: This policy is not supported on Windows RT. Setting this
OK
Cancel
Apply

[This policy doesn't work if the **Specify intranet Microsoft update service location** policy is not configured.]

Managing updates

By default, all updates will be in the **Not Approved** state unless you have changed the approval settings to **Auto Approvals** from the **Options** node. The following section provides details of approving these updates for testing or deployment, and targeting a specific set of computers (for example `Pilot_Servers`):

1. Open the **Windows Server Update Service** console.
2. Expand the **WSUS** server and then the **Updates** node.
3. Select the **All Updates** node. You will see all the available updates in the middle pane based on the product section.

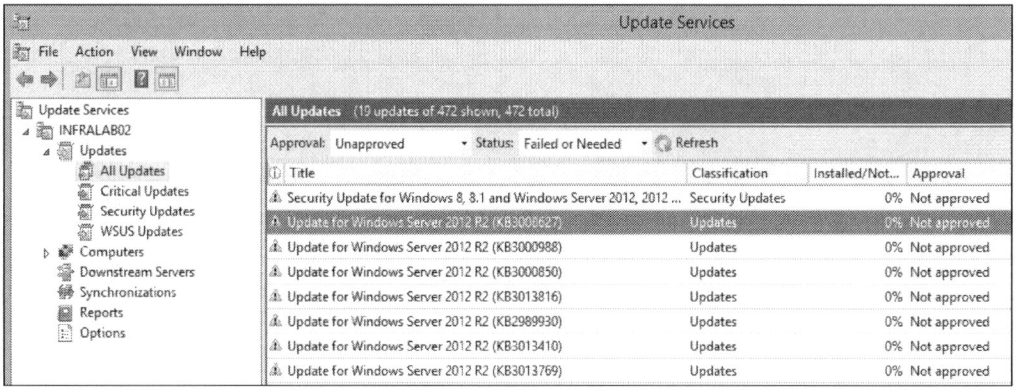

[You can modify the product and update selection by modifying the **Product and Classifications** settings in **Options** node.]

4. Unless you have **Automatic Approvals** (**Options** | **Automatic Approvals**) enabled, by default, all the downloaded updates will be in the **Not Approved** state.

5. Right-click on the updates and select **Approve**.

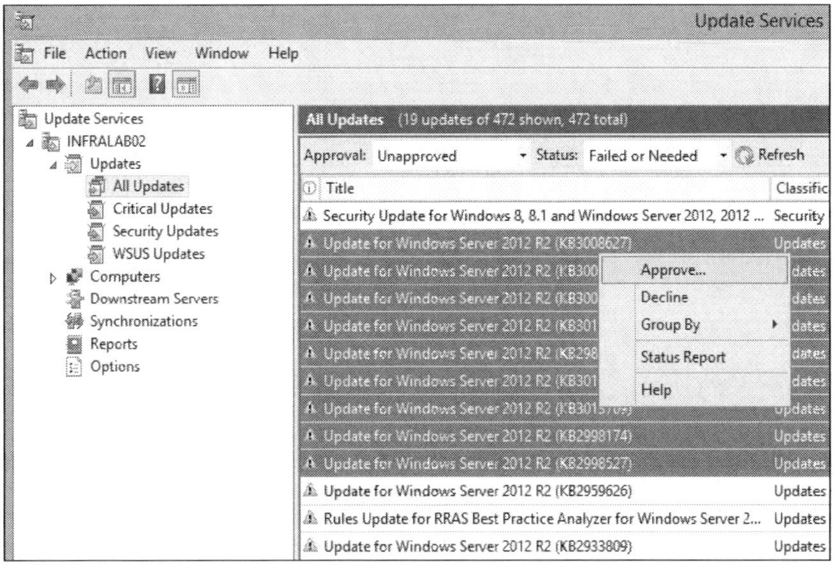

6. As a good practice, it is recommended to test and validate new updates on test machines before deployment to all production machines. You can use the previously created group in WSUS for this testing purpose. From the **Approve Update** window, select the **Pilot_Servers** group and then select the **Approved for Install** option. Click on **OK**.

7. You will see the approval progress and status in the **Approval Progress** window. Click on **Close**.

Managing the group membership

The computer group membership can be managed automatically or by using the WSUS console. The following instructions provide the details of managing and moving computers using the WSUS console:

1. Open the **Windows Server Update Service** console.
2. Expand the **WSUS server | Computers | All Computers** node.
3. Select the **All Computers** node. You will see all the computers in the middle pane. If you don't see any computers, you need to make sure the WSUS GPO is applying on to the computer and the **Status** is set to the correct state, as shown in the following screenshot:

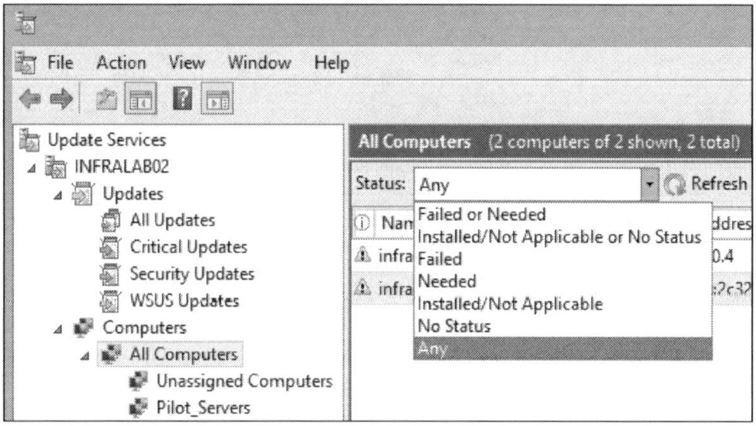

4. Right-click on the computer and select the **Change Membership** option.

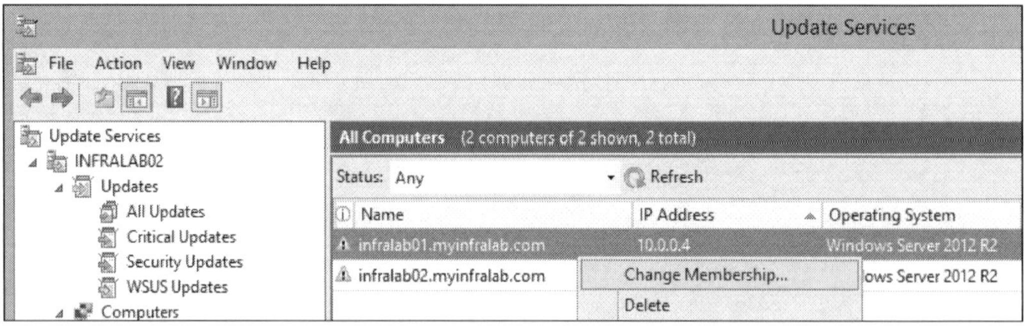

5. From the **Set Computer Group Membership** window, select the correct group. Click on **OK** to complete the operation.

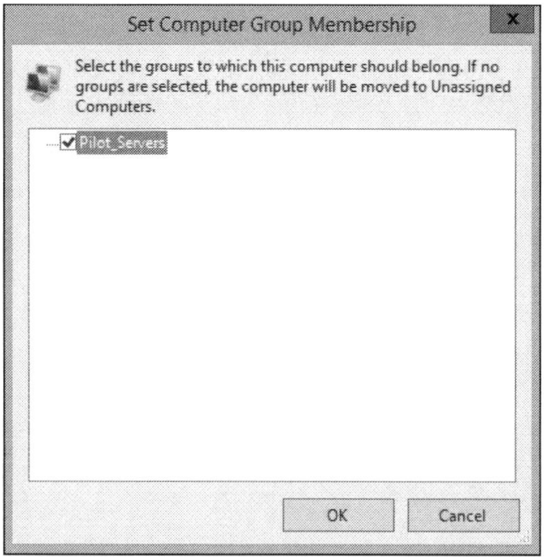
Set Computer Group Membership
Select the groups to which this computer should belong. If no groups are selected, the computer will be moved to Unassigned Computers.
Pilot_Servers
OK
Cancel

> The WSUS server and service can also be managed by using PowerShell cmdlets. The details of cmdlets can be found in `http://technet.microsoft.com/en-us/library/hh826166.aspx`.

The WSUS supports **Cluster Aware Updates** (**CAU**). The CAU is an automated mechanism that can be used to update cluster server nodes with minimal downtime. More details of this feature can be found at `https://technet.microsoft.com/en-us/library/hh831694.aspx`.

Summary

The Windows Server Update Service is a powerful tool for any organization for maintaining the updates and security patches. This is a critical path to ensure the protected state of the Microsoft infrastructure. I hope the details and instructions included in this chapter provide value to your organization when considering an automated solution for patch management, as well as maintaining a constant state of your Microsoft infrastructure from a security standpoint. I believe that at this point, you have established a steady state by applying the technologies and solutions mentioned in the previous chapters of this book. The next chapter will provide a solution to monitor the changes in Microsoft infrastructure that may lead to a security threat in your organization.

8
Auditing and Monitoring

I know it has been quite a journey and now we have reached the last chapter of this book. At this point, you have configured your servers and server infrastructure with best practices and industry-standard recommendations, which we explained in the previous chapters of this book. The current state of the server should be secure at this point. But how do you ensure that the state of the server infrastructure will be secure in the future? From an administrative perspective, the best way to make sure that your infrastructure is in compliance with the security policy is by proactively monitoring and auditing the configuration as well as the state of the servers. These activities can be automated or an administrative-driven process can be used. The goal of this chapter is to provide you with a few options for your server infrastructure auditing and monitoring needs.

This chapter has two sections—auditing and monitoring. The *Auditing* section provides the details of enabling and monitoring security events and alerts using **Group Policy Objects** (**GPOs**) from a centralized location. The *Monitoring* section provides the details of configuring a real-time alert using these alerts. This section also provides some details about monitoring solutions or products that can be used in your organization based on your requirements.

Auditing

In Windows Server, some of the auditing capabilities are enabled by default, and some are available for you to configure, based on your requirements. These options can be configured using GPOs. In this section, you will see how these auditing options can be configured and how you can forward all these alerts into a centralized location.

Default auditing policies

There are two sets of policies available in Windows Server 2012 to support auditing capabilities—Basic Auditing Policy and Advanced Auditing Policy. The Basic Auditing Policy contains nine basic auditing tasks. These polices are located in the **Computer Configuration | Policies | Windows Settings | Security Settings | Local Policies | Audit Policies** section in GPO. The Advanced Auditing Policy contains 10 different categories and contains 58 granular settings for each category. These policies are located at **Computer Configuration | Policies | Windows Settings | Security Settings | Advanced Audit Policy Configuration | Audit Policies**, as shown in the following screenshot:

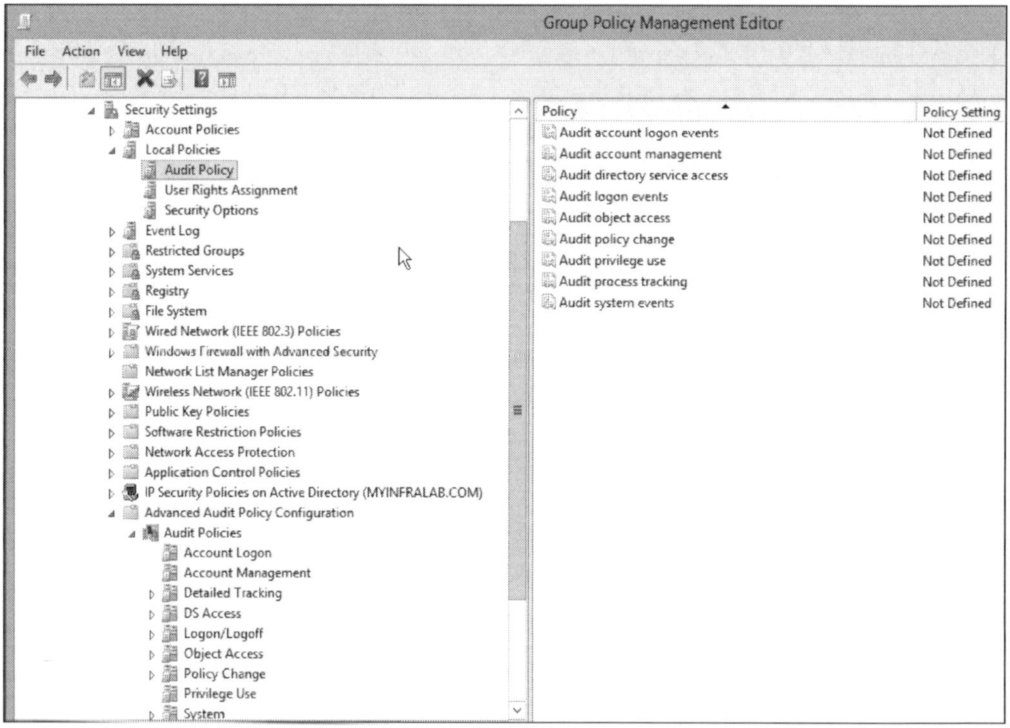

By using this policy features, you can control the auditing capabilities using **Global Object Access Auditing, System Access Control List** (**SACL**), and **Schema**. You will see the details of these configurations in the following sections.

Enabling Global Object Access Auditing – filesystem

In this section, you will be configuring filesystem-based auditing policy using the GPO. These GPO settings are located in the advanced auditing policy section in the **Computer Configuration** | **Policies** | **Windows Settings** | **Security Settings** | **Advanced Audit Policy Configuration** | **Audit Policies** | **Global Object Access Auditing** node.

In *Chapter 6, Access Control*, you have created an `HR_File_Access` dynamic policy. You will be using the same expression-based scenario to configure this auditing policy. Policies of this type are called expression-based Audit Policies in Windows Server 2012. In this section, you will be configuring the following three advanced auditing policies:

- **Object Access—Audit File System**: This policy generates an event alert each time a resource accesses the file system.
- **Object Access—Audit Handle Manipulation**: This policy generates an event alert when there is a change in the object handle.
- **Global Object Access Auditing—filesystem**: This policy generates an event alert based on your expression-based policy configuration.

The following step-by-step instructions will provide an option to successfully configure these policies:

1. Log on to a Domain Controller or member server. Open the **Group Policy Management** console.
2. Right-click on the existing policy and select the **Edit** option.
3. Navigate to the **Computer Configuration** | **Policies** | **Windows Settings** | **Security Settings** | **Advanced Audit Policy Configuration** | **Audit Policies** | **Global Object Access Auditing** node and select the **Object Access** node. Double-click on the **Audit File System** task.

4. From the **Audit File System Properties** window, select the following checkboxes:
    - **Configure the following audit events**
    - **Success**
    - **Failure** options, as shown in the following screenshot:

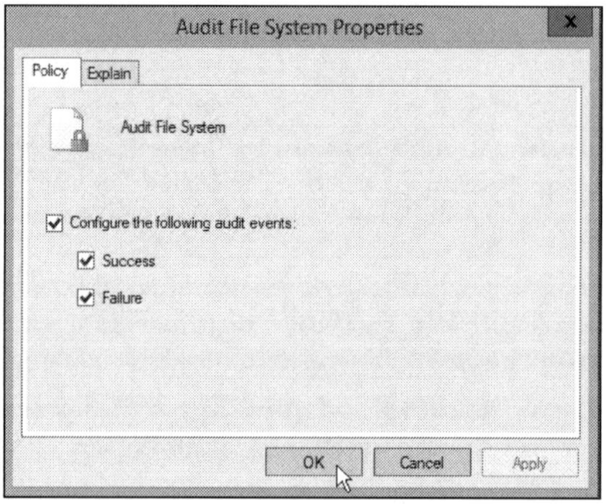

5. Click on **Apply** and **OK** to complete the configuration.
6. Double-click on the **Audit Handle Manipulation** configuration task and select:
    - **Configure the following audit events**
    - **Success**
    - **Failure** options, as shown in the following screenshot:

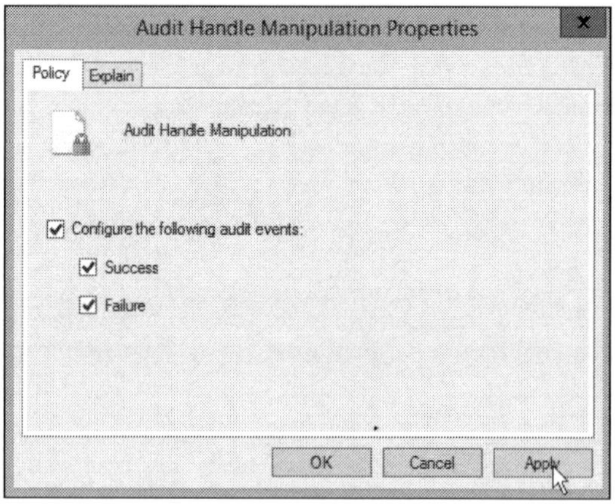

7. Click on **Apply** and **OK** to complete the configuration.
8. From the left pane, select the **Global Object Access Auditing** policy node.
9. From the right pane, double-click on the **File system auditing** task and select the **Define this policy setting** checkbox. Click on the **Configure** button.

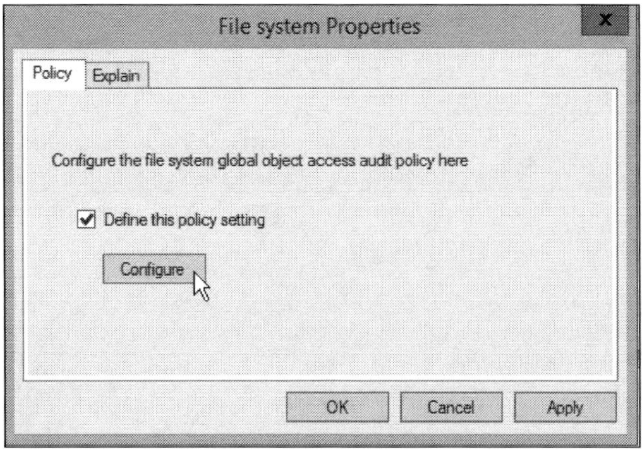

10. In the **Advanced Security Settings for Global File SACL** window, select the **Add** button.
11. In the **Auditing Entry for Global File SACL** window's **Select a Principal** option, select **Authenticated Users** as the principal.

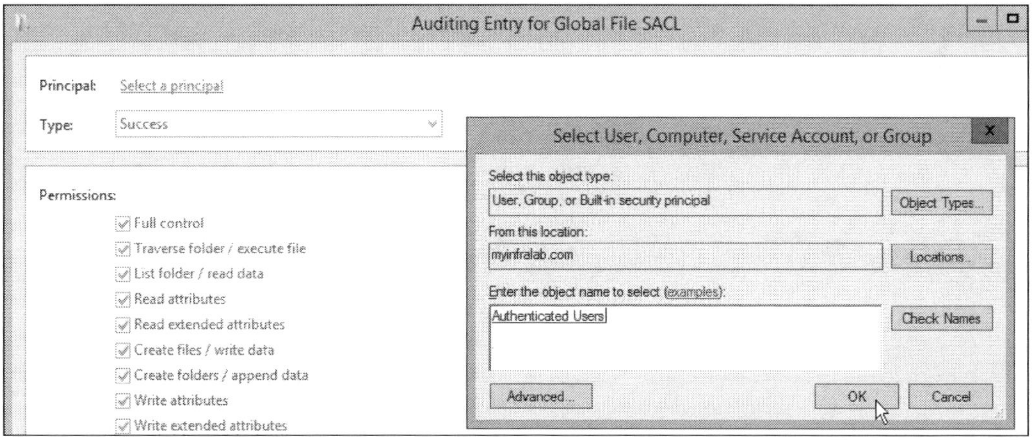

12. In the **Type** drop-down box, select the appropriate event type (**Fail**, **Success**, or **All**) for the audit.

13. In the **Permissions** section, select the appropriate permission for auditing. In the **Condition** section, select the **Add a Condition** option. In this section, you will select an expression-based policy based on your requirement. In *Chapter 6, Access Control*, you have created a dynamic file access policy for HR employees. You will be using the same expression here as well. You can create additional expression-based policies by following the instructions listed in *Chapter 6, Access Control*. In this scenario, you will be selecting the **Resource**, **Department_HR**, **Equals**, **Value**, and **HR** conditions, as shown in the following screenshot:

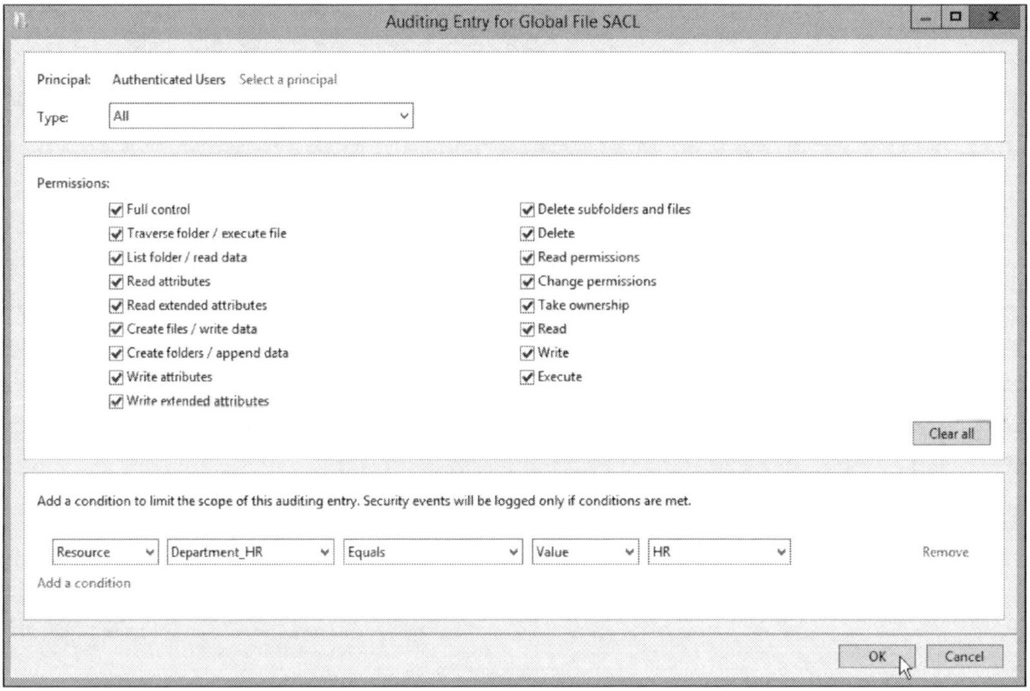

14. Click on **OK** thrice to complete this auditing policy configuration.

> The configuration details of Dynamic Access Control are explained in *Chapter 6, Access Control*. The validation of steps are included in the *Verifying the access control configuration and permission* section.

Enabling Global Object Access Auditing – directory services

This section provides the details of configuring Active Directory service-related monitoring and alerting using the Global Object Access Auditing policy. The Active Directory-related auditing policies are located in the **Computer Configuration | Policies | Windows Settings | Security Settings | Advanced Audit Policy Configuration | Audit Policies** node in the GPO. Perform the following steps:

1. Open the **Group Policy Management** console.
2. Right-click on the existing policy and select the **Edit** option.
3. Navigate to the **Computer Configuration | Policies | Windows Settings | Security Settings | Advanced Audit Policy Configuration | Audit Policies** node.
4. The following Active Directory-related auditing options categories are available in the auditing policies node:
    - **Account Login**
    - **Account Management**
    - **DS Access**
    - **Logon/Logoff**

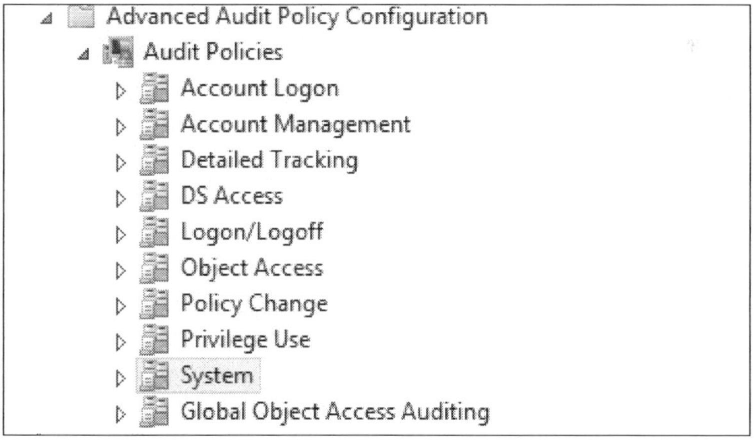

5. Based on your requirement, you can double-click on these to configure the auditing settings. Most of these settings will have **Success** and **Failure** auditing options; for example, if you want to enable the **Directory Service Change** audit, select the **DS Access** node and double-click on the **Audit Directory Service Changes** setting. Select the **Auditing event** option based on your requirements.
6. Click on **Apply** and **OK** to complete the configuration.

All these auditing details and results will be stored in the event log of the local Domain Controller. Monitoring these events from each Domain Controller can be a tedious task. In an enterprise, you need to have a centralized solution for monitoring these events. The following section provides the details of monitoring alerts from a centralized console using the event forwarding method.

Event forwarding

In the previous section, you have enabled alerts based on different categories. These alerts will be in the respective event log on a local server. In an enterprise, verifying the event log on each server can be a time-consuming task. In this section, your goal is to forward all these alerts into a centralized server for better monitoring and alerting.

By default, the event forwarding and centralized monitoring functionalities are available in Windows Server 2012. In order to achieve this, you need to create a target computer (collector), which will be your consolidated monitoring server, and a source computer (collected). The source computers will forward the configured events to the target (collector) computer. An administrator can monitor all events from the collector computer. You can also enable real-time alerting based on these events. The monitoring section in this chapter provides the details of enabling real-time alert.

It is not required to have additional tools or a console to manage these forwarded events. These events can be viewed in the **Event Viewer** itself. You will see a **Forwarded Event** node in the **Windows Log** section. Each forwarded event will have a source computer name under the **Computer** column, as shown in the following screenshot:

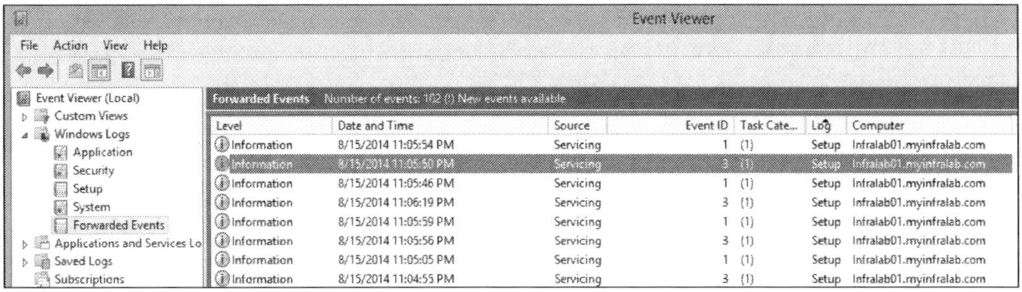

The event forwarding settings can be configured in Event Viewer as well. These configurations can be found in the **Subscription** node in Event Viewer. If you don't have any subscriptions configured, or Windows Event Collector Service is not running, you may receive the error message displayed in the following screenshot. You will be configuring all the required components for enabling event forwarding in the following sections. If you receive this message, make sure you follow the instructions listed in the configuration section.

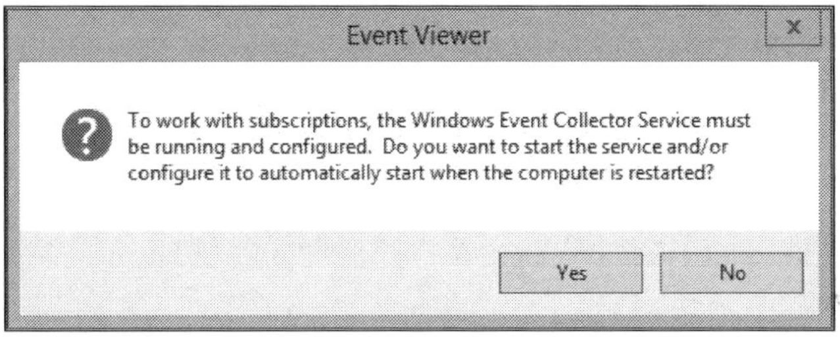

WinRM service must be running and WinRM must be set up for remote management.

Configuring the source computer

The source computer will have to forward all the events to the Collector (target) computer. This can be verified by either using the `winrm quickconfig` command, or using Group Policy Objects. These settings are available in the **Computer Configuration** | **Policies** | **Windows Settings** | **Administrative Templates** | **Windows Components** | **Event Forwarding** node section of the **GPO**. You can use the following instructions to complete the required GPO configuration for enabling event forwarding from the source computers:

1. Open the **Group Policy Management** console.
2. Right-click on the GPO and select the **Edit** option. If you are planning to create a new GPO, select the **Create a new GPO and link it here** option and then edit the GPO configurations.

3. Navigate to the **Computer Configuration** | **Policies** | **Windows Settings** | **Administrative Templates** | **Windows Components** | **Event Forwarding** node.
4. Double-click on the **Configure target Subscription Manager** setting from the right pane.
5. Select the **Enabled** checkbox in the configuration section. From the **Subscription Manager** section, select the **Show** option.

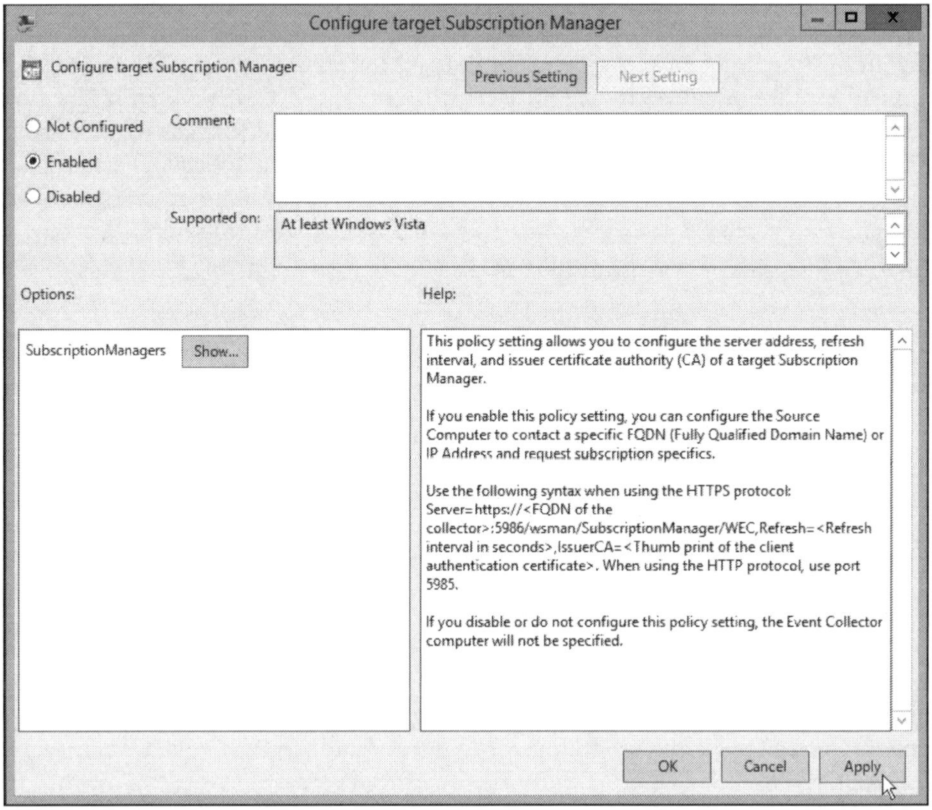
Configure target Subscription Manager
Configure target Subscription Manager
Previous Setting
Next Setting
Not Configured
Comment:
Enabled
Disabled
Supported on:
At least Windows Vista
Options:
Help:
SubscriptionManagers
Show...
This policy setting allows you to configure the server address, refresh interval, and issuer certificate authority (CA) of a target Subscription Manager.
If you enable this policy setting, you can configure the Source Computer to contact a specific FQDN (Fully Qualified Domain Name) or IP Address and request subscription specifics.
Use the following syntax when using the HTTPS protocol: Server=https://<FQDN of the collector>:5986/wsman/SubscriptionManager/WEC,Refresh=<Refresh interval in seconds>,IssuerCA=<Thumb print of the client authentication certificate>. When using the HTTP protocol, use port 5985.
If you disable or do not configure this policy setting, the Event Collector computer will not be specified.
OK
Cancel
Apply

6. In the **Show Contents** window, the **Fully Qualified Domain Name** (FQDN) of the target (collector) computer is available in the **Value** section, as shown in the following screenshot:

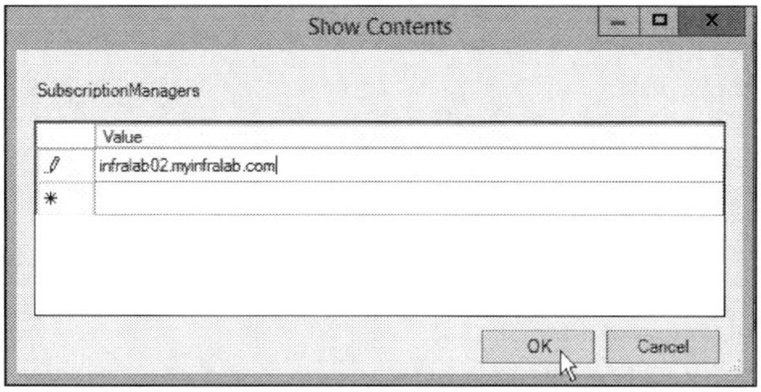

Show Contents
SubscriptionManagers
Value
infralab02.myinfralab.com
OK
Cancel

7. Navigate to the **Computer Configuration** | **Policies** | **Windows Settings** | **Administrative Templates** | **Windows Components** | **Windows Remote Management (WinRM)** | **WinRM Service** node.
8. Select the **WinRM Service** node. From the right pane, double-click on the **Allow remote server management through WinRM** settings.
9. From the configuration window, select the **Enabled** checkbox. In the **Options** section, enter `*` as **IPv4 and IPv6** filter. Click on **Apply** and **OK** to complete the configuration.

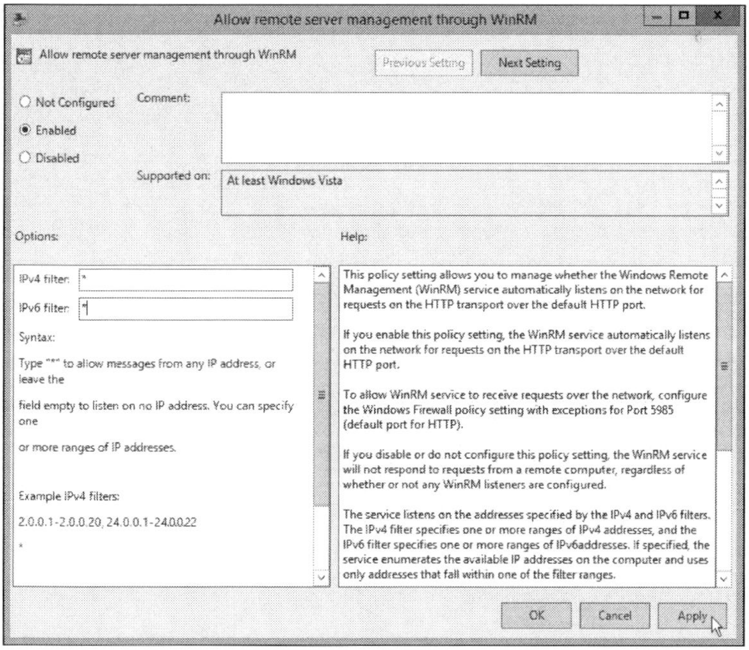

Allow remote server management through WinRM
Allow remote server management through WinRM
Previous Setting
Next Setting
Not Configured
Comment:
Enabled
Disabled
Supported on:
At least Windows Vista
Options:
Help:
IPv4 filter:
IPv6 filter:
Syntax:
Type "*" to allow messages from any IP address, or leave the
field empty to listen on no IP address. You can specify one
or more ranges of IP addresses.
Example IPv4 filters:
2.0.0.1-2.0.0.20, 24.0.0.1-24.0.0.22
*
This policy setting allows you to manage whether the Windows Remote Management (WinRM) service automatically listens on the network for requests on the HTTP transport over the default HTTP port.
If you enable this policy setting, the WinRM service automatically listens on the network for requests on the HTTP transport over the default HTTP port.
To allow WinRM service to receive requests over the network, configure the Windows Firewall policy setting with exceptions for Port 5985 (default port for HTTP).
If you disable or do not configure this policy setting, the WinRM service will not respond to requests from a remote computer, regardless of whether or not any WinRM listeners are configured.
The service listens on the addresses specified by the IPv4 and IPv6 filters. The IPv4 filter specifies one or more ranges of IPv4 addresses, and the IPv6 filter specifies one or more ranges of IPv6addresses. If specified, the service enumerates the available IP addresses on the computer and uses only addresses that fall within one of the filter ranges.
OK
Cancel
Apply

Since this is a GPO-based configuration, you will either have to wait for the GPO to be updated, or will have to run the `GPUPDATE /FORCE` command to update the GPO on the local computer.

Configuring the target (collector) computer

The next step in this process is to configure the subscription in the collector computer. The following section provides the details of configuring the subscription:

1. Open the **Event Viewer**.
2. Right-click on the **Subscription** node and select the **Create Subscriptions** option.

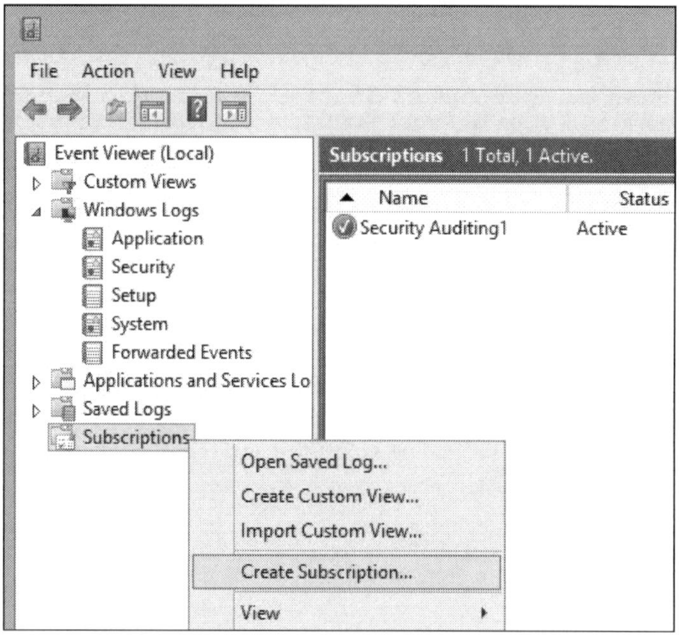

3. In the **Subscription Properties** window, enter an appropriate name for this subscription in the **Subscription Name** box. By default, these events will be in the **Forwarded Event** log. You can select a different location from the **Destination log** box. From the **Subscription Type** section, select the **Source Computer Initiated** option, and then click on the **Select Computer Groups** option.

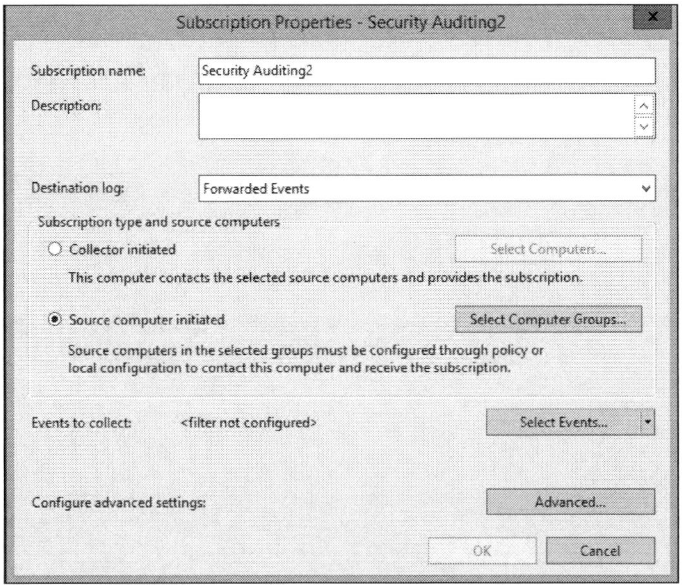

[If you are not using GPO, you can select the collector initial option to collect the events from the source computers.]

4. From the **Computer Group** window, select the appropriate group from the **Add Domain Computers** section. In this scenario, you will be selecting **Domain Computers**. Click on **OK**.

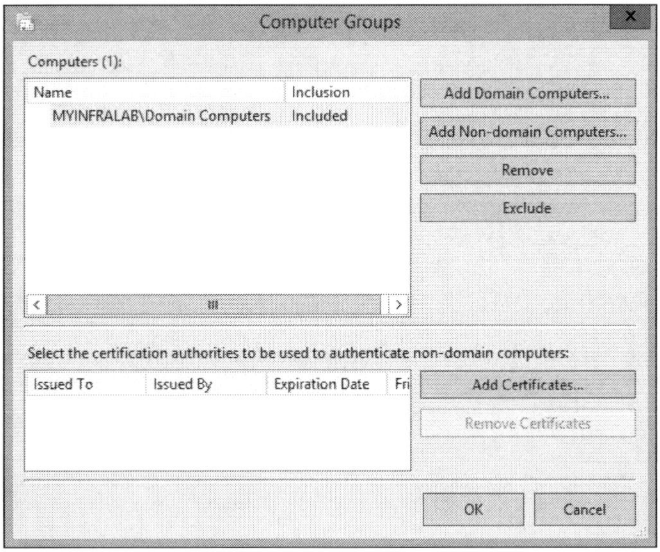

5. From the **Subscription Properties** window, click on the **Select Events** button from the **Events to collect** section to configure the event filters. Select the appropriate event filter based on your requirements. Click on **OK** twice to complete the configuration.

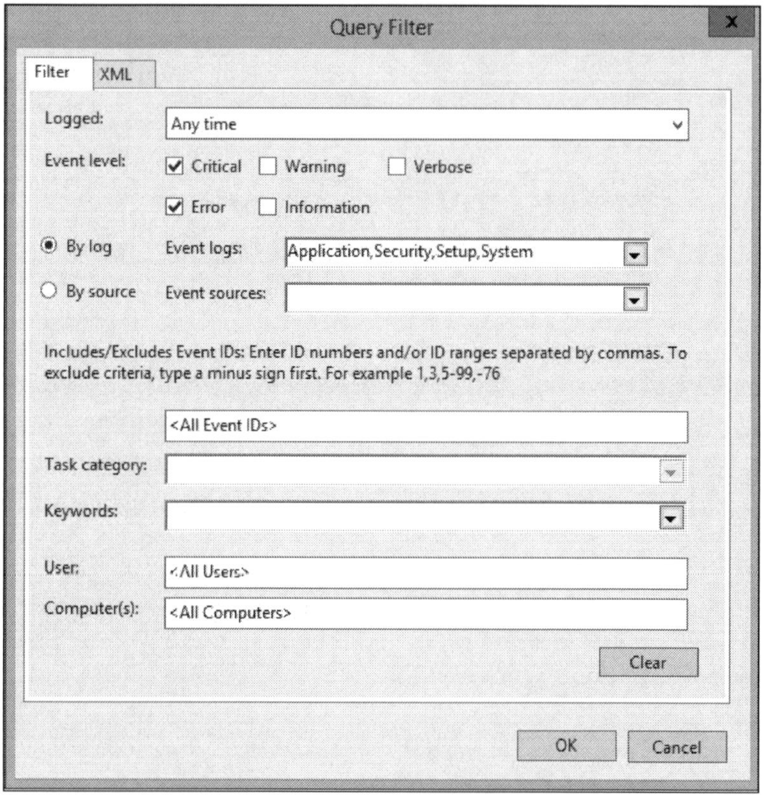

At this stage, you have completed the source and target-side configurations. All the forwarded events will be in the **Forwarded Events** node on the collector computer. Keep in mind that you may need to configure additional permissions for reading security-related events from the source computers. You can add appropriate user accounts to the **Event Log Readers** built-in group in the Active Directory to achieve this.

Troubleshooting event forwarding

Some of the basic troubleshooting steps can be performed from the Event Viewer itself.

Select the **Subscriptions** node. From the middle pane, right-click on **Subscription Name** and select the **Runtime Status** option.

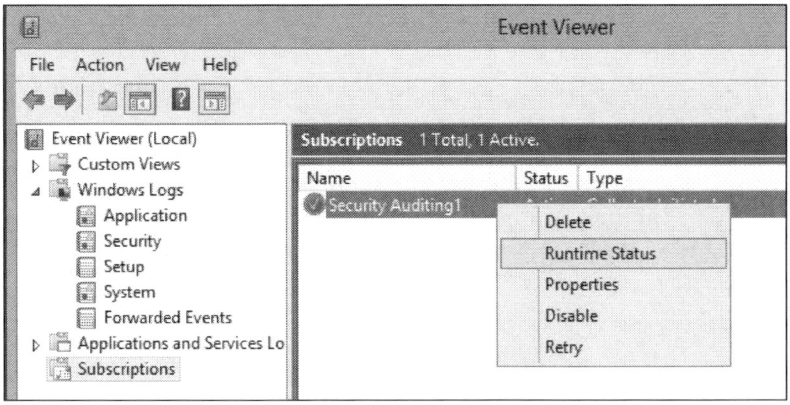

The following is an example of an error message. As you can see in the following screenshot, you will get the details of the error message at the bottom of screen. In this particular message, the error message was **Access is denied**. You can review the permissions of the service account to resolve this issue.

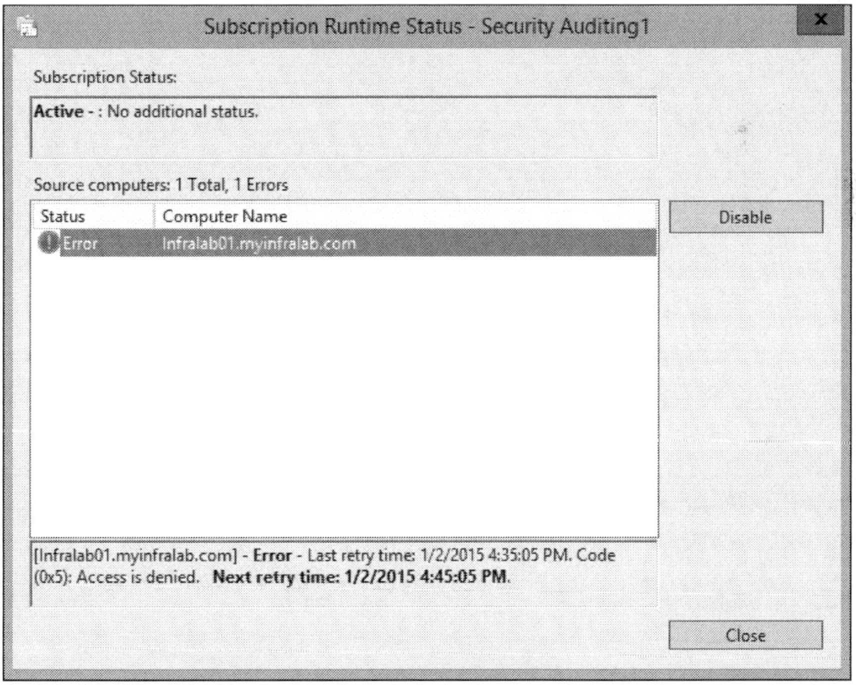

Access denied error

Monitoring

As mentioned earlier, proactive monitoring is the key to identifying and mitigating any security risk in an organization. In a large enterprise, a tool-based monitoring and alerting solution may become necessary, based on the requirements. Microsoft **System Centre Operations Manager** (**SCOM**) is an infrastructure monitoring tool and a solution from Microsoft, which provides cost-effective and reliable solutions. The details of SCOM are beyond the scope of this book. However, I would encourage you to evaluate the product in your environment to ensure that it satisfies your business and technical requirements. The details of this product can be found in `http://technet.microsoft.com/library/hh205987.aspx`.

In the previous section, you have created an event forwarding solution for all your critical events. These events are currently located in the **Forwarded Events** node of the Windows Log. Perform the following steps:

1. Open the Event Viewer.
2. Expand **Windows Logs** and select **Forwarded Events**.
3. From the middle pane, right-click on the event and select the **Attach Task to This Events** option.

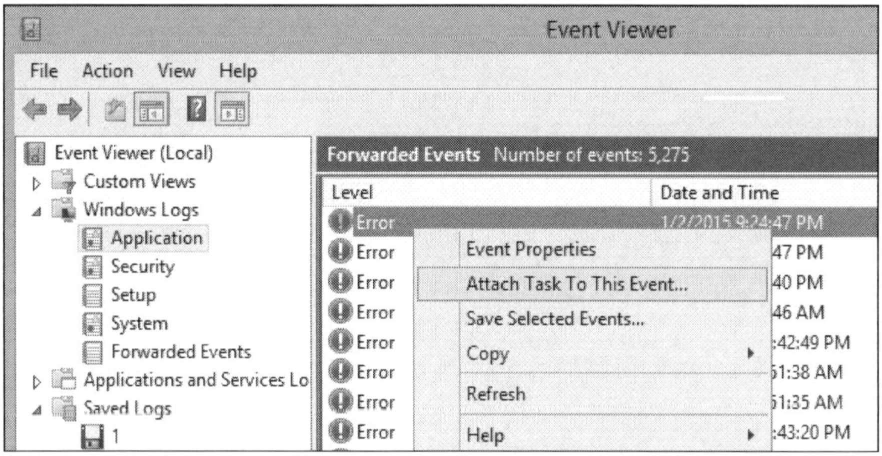

4. On the **Create Basic Task Wizard** window, enter the name for the task and click on **Next**.
5. Click on **Next** on the **When an Event is Logged** window with the default values.

6. On the **Action** window, you have three options, as shown in the following screenshot. Since **Send an e-mail** and **Display a message** are deprecated in Windows Server 2012 and later, you will be selecting the **Start a Program** option. Click on **Next**.

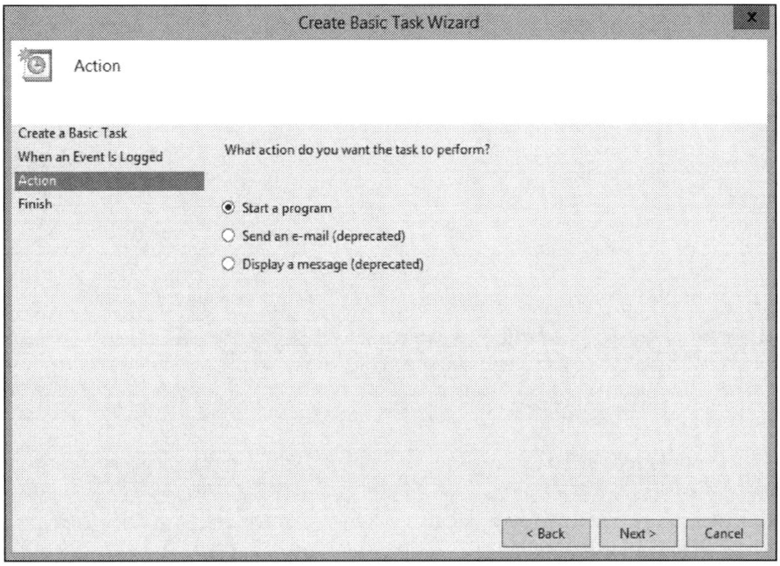

7. On the **Start a Program** window, enter the program or script name, based on your requirement. Click on **Next**.
8. Click on **Finish** to complete the configuration.
9. Click on **OK** on the **Event Viewer** pop-up window.

The administration and management of these tasks can be performed from the Task Scheduler:

1. Open the **Task Scheduler**.
2. Navigate to **Task Scheduler (Local)** | **Task Scheduler Library** | **Event Viewer Tasks**.
3. In the middle pane, you will see the newly created task.

You can modify the configuration by double-clicking on the task, or by going to the properties by right-clicking on them.

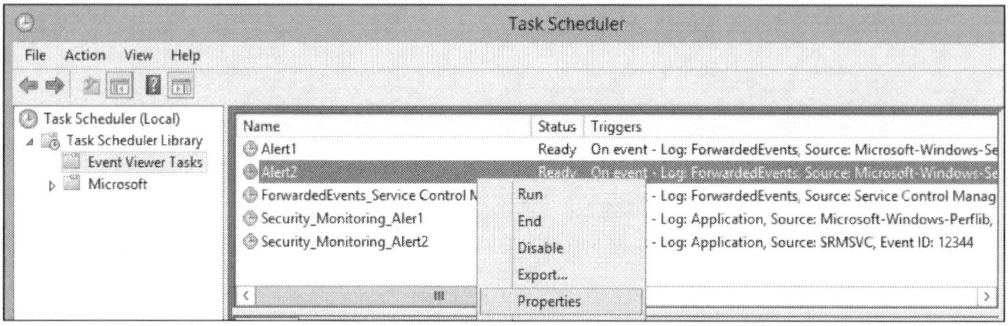

Microsoft Best Practice Analyzer

In the previous chapters, you learned a few security tools such as Microsoft Security Configuration Wizard, Microsoft Security Compliance Manager, Microsoft Attack Surface Analyzer, and so on. You may wonder why we didn't hear about the **Microsoft Best Practice Analyzer** (**BPA**) tool so far. If you execute the Microsoft Best Practice Analyzer in the beginning, you will see a lot of recommendations based on best practices. My approach was to walk you through all the available tools and configuration first, and then implement them before you run **BPA**. That way, all the best practices and industry-standard configurations will be in place, and BPA should report only a few minor recommendations. Since you have all the security configurations currently in place, it is time to run the **BPA** to validate your existing server security configurations. This task can be a part of your monitoring activity.

In Windows Server 2012 and later, BPA is a part of the operating system. Unlike other operating systems, you don't need to download or install any additional software. You can directly execute the **BPA** from the Server Manager. Perform the following steps:

1. Open the Server Manager.
2. Select **Server Role** from the left pane. Scroll in the middle pane until you reach the **BEST PRACTICES ANALYZER** section.
3. From the **Task** menu, select the **Start BPA Scan** option.

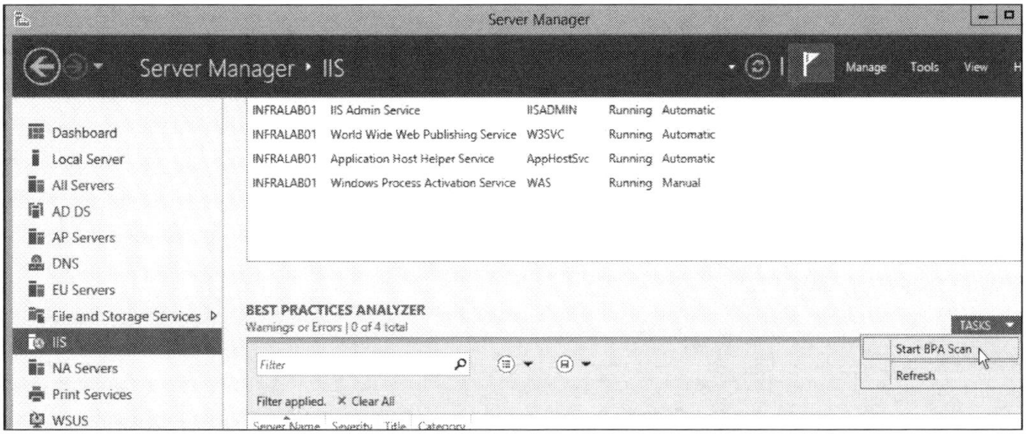

The Start BPA Scan option

4. On the **Select Server** window, select the appropriate servers. Click on **Start Scan** to begin the BPA scanning process.

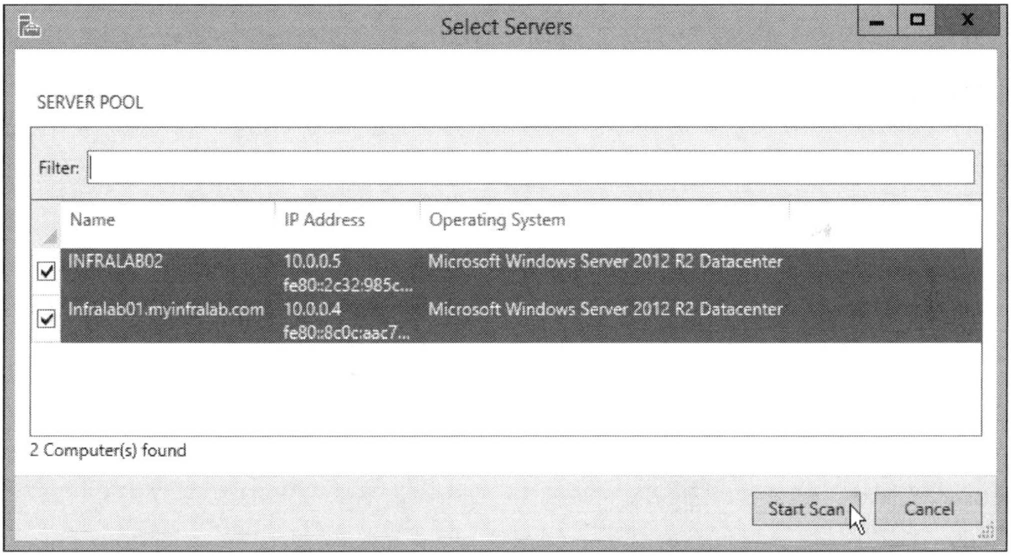

5. The result will be displayed in the **BEST PRACTICES ANALYZER** section.

You may feel that some of these recommendations or tasks may be redundant or have some overlap. This is another reason why I did not introduce this tool in the beginning of this book. As you can see in the following screenshot, BPA is reporting that DNS Scavenging should be enabled. If you remember, in *Chapter 5, Network Service Security*, we recommended enabling Scavenging for DNS zone and records. So if you follow the recommendations provided in this book, you shouldn't be seeing the DNS warning from BPA. However, it is a good validation approach from a different perspective to confirm your security configuration. This is why I consider BPA more like a validation and monitoring tool.

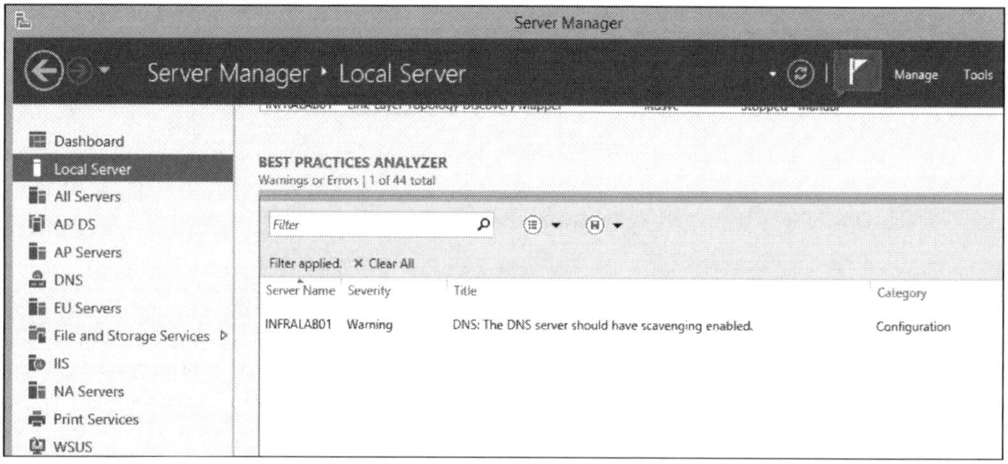

Monitoring the performance

High resource utilization, slow response, and slow performance can be indications of unusual activities on a server. The **Denial of Service** (**DoS**) or **Distributed DoS** (**DDoS**) attacks are known for consuming most the system resources. There are many ways you can identify unusual behavior from a server perspective. Monitoring performance counters on critical servers can provide some indication of high resource utilization. The monitoring of network traffic can alert you with irregular patterns of network activities.

> The details of Denial of Service can be found at `http://en.wikipedia.org/wiki/Denial-of-service_attack`.

From a server level, you can use Microsoft Performance Monitor and Microsoft Resource Monitor to monitor resource utilization and Microsoft Message Analyzer to capture and analyze the network packets. The Microsoft Performance Monitor and Microsoft Resource Monitor are built-in tools in Windows Server. The Microsoft Message Analyzer is a standalone application, and can be downloaded from `http://www.microsoft.com/en-us/download/details.aspx?id=44226`.

Summary

The goal of this chapter was to provide you with a few options and frameworks to monitor and audit your Microsoft server environment. The options provided here do not replace a monitoring or auditing solution. This can be used as a supplement to the existing options you may have in your environment. I believe I have provided you with a basic idea for proactively monitoring server infrastructure; it is now up to you to expand this basic idea to achieve the goal, based on your business and technical requirements.

As mentioned earlier in this book, security is a broad term and it has different interpretations, based on the point of view. In this book, I have provided a solid foundation for server security. I would encourage you to use this book and techniques mentioned in the book as a starting point, when considering security in your server infrastructure. I don't believe an administrator can create a security solution by just considering or learning technical details. He or she must consider polices, process, compliance, and other business aspects, along with technical guidance to effectively create a security solution. There are many places you can get a baseline and recommended polices for you server and infrastructure. I would recommend you to periodically evaluate the following sites for the updated information and guidelines:

- **Microsoft Security Research Center**: `http://research.microsoft.com/en-us/groups/security/`
- **Microsoft Security Advisories and Bulletins**: `https://technet.microsoft.com/library/security`
- **National Institute of Standards and Technology** (**NIST**): `http://www.nist.gov/`
- **Center for Internet Security** (**CIS**): `http://www.cisecurity.org/`
- **Security Technical Implementation Guides** (**STIGs**): `http://iase.disa.mil/stigs`
- **National Security Agency** (**NSA**) **Configuration Guides**: `https://www.nsa.gov/ia/mitigation_guidance/security_configuration_guides/index.shtml`

Index

A

B

C

N

O

P

R

S

T

U

W

[PACKT] PUBLISHING enterprise
professional expertise distilled

Thank you for buying

Getting Started with Windows Server Security

About Packt Publishing

Packt, pronounced 'packed', published its first book, *Mastering phpMyAdmin for Effective MySQL Management*, in April 2004, and subsequently continued to specialize in publishing highly focused books on specific technologies and solutions.

Our books and publications share the experiences of your fellow IT professionals in adapting and customizing today's systems, applications, and frameworks. Our solution-based books give you the knowledge and power to customize the software and technologies you're using to get the job done. Packt books are more specific and less general than the IT books you have seen in the past. Our unique business model allows us to bring you more focused information, giving you more of what you need to know, and less of what you don't.

Packt is a modern yet unique publishing company that focuses on producing quality, cutting-edge books for communities of developers, administrators, and newbies alike. For more information, please visit our website at `www.packtpub.com`.

About Packt Enterprise

In 2010, Packt launched two new brands, Packt Enterprise and Packt Open Source, in order to continue its focus on specialization. This book is part of the Packt Enterprise brand, home to books published on enterprise software – software created by major vendors, including (but not limited to) IBM, Microsoft, and Oracle, often for use in other corporations. Its titles will offer information relevant to a range of users of this software, including administrators, developers, architects, and end users.

Writing for Packt

We welcome all inquiries from people who are interested in authoring. Book proposals should be sent to `author@packtpub.com`. If your book idea is still at an early stage and you would like to discuss it first before writing a formal book proposal, then please contact us; one of our commissioning editors will get in touch with you.

We're not just looking for published authors; if you have strong technical skills but no writing experience, our experienced editors can help you develop a writing career, or simply get some additional reward for your expertise.

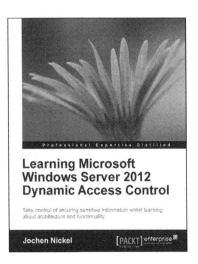

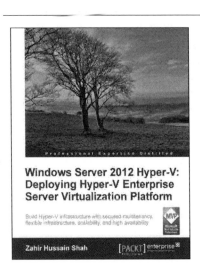

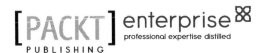

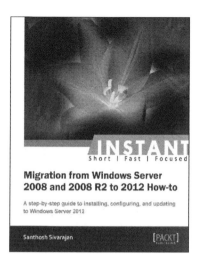

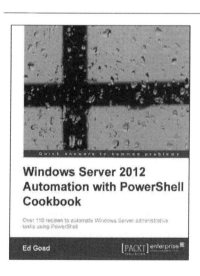

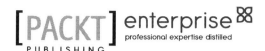

36938495R00135

Made in the USA
San Bernardino, CA
06 August 2016